SPIRITUALITY FOR THE SKEPTIC

Spirituality for the Skeptic

The Thoughtful Love of Life

Robert C. Solomon

OXFORD
UNIVERSITY PRESS
2002

OXFORD
UNIVERSITY PRESS

Oxford   New York
Auckland   Bangkok   Buenos Aires   Cape Town   Chennai   Dar es Salaam   Delhi
Hong Kong   Istanbul   Karachi   Kolkata   Kuala Lumpur   Madrid   Melbourne
Mexico City   Mumbai   Nairobi   São Paulo   Shanghai   Singapore   Taipei   Tokyo   Toronto

and an associated company in Berlin

Published by Oxford University Press, Inc.,
198 Madison Avenue, New York, New York 10016

Oxford is a registered trademark of Oxford University Press

Library of Congress Cataloging-in-Publication Data

Solomon, Robert C.
   Spirituality for the skeptic : the thoughtful love of life / Robert C. Solomon.
      p.   cm.
   Includes bibliographical references and index.
   ISBN 0-19-513467-2 (alk. paper)
   1. Spirituality. 2. Religion—Philosophy. I. Title.

BL624.S63 2002
291.4—dc21   2001047553

Printed in the United States of America
on acid-free paper

9 8 7 6 5 4 3 2 1

For Kathy,

and for Betty Sue, Paul, Sam, Jacquie,
Frithjof, Roger, Steve, and Cynthia

This is what happens to us in music: First one has to *learn to hear* a figure and melody at all, to detect and distinguish it, to isolate it and delimit it as a separate life. Then it requires some exertion and goodwill to *tolerate* it in spite of its strangeness, to be patient with its appearance and expression, and kindhearted about its oddity. Finally there comes a moment when we are *used* to it, when we wait for it, when we sense that we should miss it if it were missing; and now it continues to compel and enchant us relentlessly until we have become its humble and enraptured lovers who desire nothing better from the world than it and only it.

But that is what happens to us not only in music. That is how we have *learned to love* all things that we now love. . . . Even those who love themselves will have learned it in this way; for there is no other way. Love, too, has to be learned.

—Friedrich Nietzsche, *The Gay Science*

We are here on Earth to fart around. Don't let anybody ever tell you different.

—Kurt Vonnegut, *Timequake*

TABLE OF CONTENTS

ACKNOWLEDGMENTS

This book began as a condensation and revision of another Oxford book of mine, *The Joy of Philosophy.* (In fact, my playful working title was "Little Joy.") But once I got into it, my thinking and soon my aim quickly shifted. In *Joy of Philosophy,* I launched what I saw as an overdue attack on the mind-numbing "thinness" of too much of contemporary philosophy. I tried to balance the attack with illustrations of how philosophy could once again become richer and more full of life, more relevant *to* life. But by the time I finished *Joy* and had written the conclusion ("Has Analytic Philosophy Ruined Philosophy?"), I had moved beyond the attack mode. When I began to write this book, I saw very quickly that though the outline and structure would remain pretty much the same, the tone, and temperament and, in fact, the basic subject matter would be in stark contrast to *Joy.* (I thought of a series of Picasso's *Minotaur* lithographs I had just seen in Madrid, in which the same picture took on strikingly different and even opposite meanings depending on a few extra lines, textures, and variations in the inking and coloring. So I do not apologize if some of this seems familiar to readers of my earlier book.) Here, I allowed myself to enter what I had previously considered forbidden, or in any case inhospitable territory, the realm of spirituality.

I characterize my efforts here as a "search" and certainly intend to be open-minded. Nevertheless, three presumptions I knew I would not give up were (1) the idea that spirituality has a lot to do with thoughtfulness, (2) that spirituality is not at odds with, but rather in cahoots with science, (3) that spirituality is by no means limited to religion much less sectarian, authoritarian religion. These presumptions in turn prompted my affirmation of what I call naturalized spirituality and my summary Hallmark-card phrase, "spirituality as the thoughtful love of life."

Confucius says, "Learning without reflection is a waste, reflection without learning is dangerous." I realized that I had a lot to read—much of which, I must say, I found silly and simple-minded. But I had already steeped myself for 30 years in some of the richest philosophical literature in the West, and bits and pieces from the East as well, so the lion's share of the work fell to reflection. But that still left me wrestling with spirituality pretty much on my own, which is probably as it should be. While steeped in some of the philosophers I have always loved, I will not pretend to have mastered even a small part of the vast literature on spirituality, and I will no doubt only repeat in a clumsy and impoverished way the insights and wisdom of many more profound and spiritually enlightened thinkers. But that is the way the cookie crumbles, according to an old and wise Buddhist proverb. I only hope that some of my readers are guided and edified by these meditations as I was as I wrote them.

I was never alone. I owe special thanks to my good friends Betty Sue Flowers, who has spoken with me often on these issues, Paul Woodruff, who was exploring the kindred concept of reverence just as my own interest in spirituality was perking. Sam Keen has been gently prodding me along this path for years. Jacquie Thomas often talked to me about matters I did not understand but kept my curiosity alive. Frithjof Bergmann moved me, spurred my love of philosophy, and earned not only my lifelong gratitude, but taught me indelibly that precious sense of *teacher* that many traditions have identified at the very heart of spirituality. Roger Ames and Stephen Phillips continue to make me more conscientious about Chinese and South Asian philosophy. A few of my colleagues at Texas have continued to remind me how vicious and intolerant self-righteous, sectarian religion can be, especially when combined with hypocrisy and paranoia. My wonderful editor (as well as part-time spiritual gadfly) at Oxford University Press, Cynthia Read, encouraged the project from the first.

But most of all, my most profound thanks to Kathy Higgins, my spiritual partner in life. (Until a year or so ago, I never thought that I would utter such a phrase.)

PREFACE

It is in our wild nature that we best recover from our un-nature, our spirituality. . . .

—Friedrich Nietzsche, *Twilight of the Idols*

This being a book on spirituality, let me begin with a confession of sorts. I have never understood spirituality. Or rather, I never paid much attention to it. When the subject was introduced, I made a convenient excuse to leave, perhaps expressing myself inwardly with a muted groan, expecting what followed to be platitudinous if not nonsense. Even when I was an aspiring young philosopher with poetic inclinations, I found most of what passed as spirituality something of a sham, fueled by pretension and dominated by hypocrisy. Moreover, I was not brought up to be religious. I was brought up to be "moral" along the lines of what evangelical polemicists have taken to calling secular humanism. Growing up as one of the very few kids with a (albeit nominal) Jewish affiliation in an overwhelmingly Protestant community meant that religion always appeared as a threat to me. Hitler and the Holocaust were always in the background. So religion seemed to me to be something dangerous, an impersonal source of suspicion and sometimes outright hatred based on nothing other than what seemed to me to be a set of abstract and arbitrary categories.

In retrospect, I realize that I was missing out on something important, throwing the baby out with the bath toys, so to speak. I was conflating spirituality and religion, and the very worst of religion at that, and I was denying both of them in accordance with fears and prejudices I had carried with me since childhood. Of course, I still have to confront the uncritically self-righteous and often sectarian attitudes of those who pride themselves on being religious, who look down with contempt on anyone who does not accept the same beliefs and affiliations that they do. (Today this intolerance goes by any number of more respectable-sounding names, for instance "exclusivism.") I am still surrounded by the soft-spoken, sometimes brain-dead but benign "new consciousness" pap that passes itself off as nonsectarian spirituality—from pyramid power and *feng shui* to channeling and the latest *Celestine Prophesy*. (I would not want to paint all New Age thinking with that brush, however—there are many important and promising ideas to be found there.) But between my disgust for self-righteous hypocrisy and my disdain for mindless New Age platitudes, I mistakenly rejected what I now see as an essential dimension of life. Spirituality can be severed from both vicious sectarianism and thoughtless banalities. Spirituality, I have come to see, is nothing less than the thoughtful love of life.

Let me say once and for all at the start of this book, spirituality does not mean and is not restricted to belief in the Judeo-Christian-Islamic God, and belief in God does not constitute spirituality. To be sure, for most Jews, Christians, and Muslims, belief in God is an essential component of spirituality. But even so, it is not necessary to be religious—much less to belong to an organized religion—to be spiritual. We all know people who claim and believe themselves to be devout, but are as devoid of spirituality as an empty Styrofoam cup. There are many millions of people, ten million Buddhists for example, who are exquisitely spiritual without the aid of a Judeo-Christian Jehovah, or Islamic Allah, or for that matter even a church or a political action committee or lobbying group. I reject neither the Judeo-Christian-Islamic tradition nor the Judeo-Christian-Islamic God, of course, but I am skeptical and must wonder if having been brought up with a certain set of institutionally sanctioned ideas is proof of their absolute truth. This is no argument against them either. But I would think such mere contingency ought to carry with it both humility and tolerance of other perspectives.

This is not to say that spirituality is not at home in organized religion. Of course it is. For billions of people one is unimaginable without the other. But I am sure that I am not alone in thinking there is also a home for spirituality outside the walls of the world's established religions, in the individual soul, some might say. But it is just such concepts as individual and soul (plus spirituality, of course) that I want to scrutinize here. Nevertheless, my search in this book is for a nonreligious, noninstitutional, nontheological, nonscriptural, nonexclusive sense of spirituality, one which is not self-righteous, which is not based on Belief, which is not dogmatic, which is not antiscience, which is not other-worldly, which is not uncritical or cultist or kinky. I might be unkindly compared to the proverbial drunk looking for lost car keys under a streetlight, because that is the only place he can see. So be it. It is a good first place to look.

I have a dear colleague named Paul Woodruff with whom I often team-teach undergraduate courses. Over the past few years, we have jointly expressed our growing frustration at the extent to which the notion of spirituality (or, in Paul's case, what he calls reverence) has been hijacked by organized religion, New Age eccentrics, and divisive sectarians, and the extent to which so much of current day religion is mindlessly ahistorical, focussed on eternal truths, and therefore oblivious to the rich and violent history—and the current day faddishness—of much of what they believe. Indeed, I share with Bertrand Russell the conviction that the history of western religion is a horror story, a history of intolerance, persecutions, and massacres, what the philosopher Hegel called "the slaughter bench of history." This is not, I now believe, a sufficient reason to reject religion, but it is a very good reason to reject those restrictions on faith that would render irrelevant such vile remembrances. Santayana famously said, "Those who do not know history are condemned to repeat it." Hence those who share my anxiety about current trends in American religiosity will agree that the Inquisition and the Holocaust will and must never become "mere history."

For most of my life, I have been dismissive of both spirituality and religion. I say this to clarify the perspective and the starting point of this book. No doubt many of my readers may think me simple-minded, trying to recover what I should have learned had I been rightly raised in the conventional matrix of religion, ritual, and belief. Others, my science and most of my political friends, will think me benighted, or perhaps something of a sellout, for giving up my lifelong down-to-earth scientific and admittedly hyperrational way of thinking about things. But if the very idea of spirituality seemed to me to be contaminated by sectarian religion and by uncritical and antiscientific thinking, my view of life, which manifested in my becoming a philosopher (it did not come *from* philosophy) pointed to something else. Spirituality is not just organized religion. Nor is it antiscience, un- or super-natural. There is a *naturalized* spirituality that I have always had a glimpse of, and this is what I want to pursue in this book.

About a dozen years ago, my life began to change. For one thing, I was growing increasingly disillusioned with what I loved, philosophy, or at least with the way philosophy was being defined and taught at our leading universities (including my own). What had originally been conceived as the love of wisdom had become a tedious technical enterprise, appealing more to students with affective disorders than to those who were seeking the meaning of life. Philosophy utterly ignored the emotional side of being human, and I began to feel that as professionally practiced, it had betrayed the very spiritual aspirations that had defined it since its beginnings in the Indian Vedas and the early philosophy of the Greeks. As professional philosophy has gotten even more narrow and exclusive, I began studying and appreciating the more varied philosophies from around the world, including Chinese Taoism, South Asian Buddhism, and the tribal religions of the South Pacific. It became more and more obvious to me that philosophy could not be severed from questions about spirituality and that what has come to be called the philosophy of religion could not long survive in the rarified air of abstract proofs and propositions in which it had been defined. "Worldly" religion came to mean two things to me. It represents the many religions of the world (and thus religious pluralism) and also religion that really matters, not just as an intellectual exercise but as a concrete way of coming to grips with life and the world.

I had long insisted that philosophy be sharply separated from religion, but now I began to feel that I had overemphasized this point and once again had confused religion and spirituality with sectarian proselytizing. Reading the works of the Danish philosopher, Søren Kierkegaard, I started to appreciate just how excessive the emphasis on *belief* had become in contemporary philosophy and theology. I also realized that the philosophical overemphasis on critical thinking had taken a devastating toll on the emotional engagement, personal devotion, and commitment that lies at the heart of every religion and in the heart of almost every beginning philosophy student. What I started to feel, at first very uncomfortably, was that "spirituality" was a good way of talking about the broader more inclusive conception of philosophy I was seeking. Spirituality, as I conceived of it, embraced both emotion and rationality, both philosophy and religion. But while religions seemed (and still seem) to me to be overly parochial and exclusive (whether or not they have gone global and enjoy worldwide success), spirituality, while admitting of any number of local variations, remains truly nonsectarian and international. I now think that it is what philosophy, the love of wisdom, is all about.

What happened then was most important. After many experiments, experiences, missteps, foolishness, and the long hard process of maturing (immaturity being the dominant trait of philosophers), I met and slowly married my wife, Kathleen Higgins. I say "slowly married," an odd phrase to be sure, because I did indeed wade, wriggle, and writhe into the beautiful life we now share. Some of this may have had to do with the usual male fear of commitment or more accurately, *twice burned thrice shy*, but much more importantly, it took me quite some time to begin to appreciate and to understand Kathy's profound sense of spirituality.

By way of tantalizing my readers (and perhaps provoking them to look at her books too) I note that Kathy was raised a pious Catholic, and like many pious young Catholic girls, she intended at one time to become a nun. She is now one of the better-known Nietzsche scholars in the world, and as anyone who knows even a smidgen of philosophy knows, Nietzsche is the most vehemently anti-religious, anti-Christian philosopher in the Western canon. Kathy retains and "religiously" practices her Catholicism, but she nevertheless de-

xiv

fends the great "God is dead" philosopher. How she manages this is a secret we save for those students who successfully complete their Ph.D.s with us, but the point, simply put, is that her Catholicism—and her love of Nietzsche—consists of a deep spirituality. It has taken me a long time to even begin to understand what this is, and it is my attempt to understand it, perhaps more than anything else, that drives me to write this book. In that sense, it is a work of love, although love is but one of the passions that will be expressed and discussed in these pages.

I have said that spirituality is not confined to religion, but I have not yet said much of anything about what a naturalized spirituality would be. Perhaps a good place to start would be to use an experience that most of us have had, perhaps often, and that is the experience of spirituality in music. I refer particularly to music that we say sweeps us away. Needless to say, some sorts of music are more conducive to such experience than others. But I would not too quickly dismiss the experiences evoked by even the most street-wise forms of rock-'n'-roll, grunge music, and gangsta-rap, much less the often profound responses we have to jazz and folk music. What is essential, as the philosopher Schopenhauer suggested many years ago, is that music takes us out of ourselves. It allows us to escape from our worries and desires (though here the *lyrics* of the music must surely be taken into account). It transports us to a larger universe and forges a community with our fellow listeners. Indeed, the most neglected cross-cultural universal in philosophy would seem to be the human need for music, however varied the modes and styles may be.

A different example of naturalized spirituality can be found, not surprisingly, in nature, if only we would look for it. Whether one sees the world as God's creation or as a secular mystery that science is on the way to figuring out, there is no denying the beauty and majesty of everything from mountain ranges, deserts, and rain forests to the exquisite details in the design of an ordinary mosquito. Whether or not we pay attention, Nature, uninvited, inflicts itself upon us, through the staggering force of a hurricane or an earthquake, curiously designated by Godless lawyers and insurance adjusters as "acts of God." When I was young, before philosophy, I was a gung-ho biology student (back in the days when the genome project was still science fiction). What I discovered, even then, was that what I loved about science was *nature*, not so much the quest for ultimate truth much less the Frankensteinian drive for power, but the very wonder of it all. Through my fascination with bugs and critters and microbes and plants of all sorts I found, as Schopenhauer found in music, a way to get out of myself, a way to escape from my insecurities and my often painful self-consciousness. Science—or rather, my fascination with nature—transported me into a larger universe and forged a global community with my fellow naturalists. But the important point is that this larger universe was *this* universe, this world, this nature, not supernature. The place to look for spirituality, in other words, is *right here*, in our lives and in our world, not elsewhere.

Closer to the heart, spirituality is to be found in our grandest passions, love in particular. Petty and jealous love do not qualify, of course. But no one who has experienced expansive, romantic love would deny that the feeling is deeply spiritual. There is also spirituality in our sense of humanity and camaraderie, in our sense of family (which is not for a moment to deny that family life can be complicated and difficult), and it can be found in the best of friendships. There is awe and spirituality in the sense that we are not in complete control of our lives, that there are forces that determine our course that we do not understand that nevertheless seem to have some purpose. (I am no longer loathe to call this "fate.") In a recent interview, scholar Ann Douglas described her recovery from alcoholism in terms of the feeling that "something intervened in my life." She said, "I choose to call that God. I really don't know any other way to describe it" (*New York Times,* Oct. 17, 1998). I don't know what to call it either, but I do not want to invoke monotheism by calling it "God." Even "Spirit" is too suggestive of a singular and supreme being. So I will stick with spirituality, or what I call naturalized spirituality, and try on my own to rediscover it through philosophy.

SPIRITUALITY FOR THE SKEPTIC

INTRODUCTION:
IN THE SPIRIT OF HEGEL

It is not difficult to see that ours is a birth-time and a period of transition to a new era. Spirit has broken with the world it has hitherto inhabited and imagined. . . . It is indeed never at rest but always engaged in moving forward. . . . The frivolity and boredom which unsettle the established order, the vague foreboding of something unknown, these are the heralds of approaching change.

—Georg Wilhelm Friedrich Hegel, *The Phenomenology of Spirit*

Twenty years ago, when I was wrestling with the rather impenetrable prose of the German idealist G.W.F. Hegel, I tried to capture his grand vision of the human cosmos, which he summarized in his first and greatest book, *Die Phenomenologie des Geistes*, as "Spirit" (*Geist*). The result of that wrestling match was the fattest book I have written (or will ever write), a 600 page tome entitled *In the Spirit of Hegel*. It was a gigantic departure from my former views and temperament, which I would still summarize as "existentialist." In other words, my philosophy was heavy on the notion of personal responsibility, adamant about the significance of individual choice and decisions, outspokenly individualistic if not also eccentric, and emphatic about the importance of the passions in human existence, including not only such lovely emotions as love and compassion, but also dark moods and emotions such as despair, resignation, anger, and angst.

Hegel, by contrast, took great pains to downplay the importance of the individual and to stress instead the primacy of the social and his all-embracing comprehension of the world as Spirit. In contrast to the existential emphasis on angst and taking control of our lives, Hegel talked about "destiny" and "fate" and pointed out the futility of individual decision-making in the face of the overwhelming forces of the "Spirit of the Times," (*Zeitgeist*). He embraced the passions—his "dialectic" has been called a "logic of passion"—but the passions are suprapersonal, the passions of an age or a "form of consciousness," hardly individual at all. They are the passions of being caught up in life, even "swept away," the very opposite of the "take charge" resolutions of the modern existentialist. The Hegelian picture is brutally portrayed by Leo Tolstoi in his great philosophical novel *War and Peace*, where even Napoleon is the pawn of forces he cannot control and does not even comprehend.

The contrast and confrontation between Hegel and existentialism remains emblematic of the dominant philosophical problem of our times. For all of the convolutions of postmodernism, the excitement and furor over the global economy, and exhortations about "the new world order," that which remains intractable is our personal and collective need to get straight about our place in the world. How are we to live and how should we cope with overwhelming difficulties and tragedies in life? How should we think about and deal with death? These are not Western as opposed to Eastern or Third World questions. These are the universal questions that face the most sophisticated and advantaged folks in the world and the peasants of China, the untouchables of India, and the inhabitants of the smallest villages in Africa, the Amazon basin, and the tropical South Sea Islands. The near instantaneous trafficking of global information brings the options and tragedies of human life to our every doorstep.

Hegel, in his times, anticipated with a mix of hope and anxiety the unification and liberalization of Europe under Napoleon. In our times, by contrast, it is quite literally the world that is to be unified. Not by conquest—that has been tried and has failed many times. And not just by commerce, although that, to be sure, is one of the dynamic forces at work in the world these days. In our times as in Hegel's, the world is to be unified first and foremost in human consciousness, in the way we think about ourselves and our places in the world. In our individual lives, these Hegelian concerns remain existential. But they nevertheless demand that we keep in mind some sense of the "big picture." How can we both respect ourselves and adopt the kind of humility that puts us in our proper place in the world? How can we learn to think of ourselves in terms of our relations with other people, in terms of compassion and shared Spirit, as opposed to our acquisitive individualism? How can we come to terms with the awesome and sometimes terrifying forces in the world without reducing them to economic, political, conspiratorial, or apocalyptic simplicities? How can we cultivate the grand passions and exorcise (or at least limit the damage of) the petty ones? How can we maintain a sense of the big picture while we are so caught up in our hopes, fears, aspirations, and the tempers and fashions of the times? Those seem to me to be the questions that lead us to spirituality, and this seems to me to be the perennial task and responsibility of all of us, but especially of philosophers.

Spirituality, like philosophy, is coming to grips with the big picture and with it our need for a larger sense of our lives. As an existentialist, I have always been concerned with the action-oriented questions: What should I do? How should I live *my* life? What should I make of myself? Accordingly, I felt obliged to remain wholly secular and more than a bit profane. Even my interpretations of Hegel were light on Spirit, which I mainly construed in terms of social membership and shared values. Not that some existentialists haven't contributed mightily to our conception of spirituality. The names Kierkegaard, Buber, and Tillich immediately come to mind. But I was captivated by Friedrich Nietzsche and Jean-Paul Sartre, whose atheism and harsh denunciations of religion dominate both their philosophies and their reputations. In recent years, however, I have come to see another side of Nietzsche (and even of Sartre), and a powerful affinity between Hegel and Nietzsche. Nietzsche may have rejected religion in many of its forms—particularly its more sectarian and hypocritical manifestations, but he never rejected spirituality. On the contrary, and like Hegel, he attempted to "revalue" and revise our concept of spirituality. Or to put it a different way, what both Hegel and Nietzsche tried to do was to *naturalize* spirituality, to get away from "other worldly" religions and philosophies, and to reappreciate or "reenchant" everyday life. The idea is to recombine spirituality with science and nature rather than play them off against each other. Thus for Hegel, nature is spiritual and spirituality is nothing less than nature fully developed in us. For Nietzsche, spirituality is as much a matter of "physiology" as it is a function of the (necessarily embodied) soul. Spirituality thus naturalized is what I want to grapple with in this book.

I am a philosopher. (As Kurt Vonnegut writes in *Timequake*, "I have to be.") I am not a spiritual thinker, much less a spiritualist or a religious advocate of any kind. But it seems to me, at least as a philosopher, that if spirituality means anything it means *thoughtfulness*. It does not mean thought without feeling, needless to say, and not any thoughts or any kind of thinking, of course, but thoughts about the meaning of life and the profound feelings that such thoughts engender. Spirituality, like philosophy, involves those aspects of our lives that are not reducible to career strategies, personal psychology, civic responsibilities, the fluctuation of our economic or romantic fortunes. Spirituality, like philosophy, involves those questions that have no ultimate answers, no matter how desperately our various doctrines and dogmas try to provide them. But philosophy has too long been absorbed in its own precious puzzles and paradoxes. As Nietzsche said a century ago, "Philosophy reduced to 'theory of knowledge'—that is philosophy in its last throes." Anyone surveying the same desert terrain today can only conclude that, although it is teeming with life, it has become more desiccated than ever.

To say that what interests me is spirituality is thus above all to put at arm's length all of the clever philosophy that scoffs at the big questions or reduces them to mere puzzles and paradoxes. Death and tragedy, for example, provoke unavoidable questions in even the most thoughtless among us that we cannot answer no matter how thoughtful we are. But all too often, in our cleverness, we contrive any number of curious puzzles and paradoxes about nonexistence. These are evasions rather than confrontations with the inevitable. It is not merely asking the questions that brings us into the realm of spirituality, but the realization that there are no ultimate answers to these questions. Even if we share a dogma with millions, the questions remain and the answers are to each his or her own.

An ominous warning here is Tolstoi's story *The Death of Ivan Ilyich*, in which an ordinary man who has "done everything right" and shared in the beliefs of his society comes to face the big questions, by himself, as he is dying of cancer. But such an exit calls forth a deep regret, namely, *Why was I not asking these questions all along?* The mayor of New York City was recently diagnosed with prostate cancer in the midst of a heated election. A man not known for his sensitivity, he nevertheless wisely declared to the press, "It makes you think about the really important things. It makes you think about what you should have been thinking about all along."

Without for a moment denying that spirituality requires thought and thoughtfulness, it nevertheless has everything to do with passion and the passions of life. The fear of death, grief, and despair are not themselves spiritual emotions, but they often serve as preconditions or anticipations of spirituality and can become spiritual as we think about them, as do joy, love, and certain kinds of trust and gratitude. But just as thoughts without feeling do not constitute spirituality, dumb feelings no matter how exhilarating without adequate thought do not either. Spirituality means to me the grand and thoughtful passions of life and a life lived in accordance with those grand thoughts and passions. Spirituality embraces love, trust, reverence, and wisdom, as well as the most terrifying aspects of life, tragedy, and death. Thinking of spirituality just in terms of our terrifying realization of loss of control and impending death is morbid, but thinking of spirituality only in terms of joy or bliss is simple-minded, a way of (not) thinking that is rightly summarized as "la-di-da." If it is passion that constitutes human spirituality, it must be the whole spectrum of human passions—and thoughtful passions—that we must consider. Thus when I have to summarize naturalized spirituality in a single phrase, it is this: *the thoughtful love of life.*

Spirituality, I will argue, is ultimately social and global, a sense of ourselves identified with others and the world. But ultimately, spirituality must also be understood in terms of the *transformation* of the self. It is not just a conclusion, or a vision, or a philosophy that one can try on like a new pair of pants.[1] How we think and feel about ourselves has an impact on who we actually are. The grand thoughts and passions of spirituality do not just move us and in-form us, or supplement our already busy day-to-day existence. They change us, make us different kinds of people, different kinds of beings. Thus Hegel insists on the "strenuousness" of the realization of Spirit. Spirituality is a process. The self is a process, and spirituality is the process of transforming the self.

Some brands of spirituality insist on the abandonment of the self. Conversely, I want to say that spirituality is the expansion of the self. Some brands of spirituality focus instead on the soul, that metaphysical nugget at the core of each of our being. To the contrary, the soul is not something fixed and eternal, but is as fluid as our lives are. Nevertheless, the language of soul implies a depth that the language of self does not. A recent book summarizes the whole drift of modern philosophy as a move "From Soul to Self."[2] Following Hegel and Nietzsche, I would like to explore a reversal of this trend, the transformation of modern self back to something more soul-like in a naturalized spirituality, the thoughtful love of life.

1

FROM PHILOSOPHY TO
SPIRIT AND SPIRITUALITY

Zi-lu asked how to serve the spirits and the gods. Confucius replied, "Not
being able to serve other people, how would you be able to serve the spirits?"

Zi-lu said, "May I ask you about death?" Confucius replied, "Not yet understanding life, how could you understand death?"

—Confucius, *Analects*

The word "spirit" conjures up many images. Spirit, first of all, evokes
spirited, being enthusiastic, passionate, devoted. More generally, it refers to states of mind, "being in good spirits" or "needing one's spirits
raised." It also suggests a series of contrasts, most obviously, between spirit, or
soul, or mind on the one side and the material world and the merely physical
human body on the other. (Thus the word "*Geist*" in German and in Hegel's
title is sometimes translated as "mind.") It is worth noting that Hegel ultimately
rejected all such contrasts, insisting that the body and the mind were one, and
the whole of nature is Spirit. So, too, Nietzsche tried to conceive of even the soul
as physiological, following the world view of Homer and the ancient Greeks,
but it would be an enormous mistake to confuse such naturalism with scientific
materialism, that is, the reduction of mind, soul, and spirit to the neurological
nuts and bolts of a soul-less biology. (Nietzsche said, "Do we really want to
permit existence to be degraded for us like this—reduced to a mere exercise for
a calculator."[1]) Both Hegel and Nietzsche rejected a concept of soul that was
anything other than this-worldly and natural, but neither could tolerate a soul-
less world, a world without spirit and spirituality.

"Spirit" also conjures up a nonmystical shared passion, as in such mundane phrases as "team spirit" and the "spirit of the times." It is in this sense a
distinctively social conception, as is evident also in more down-to-earth in-

8

terpretations of the "Holy Spirit" as the bonds of mutual feeling in a spiritual community. Hegel's early philosophy celebrated the "folk spirit" of the early Greeks, in contrast to what he saw as the alienating otherworldliness and "positivity" of contemporary Protestantism. In his more mature work, he contrasted the spirit of folk morality to the abstract rules and hyperrationality of modern morality. In his politics, too, spirit is what encompasses all of humanity, in contrast to the particularity of states, and it is this same world-spirit that transcends the childish sectarianism of contemporary religion. Whatever else it may be, spirit is social. It represents our sense of participation and membership in a humanity and a world much larger than our individual selves. This is even more important today than it was in Hegel's times. In his day, he saw the dawning of an international Europe. Now, we have all come to see the reality of a global humanity as well as the emerging specter of the earth itself as a shared but deeply endangered homeland.

"Spirit," in its most dramatic employment, refers to a realm that is supernatural, a realm of "spirits:" muses, gods and goddesses, angels, devils, and— sharing our secular space—ghosts. I know nothing of this realm (except what I read in the bookstores and see in the movies), so I have nothing much to say about it. Aesthetically and politically, I much prefer the idea of a richly populated spirit world than the lonely image of one true god. But however attractive such rich imagery may be, it too readily projects spirituality away from us and locates it somewhere else. The spiritual world is nowhere but *here*, whatever "here" refers to. *We* are Spirit, and the independent status of so-called spirits is not something I want to speculate about here.

Moving from the ethereal to the vulgar, "spirits" also refers to spirits, those high-alcohol drinks that, in their initial effects at least, tend to make most of us rather spirited. Hegel refers to his own work as a "bacchanalian revel," a carefree drunken festival. Nietzsche similarly refers to his philosophy as "Dionysian." (Bacchus was the Roman equivalent of the Greek Dionysus, the god of wine, among other things). To Nietzsche, the Dionysian referred to "letting go," to losing one's sense of rational individuality and gaining a sense of oneness with the larger cosmos. To Hegel, the revel meant letting our thoughts and feelings follow their natural course, which he thought would naturally lead to the recognition of ourselves with others and the world as Spirit. The intimate links in ancient Greek religion between the two kinds of spirits, gods on the one hand and booze in the other (contrasted with the antipathy to inebriation in a good deal of modern religion), should give us an important insight. Spirits are not other beings but rather the Spirit is in us, especially when we have drunk of our lives to the fullest.

"Spirit," which sounds like a name, ultimately signifies spirituality, a property, an aspect, a state of mind, a mode of being. This is too often thought to be the exclusive province of religion. But again, spirituality and religion are not the same. Although one might identify spirituality in terms of what John Dewey once called a "religious attitude," spirituality is a much broader concept than the rather specialized notion of religion. Despite the glib exclusivity of too many religious demagogues who insist that spirituality is synonymous with their (and only their) religion or sect, there are many meanings as well as modes of spirituality and no religion has an exclusive or even a special right to consider itself the true path to spirituality. Spirituality is a *human* phenomenon. It is part and parcel of human existence, perhaps even of human nature. This is not to deny that some animals might have something like spiritual experiences. But spirituality requires not only feeling but thought, and thought requires concepts. Thus spirituality and intelligence go hand in hand. This is not to say that intelligent people are more spiritual, but neither is it to buy into a long tradition of equating spirituality with innocence misconstrued as ignorance or even as stupidity.

To experience the world in terms of something more than immediate stimuli (that is, things to eat, things to avoid, things to be done) is already on the way to spirituality. But spirituality also requires the critical question, "Why?" It requires a sense of the future and of the significance of the past. It requires a recognition of death (one's own and of others), and consequently of the contingency and preciousness of life. It requires an awareness of the tragic, of the awful possibilities that face and eventually befall us. It requires a keen conception of self, not just consciousness or mere awareness but self-consciousness and self-reflection, the impulse toward "an examined life." The self is not just (as Wittgenstein once noted) the frame of our world, but something both substantial and mysterious. Not only can we never know with certainty all that is in the minds of others (even those closest to us), but we can never know with total confidence what is in our own hearts either.[2] Both self and consciousness invite a sense of mystery for which "soul" is merely a verbal pacifier. (Jean-Paul Sartre captures this mystery by way of a number of metaphors of evasiveness, for instance the paradoxical slogan, "I am what I am not and I am not what I am.")

Again, I do not want to deny that animals, perhaps elephants, apes, whales, and some of our favorite pets might have some such awareness, of death, of tragedy, of self. But at the very least, their awareness seems to be more limited and less articulate than ours. This is not the place for species chauvinism, however, on the contrary, if spirituality means anything, it certainly includes a certain kindred spirit with our animal colleagues in life, whether or not they have the same awareness or anything like the sense of spirituality that we do. Toward the end of the nineteenth century, the Swedish artist Richard Bergh wrote, "Has Nature a Spirit? Yes, insofar as the beholder of Nature has one. Man instinctively locates an inner life, resembling his own, behind the changing contours of Nature's exterior."[3]

This is a view that has grown rather unfashionable, not least for its apparent anthropocentrism. But it is starting to show signs of recurrence, especially in the deep ecology and Gaia movements of recent years.[4] The point, which I share with Hegel and Nietzsche, is to cast the net of spirituality as widely as possible. In that sense, we can qualify what I said above by insisting that, whatever spirituality may be, it cannot involve *only* humanity (or the relationship between human beings and God, gods, or goddesses.) Spirituality is all-embracing, including much (if not all) of Nature and the natural world. As for those tendentious conceptions of spirituality that would limit the spiritual world to the members of one's own sect and their special relationship with God, I can only propose that that is the very antithesis of the inclusiveness that spirituality demands.

Spirituality is often conflated with mysticism. To be sure, many mystics have been extraordinarily spiritual people, and even ordinary and naturalized spirituality may involve a sense of the ineffable and the infinite. But ineffability—the inability to submit an experience to analysis—is hardly an adequate excuse for some of the banal vacuities that pass as spiritual wisdom these days. Furthermore, we should distinguish carefully between the mystical insight that we are "One" with God or the world, and the fallacious follow-through that we are therefore incapable of understanding or analyzing what this means. Thus Hegel attacked the romantics and "intuitionists" of his day for reducing spirit to vacuous monism (making a famous crack against his romantic friend Schelling, "the night in which all cows are black.") And Nietzsche lampooned the romantics of his day (a half century later), noting that "they muddy the waters to make them look deep." One can accept mysticism wholeheartedly (whether or not one has had a mystical experience oneself), but nevertheless deny that ineffability is the first and last word in the search for spirituality. (It is the *last* word only in the sense that it signals a refusal to go on.)

It is true that spirituality is opposed to the merely technical, the merely perfunctory, and the nit-picking argumentation that refuses to accept anything as a living whole and insists instead on dissecting the lifeless pieces. But although it escapes narrow analytic categories and is less available to argument and "proof" than a limited empirical hypothesis or a mathematical proposition, the fact that spirituality lacks apt categories is no reason to say that it is irrational or indescribable. Kant elegantly pointed this out in his contrast between our scientific knowledge of the world and our intuitive extrascientific vision of the world as teleology (as God's design, as a "regulative ideal.") One might argue that one can appreciate that vision only through poetry. But then let's be sure that it is philosophical poetry—and perhaps if possible poetic philosophy too.[5]

At the very minimum, spirituality is the subtle and not easily specifiable awareness that surrounds virtually everything and anything that transcends our petty self-interest. Thus there is spirituality in nature, in art, in the bonds of love and fellow-feeling that hold a community together, in the reverence for life (and not only human life) that is the key to a great many philosophies as well as religions. This does not mean that spirituality is a form of selflessness (or egolessness). Spirituality, I want to argue, is an expanded form of the self, which is emphatically not to say that it is an expanded form of selfishness. Rather, as many Buddhists have long argued and Hegel more recently, it is that passionate sense of self-awareness in which the very distinction between selfishness and selflessness disappears.

Spirituality, Religion, and Science

I do not want to suggest that spirituality and religion are opposites or antagonists. But they are at least sometimes at odds, as in the petty sectarian demonizing that is all too visible in some contemporary religious circles. The conflation of spirituality and religion sometimes turns on the idea that both consist primarily of *beliefs*. But spirituality, at least, is not primarily a matter of beliefs (although it certainly involves beliefs). It is rather a way (or a great many ways) of experiencing the world, of living, of interacting with other people and with the world. It involves a set of practices and rituals, not necessarily prayer, or church services, or meditation, or prescribed rituals of purification but any number of ways, whether individual or collective, of thinking, looking, talking, feeling, moving, and acting.

Religion, by contrast, is primarily *belonging*. This is not, of course, the usual characterization of religion. The usual characterization, one that is embedded in Constitutional law as well as common sense, is that religion is a matter of belief, and that the identity of each religion is a function of its particular beliefs (and how those differ, however slightly, from the others). I would argue that for the most part beliefs are secondary, at best. I think that it is safe to say that many adherents to the major religions of the world do not understand the beliefs of their particular religion, its theology. Nor do I think that such understanding is necessary to either religion or spirituality. Indeed, it has often been argued (and not just by critics of religion) that the beliefs of various major religions are unintelligible. For instance, the existentialist Danish Christian philosopher Søren Kierkegaard insisted that the central beliefs of Christianity were "paradoxes" and literal nonsense, but that was no obstacle to a committed Christian. What made a person a Christian, according to Kierkegaard, was *faith*, "passionate inwardness" and not belief.

Moreover, the acceptance of such beliefs—and many of these are abstract metaphysical claims that would daunt even the most speculative philosopher—can hardly be based on anything other than group membership (or the desire for group membership). This is what is so very impoverished in those "philosophies of religion" that would reduce faith to beliefs, propositions to be "proven" (or at the very least, rendered "indefeasible"). While I do not doubt that philosophers who practice this sophisticated craft are as devout as they claim to be, I sense a severe disjunction between their theological efforts and their devotion. Most religious beliefs are more like club passwords or code words than propositions that can be explicated or defended. The difference between the beliefs of one sect and another, or even between one major religion and another, may be all but indistinguishable to a neutral observer. Indeed, the perennial and welcome attempts at ecumenicalism typically emphasize the similarities between different faiths, even insisting that God (or gods) are identical and simply referred to by different names (Jehovah, Yahweh, Allah, Brahma, the Godhead). Thus belonging is expanded from sect and faith to humanity, and that is where religion meets up with and joins spirituality.[6] Spirituality may rest with the individual, but it embraces (whether or not it is openly shared with) everyone else, and with the world as well.

One reason for de-emphasizing the role of belief in spirituality and religion is to undermine the false and often tragic battle between science and religion. (I would argue that spirituality and science at their best are kindred spirits and not at all opposed.) Science, to be sure, is largely about belief, backed by the evidence of the senses. But if religion is defined primarily in terms of belief, there is inevitably a clash between religion and science, whether on the most general level (whether everything including the origins of the world and of life can be adequately explained by science) or on the more particular level (why there are so many species of beetles, how such miracles as the eyeball or the immune system could have come about). Most scientists and theologians are willing to call a truce regarding the general questions. Few scientists deny that there will always be some open, ultimate questions and very few (though very well publicized) religious fanatics insist that the hard evidence of science be simply dismissed. In fact, the advance of science has often been the stepchild of theology, for if the world is God's creation, it is out of respect for God that one seeks to know its intricate workings. Spirituality, in its effort to embrace the world, naturally seeks to know more about the world it embraces.

Science and religion involve not so much opposing beliefs or belief systems as different ways of looking at the world. One might call these "knowledge" and "faith" respectively, but I think that this traditional dichotomy is highly misleading. If faith is taken to be a mode of belief, then it is not at all clear that the conflict with science is avoided. But if faith is taken to be something more like Dewey's "religious attitude," a reverent way of experiencing the world and appreciating and feeling gratitude for its (and your) existence, then there is no conflict at all. Science may insist on hard-boiled causal explanations. Religion prefers an animated and purposive view of the world. But as the great philosopher Kant argued two centuries ago, these are complementary and not at all in conflict, so long as we get over the need to interpret religions as alternative systems of knowledge. As Kant famously noted, "Science is the organization of knowledge, but wisdom is the organization of life." And in this vein, we might note that spirituality and wisdom are ultimately one and the same.

On the more practical level, of course, the mistaken conflict between science and religion as alternative belief systems threatens to turn already badly educated students into ignoramuses. The so-called science of Creationism (as opposed to the perfectly reasonable religious attitude that perceives the world as God's creation) is one of the most absurd mistakes in the history of religion. I respect those who struggle to reinterpret the Bible (for instance, the six days of creation) to fit into the most up-to-date findings of geological and evolutionary science. I can even respect those who refuse to believe in evolution because it so threatens a world-view they have embraced since childhood. But I have nothing but contempt for those well-educated sophists who break all canons of intellectual and argumentative integrity in pursuit of a purely political agenda. For example, using quotes from squabbling evolutionists snatched out of context and made to sound like criticisms of evolution as opposed to objections to this or that particular evolutionary hypothesis. Then there is the infamous manufacturing of evidence. My favorite is the juxtaposition of "fossils" of dinosaur and human footprints in Glen Rose, Texas (about 50 miles south of Fort Worth). According to the Institute for Creation Research, such "evidence" proves that Darwinism is wrong, Genesis correct. But religious devotion notwithstanding, I do not understand how someone living in the third millennium can believe that the world is only a few thousand years old (talk about the antithesis of spirituality, which celebrates the great expanse of the cosmos). More sophisticated are the "Intelligent Design" folks, who merely weave a web of possibilities without bothering to mention the obvious sectarian goals of their mission.[7] (Why suppose that the only alternative to Darwin is Genesis? What about all the rich creation stories from Asia or the rest of the world? For that matter, wouldn't extra-terrestrials also count as intelligent designers?) But the offense is not so much crude fraud and hypocrisy as it is the severing of spirituality from its natural home, the intellect and scientific curiosity. If spirituality, like science, does not begin with wonder, can it begin at all?

A vision of the world as spirit and a sense of spirituality may or may not be scientific, but at no point need it contradict the claims of science. Spirituality may encourage us to take life and the very existence of the world as a gift, even as a miracle, so long as this isn't taken as an excuse to close the door on scientific curiosity and inquiry. The mistake of Creationism, by contrast, is that instead of embracing spirituality, it opts instead for "us" versus "them" mentality with "them" representing virtually everyone with a post-Medieval view of the world. In the end, the result only makes religion look stupid.

Here, as elsewhere, I am wary of committing what I have long called the "transcendental pretense."[8] The transcendental pretense is not only invoking (transcendent) authorities who would impose their commandments or the "One Way" upon the world, but also and more so those who would insist that their perspective on the world is *the* correct perspective. This includes the scientific as well as any religious world-view. With that in mind, I should be humbler than I may often seem, and my enthusiasms should never be taken for dogmatism. (Although remembering this is my responsibility and not the reader's.) In these reflections, there is always room for alternative views, many of which I have neither considered nor thought of. In questions of life and death, the very flux of life requires constantly evolving points of view.

Being and Doing: Spirituality, Society, and Ritual

Another reason for de-emphasizing belief is that it is an impoverished version of either religion or spirituality that would relegate both social life and social rituals to the realm of the inessential. Thus Immanuel Kant (a pious Christian) and other philosophers who have tried to naturalize religion (that for them is really to *rationalize* religion) by reducing it to a small set of essential beliefs and eliminating what they disdainfully called "superstition" on the one side and "mere rituals" on the other, impoverish religion more than they improve it. What Kant failed to appreciate, at least in his philosophy, was the extent to which religion is first of all a social phenomenon, not a matter of belief. Insofar as it is a social phenomenon, religious practices and rituals are of primary and not merely secondary importance. Here again, we should note the differences between just going through the motions and those heartfelt routines whose virtue is their familiarity and intimate association with the most spiritual passions. The Chinese concept of *li* beautifully defines this notion of ritual. Ritual is not merely something one *does* (that is, just going through the motions) but rather something one *lives*, and it involves everyday actions and not only special services and sacraments. Spirituality is a philosophical oddity in that it requires action as part of its very essence. It is a mode of doing as well as of being, thinking, and feeling. It requires understanding, but this is not the same as (nor is it opposed to) the understanding that comes through science by way of belief.

Like scientific understanding, spiritual enlightenment does not come all at once. It requires attention, work, development, and time. Even being "born again" is not so much an instant transformation as the beginning of a long, involved process. Ritual and practice are not only the expression of spirituality, but the means to its realization through repetition and familiarity. Even the platitudinous wisdom of such simple slogans as "take time to smell the flowers" and such simple routines as taking a walk in the woods suggest such a sense of ritual and repetition. So do the standard rituals of romance, a quiet dinner alone, the repetition of pet names, the giving of small gifts. To insist that spiritual rituals must be religious rituals or to deny the importance of ritual altogether is to ignore both the reality of spiritual development and the significance of individual inventiveness and ingenuity. But the best of religion *is* spirituality, and the heart of spirituality is heartfelt activity filled with intelligent feeling, action, reason, and passion together.

One of the mistaken distinctions between spirituality and religion, which works to the great favor of religion, involves the idea that religion is available to everybody while spirituality is something rare and special, limited, perhaps, to a few saints and gurus. But spirituality naturalized is not just for the chosen few. It is nothing less than the realization of what is best in all of us (although what this is may vary considerably from culture to culture and even from person to person). One reason for supposing that spirituality is so rare is thinking that it requires extraordinary, even superhuman sacrifices. But spirituality should not be confused with the renunciation of the material, sensual, and social joys of life. It does not require becoming a hermit, an eccentric, or an ascetic. It does not require the refusal of comforts, luxuries, and erotic delights. And it does not mean solitude. Solitude may be necessary—in small doses—for spirituality. However, spirituality is ultimately not solitudinous but social. Søren Kierkegaard proved himself not only an eccentric but dangerously misguided when he put all of his emphasis on "the individual" and dismissed with utter disdain both the social dimension as well as the rituals of religious worship. Not only is spirituality not restricted to the very few, it is spirituality and not always religion that calls on us to embrace others and love our neighbors as ourselves. That means not only *as we do* ourselves but, literally, *as ourselves*, that is, as spirit.

Of all of the rituals that have defined the pursuit of spirituality, the one that I find most central and most directly instrumental is philosophy itself. Philosophy, we often have to remind ourselves, is a social practice. It is not (as the cartoon version would have it) an isolated sage sitting on some unidentified mountaintop confronting the universe in thought. Socrates surely deceived himself when he fantasized his soul, contemplating unencumbered by others, throughout eternity. He, more than any other philosopher, demonstrated the social nature of philosophy and those rituals of conversation called *dialectic*. I have also come to think that spirituality may even be the ultimate goal of philosophy as truth comes increasingly under fire and consequently more trivialized. (Compare, for example, the rich conceptions of philosophical truth that dominated Plato's and Hegel's philosophies.)

Identifying philosophy with spirituality is, I admit, reactionary. But it is a reaction not against truth or science, but against the "thinning" of philosophy to the point where it has become all but irrelevant to the rest of the academic, cultural, and intellectual world, not to mention the larger community of humanity.[9] This doesn't mean that I have found religion or that I've given up on philosophy. In fact, it is very much a return to all of those earlier wisdom-oriented conceptions of philosophy that dominated the discipline from the ancient Indian Vedas through the religious philosophies of the late Middle Ages and much of modern philosophy as well. But since the Western Enlightenment (a movement that was strangely homonymous with the religious enlightenment celebrated in the East), not only religion but spirituality has been on the defensive.

Since then, spirituality and philosophy have so often been thought of as antagonists, at least in the West, that mentioning them in the same breath shocks and outrages many philosophers. I know I would have been shocked and outraged until recently. Spirituality, like sentimentality and superstition, is too often something sham, something cheap, something with enormous pretensions devoid of content. Philosophy, meanwhile, has become untranslatably technical and "scientific." Between the well-heeled spiritual pundits on the media circuit and the brilliant technocrats locked away in philosophy seminar rooms, the throngs of humanity who are searching for that big picture find themselves with a pretty poor choice. Thus, even the most wacky New Age religions get to fill many hearts that might much better find their own fulfillment, if only they were encouraged to do so by the discipline that was once the mother of all disciplines, and of spirituality too.

Imagine There's No Heaven: Naturalizing Spirituality

When I say that I want to naturalize spirituality, as Hegel and Nietzsche did, I thereby reject the notion that spirituality refers us to the supernatural. The supernatural is that which transcends scientific explanation and is inaccessible to ordinary experience (although I do not dismiss the real possibility of experiences that defy scientific explanation and transcend the ordinary). But what I have in mind is more of an ethical and aesthetic than a metaphysical or scientific aim, namely, to reject any view that minimizes the value of life in favor of some other kind of existence or value. This is not to say that nothing is more important than one's life (love and honor, for example, may well count for more). It is to insist that *this* life, with all of its joys and troubles, is the only life worth thinking about. Some of the most vocal supporters of the "right to life" seem to be remarkably indifferent to many of the values and qualities *in* life. (Family services, educational facilities, and child welfare laws tend to be inversely proportional to "pro-life" and "traditional family values" legislation in a great many states.[10]) For such "pro-life" advocates (and I do *not* mean all of those who oppose abortion), life itself becomes an abstraction, something just to be defended *on principle*. A small but dangerous minority has demonstrated that they are more than willing to kill to defend this lifeless principle.

What counts as "this life," of course, is open to considerable question. Reincarnation, as classically conceived, might count as a continuation of this life in other forms. Most popular depictions of Heaven and Hell are quite distinctively described as a continuation of not only the same soul but the same person, with a great many of his or her personality and worldly attributes, excepting material goods. "You can't take it with you" refers only to one's money and property, not to one's memories, one's virtues, or, one hopes, one's sense of humor. (Consider those "Heaven and Saint Peter" jokes, e.g., "a surgeon went to Heaven, and met Saint Peter . . .," "a lawyer went to Heaven and . . . ." "Mother Theresa went to Heaven and . . .") Of course, it's tempting to take a stronger line here, and say that only insofar as we actually *experience* this continuation of life does it count as life at all, much less the *same* life, but the issues here are both sufficiently confused and sufficiently exotic so that we can better talk about naturalized spirituality without them. What interests me is spirituality *in* life. I would be interested in a reincarnated or heavenly soul only insofar as it has the same essential attributes as a flesh and blood person who is still enjoying his or her original, earthly existence.

Naturalism has become a term with many meanings among philosophers, from technical issues about the nature of justification and the relationship between facts and values to a general endorsement of the scientific method. It is not necessarily a celebration of science or scientific explanation (neither does it preclude them), but a rejection of the external or "transcendent" imposition of values, rules, and meaning. There is all the difference between believing that it is wrong to kill or steal because the Lord God commanded us not to do so and believing that it is wrong to kill or steal out of respect for other people, or for the social order, or because one realizes the consequences of killing or stealing, or simply because we were taught that such behavior is wrong and we find ourselves "naturally" repulsed and outraged by its commission. It is the difference between relating to one another by way of some transcendent authority and relating to one another on our own turf and terms, according to our own values. It is also the difference between life's having a meaning because there is a God or a future heavenly existence and life's having its own meaning.

Consider a value such as *equality*. It is one thing to say, as our Declaration of Independence famously says, that all men are *created* equal, or to say, as is routine in our culture, that everyone is equal before God. It is something quite different to note, as the English philosopher Thomas Hobbes does, that "men are of more or less sufficiently similar in strength and cleverness that they are equally capable of killing one another." Or, more in line with our experience, we believe (on wholly naturalistic grounds) without appeal to any imposed ideal that there is something of worth in virtually every human being. Every human being (and not necessarily *only* human beings) has many of the same emotions, enjoys many similar pleasures, suffers much the same pains and liabilities, and is therefore worthy of some respect and fair treatment. We do not need to be told by a higher authority that we are created equal. It is enough that we discover and mutually develop intuitions and institutions of equality and, even more important, of mutual respect.

Supernaturalism need not involve any transcendent God, gods, or goddesses. There is a supernaturalism invoked by philosophers, even rigorously naturalistic philosophers, that imposes supernatural demands on us. (I am not just talking about *ideals*, which by their very nature may be approachable but not actually achievable. Consider this from Kant, the epitome of the modern philosophical idealist: "One cannot hope to make anything perfectly straight out of such crooked timber as humanity."[11]) But Kant also tells us that reason is a God-given but autonomous faculty which dictates to us moral laws not based on experience, or feeling, or upbringing but valid for their own sake. As has often been pointed out, most famously by Hegel only a few years after Kant, such an ethic tends to find itself detached from the real world of human behavior, and thus it has to resort to subterfuge to sneak back into our world.

One even finds such a "supernatural" view of reason in unflinchingly secular philosophy. For example, one of the most ethical and most misunderstood of contemporary philosophers, Peter Singer (Australian, now at Princeton), defends a vision of reason similarly detached from our experience, feelings, and humanity, even in the name of that very humanity.[12] Singer argues that reason dictates a rule of universal equality such that each of us should feel obliged to give away most of our belongings to the impoverished of the world and give no special attention to ourselves or our close kin, friends and neighbors. It is undeniably a noble sentiment, and a healthy prod for those of us who do indeed devour much more than our share of the world's resources. But as Bernard Williams has commented on Singer's philosophy, "People just aren't built the way Peter thinks they should be." They do care about their families and friends more than they care about strangers. They do feel entitled to goods without reference to the statistical state of the distribution of goods throughout the world. For that reason, I call Singer "Saint Peter," an irony to be sure, for this very secular philosopher[13]. But such a will to the otherworldly may be found in even the most secular of thinkers.

Naturalism is not the same as materialism, both in the ordinary sense of an emphasis on the material goods in life and in the philosophical sense that only matter (and energy) exist. If *all* one cares about is sex, money, fast cars and rock-n-roll, there is hardly a case to be made for spirituality. But the fact that one enjoys or even adores the comforts, luxuries, and thrills of life is not an argument against or necessary obstacle to spirituality. In some cultures, spirit has been closely identified with sex, and, quite often, with one or another version of that culture's more expressive music. Moreover, most religious movements are not opposed to money and luxury, and many have ambitions for political power too. Asceticism, as Nietzsche argues, is by its very nature unnatural. (Nevertheless, it may have a natural explanation.) Naturalized spirituality is not opposed to but embraces the material world, the appetites, sex and sensuality, the body, and possibly even fast cars, money and luxury, all in their proper place. One need not live in a sackcloth to be spiritual, as the Buddha finally discovered in his explorations.

Self-Actualizing Spirituality

At the risk of being cryptic or paradoxical, I want to suggest that spirituality is *self-actualizing*, that is, it comes into being by being believed in. This is, of course, the claim of a great many established religions—not only that one becomes a believer by believing (that is a tautology) but that (in some sense) the belief becomes *true* by the fact that it is believed in. This is not the patent nonsense that the harshest critics would make it out to be, nor is it the miraculous revelation that less scrupulous evangelists would suggest. Nor is it simply a version of Kierkegaard's celebrated "objective uncertainty," in which we are free to impose our subjective truths if only because there is no possibility of our being shown to be right or wrong.

Spirituality as self-actualizing is to be understood rather as a version of the psychologically familiar self-fulfilling prophecies (although the word "prophecies" may be unfortunate in this context). Thinking positively, having confidence in oneself, and believing you can do it are all examples of this familiar phenomenon. (I still remember one of my favorite childhood "Golden Books," *The Little Engine that Could*.[14] The onomatopoetic refrain "I think I can, I think I can, I think I can" has carried me through a good deal of my more adult life.) It is not so much that thinking makes it so. It is rather that adopting a stance that eschews the most debilitating doubts and discouragement makes success at least more likely (assuming that is, that one has the skills or talents or possibilities to begin with).

Spirituality may not be an achievement or a success in the sense that winning a track meet, doing well on an exam, surviving an ordeal, or getting over the mountain is an achievement or a success. But spirituality is adopting a framework or a positive attitude in which all sorts of possibilities open up that may not have been evident before. In a sense, one does not literally *make* anything true. The facts of the world remain pretty much as they were before. Nevertheless, everything changes. The world is born anew. This is not to say that we are in the realm of mere wishful thinking, much less self-delusion. In religion, it has often been argued that one gains faith by having faith. This doesn't mean that God suddenly exists, nor does it imply even the weaker (and still dubious) claim that God comes to exist *for you*. It is important to hold onto the common sense distinction between something's being true and simply believing or having faith in something. Thinking that one is in love is not the same as being in love, and believing that one has self-confidence is not the same as having self-confidence. Needless to say, thinking that one has an aptitude for mathematics, or scholarship, or deep thoughts, is by no means the same as having any such aptitude. But *being* in love changes the world, or at least one distinctive aspect of the world, and if we do not generally think of love as an achievement (more often as a matter of "falling"), perhaps that is one of the first things to reconsider on the way to spirituality.

Hegel tells us that Spirit is self-reflection and comes to be in the conceiving of Spirit. Again this is not a matter of "belief," but a way of "constituting" the world in a certain way, experiencing it (and oneself) as spiritual. Consider a now classic account of the origins of consciousness by Princeton psychologist Julian Jaynes.[15] Consciousness, he tells us, comes into being through our becoming conscious of ourselves *as* conscious. This is not to say—this would be absurd—that we are alive and perceptive and capable of feeling pains, sensations, and the like just because we believe that we are. But consciousness is something more than mere perception and sensation. It is something more than reasoning too, if by that we mean only the solving of problems, all of which can and does go on without becoming conscious in the critical sense.

To be conscious is to fulfill some fairly complex conceptual conditions, including having a concept of mind, a concept of the "I," and the narrative ability to tell certain sorts of stories. One need not accept all of Jaynes's conditions, nor need we explain them here in order to acknowledge the important point that self-reflection in some sense is not something added to consciousness but is its very precondition. To put it differently, certain concepts are necessary not only to describe consciousness, but as antecedent conditions for there even to *be* consciousness.[16] Consciousness exists, one might say, only insofar as conscious creatures have a concept of consciousness, that is, have a conception of themselves as conscious, a conception of an "inner life." In other words, believing that one is conscious (as Descartes famously discovered) is to this extent a self-fulfilling prophecy (although Descartes made the mistake of thinking that we thus *discovered* our self-consciousness rather than constituting it). So, too, achieving spirituality requires, as its precondition, gaining (constituting) some sense of oneself as spiritual.

Jaynes's emphasis on "narrativity" in consciousness is particularly important, and once again we find Hegel, 170 years earlier, making much the same point. To be conscious is not just to be conscious of the present moment. It is to have something of a sense of time, the passage of time, a sense of backward and forward, a history. But history too comes into being only with its realization in thought, that is, the thinking of it. This was a central aspect of Hegel's philosophy, the realization that *adopting* a sense of history in some sense created the history that one was adopting. ("The only thought that philosophy brings to history [is] the thought that Reason rules the world, and that world history has therefore been rational in its course." [17]) It has often been said, though it is something of a wild exaggeration, that Hegel brought history to philosophy, or even that Hegel *invented* history. Of course, philosophy already had a long history, long before Hegel ever came on the scene. But history, too, is one of those self-creating concepts such that thinking it makes it so. (One might challenge the common equation of spirituality and eternity by noting that it is only because we have a sense of history and change that we have any sense of spirituality at all.)

The link between consciousness, spirituality, and history might be furthered by an analogy. Dan Dennett points out that lions and zebras have a history in that they have been around for a long, long time. [18] But lions and zebras surely do not have a history in the sense that we have a history. They may have memory (perhaps even collective memory, in some sense). But they do not have a history both because they do not *know* that they have a history (they keep no records) and they have no vision of their species' own development. We might deny that lions and zebras lack both consciousness and spirituality (no matter how spiritual your cat seems to be as he or she stares contentedly into space), not because they are not intelligent or sensitive creatures, but because they do not have a language adequate to self-conception, self-consciousness, and the enlarged and enriched consciousness of spirituality.

History, consciousness, and spirituality are all self-actualizing concepts. To have spirituality, therefore, is to adopt a spiritual stance, a certain attitude, set of emotions, and concepts that are both conducive to and constitutive of spirituality. In a strict sense, to do so is not to make anything true or new in the world, except for the fact that you have adopted a spiritual stance. But the perspective from which one perceives and conceives of the world and everything in it may nevertheless transform the world in what Jean-Paul Sartre calls a "magical" way, and thus make an enormous difference to how one lives and how one behaves, not to mention how one feels, even if the concepts that constitute our spirituality are already available to us and perfectly natural.

Spirituality as a Larger Sense of Life

For what is your life? It is even a vapour, that appeareth for a little time,
and then vanisheth away.

—New Testament James IV, 14

Life may be brief, but spirituality is a larger sense of life. What this means
need not be taken in any sense that diminishes the significance of life. So I put
heavy emphasis on *life*, not on anything beyond or other than life. Like Hegel
and Nietzsche, I think that the ultimate value in both philosophy and religion—
and the essence of spirituality—is the value of life. This is not to advance any
particular moral or political agenda, much less to weigh in dogmatically on
some hotly emotional sectarian debates. Nor is it to say very much that has
concrete value for settling ethical issues in general.[19] But it is a way, a kind of
philosophical beacon, to remind us of what it is that really counts, not fidelity to
any God or gods but *living well*. Of course, fidelity to one's ideals is a part of
living well, and living well cannot without violence be separated from doing
good in life. Yet living well can be too easily vulgarized into living luxuriously or
simply enjoying oneself. This is why that otherwise admirable philosophy, Utilitarianism, has always gotten such bad press. (German philosophers since Hegel
have always found it "vulgar" and devoid of spirituality. John Stuart Mill, its
most famous advocate, thus felt compelled to defend his thesis against "vulgar
interpretations.")

Living well is not about comfort and luxury, although it certainly need not
exclude such things. Nor is living well just about enjoying oneself, although to
be sure (as Aristotle argued) one could not easily be said to be living well if his
or her life was devoid of pleasure and enjoyment. But living well is also more
than just doing the right thing, as Tolstoi's Ivan Ilyich came to understand. It
is not just taking pleasure but (as Mill argued) taking pleasure in the right
kinds of things. "Better a Socrates dissatisfied than a pig satisfied," he famously
comments in *Utilitarianism*. *Life* is dissatisfaction and suffering as well as joys
and accomplishments. Living well means living a rich life, and a rich life is by
its very nature more than just comforts, luxuries, and enjoyment.

To put this emphasis on life in another way, one might say that *the meaning
of life is life itself*. Life's purpose is not the pursuit of some further life (and if
this were so, what would *that* life have as its purpose?) Nor is life the meaningless struggle for survival and existence lamented by particularly sourpuss
Darwinians and pessimists like Arthur Schopenhauer. Life's significance is
not to be measured by something outside of life but by how one lives and
appreciates one's life in its own terms. But those terms include one's place in
and identity with the larger world, not the solipsistic or selfish promptings of
narcissism or selfishness. Both Hegel and Nietzsche took life to be defined by

some larger purpose, but not some purpose to be found beyond life. In Hegel's case, this purpose was the realization of spirit in its fullest, the recognition of ourselves as an integral part of a cosmic whole. For Nietzsche, this purpose was the transcendence (self-overcoming) of the individual in the realization of higher goals and ideals. In place of the dubious purpose of transcending life, let us defend the ideal of transcending ourselves *in* life.

For Nietzsche, as for Schopenhauer and other romantic thinkers, there was no link between life and spirituality more exemplary than music. For Schopenhauer, music was the direct manifestation, not simply an "expression," of the cosmic Will that pervaded all of life. For Nietzsche, the Pythagorean notion of the "music of the spheres" was something to be taken seriously, as a conception of life if not as a principle of astronomy. As a young man, Nietzsche admired the music of Richard Wagner in this regard. When he was older, he rejected Wagner (as "decadent") but continued to celebrate the Dionysian in music (for instance, in the late Beethoven). But Nietzsche's celebration of spirituality in music opens up a contemporary analogy, although Nietzsche would not have known what to make of it. The analogy is with a particular and a peculiarly American form of music—jazz. Jazz is synthetic and social, bringing many voices and people together. It is eclectic, borrowing from everywhere and everything, from childhood nursery and folk songs to Australian Aboriginal music. It is pluralistic. There is no correct form of jazz. It is improvisational, spontaneous, all of those voices responding to one another (and to the audience), building upon but never bound by what has come before. It is complex, it thrives on counterpoint , and it is richly random and unpredictable.

Spirituality can be simple, constrained, and univocal as well as multivocal, unconstrained, and complex. It is hard to conceive of spirituality without musical accompaniment, even if it is only the silence of the skies or the whoosh of wind through the leaves on an autumn day. Then again, it was Pythagoras who insisted that the seeming silence of the skies was actually "the music of the spheres," which could be heard only by the gods. The spirituality of music is everywhere, if only we would listen for it.

Listening to music, we so easily get outside of ourselves. We even feel transported. But it would be a mistake to take this in out of this world terms. Rather, music brings us together. It is by its very nature social and sensual (if not sexual as well). The way music moves and excites us, to dance, for example, is not just a natural *individual* response. It is naturally a social response, and it has been rightly said that virtually every culture enjoys and prizes music as a social medium, whether it is in the ecstasy of group dancing and singing or the passive collectiveness of the classical Western concert hall. Musical experience is by its nature secular, except, of course, when the music is explicitly religious—or the surroundings are—and there is then some other text that dictates our interpretation. (The refusal of some religions to endorse music in a religious setting reminds us that the relationship has not always been a cooperative one. Plato chased the flutists along with the poets out of his Republic. In Islam—chanting the Qu'ran is not considered music, however musically beautiful it may be.)

Music is expressive of the entire range of human emotions, from joy to despair, and it is both the sociality and the sensuality of music that makes it such a suitable paradigm—or at least a useful metaphor—for naturalized spirituality. Spirituality, like music, is a celebration of life, and we feel it in our bones. To think of ourselves reductively as spiritual beings, that is, as potentially free-floating souls that would be better off without the encumbrance of our bodies, is to demean ourselves and misunderstand spirituality. It sounds like contemporary tripe to say that our bodies are spiritual, but there is real truth to that. Just listen to a piece of music while forbidding your body to respond in any way. Many traditions (and Nietzsche) have found it impossible to think about spirituality without dancing.

Spirituality, I said, is a larger sense of life. It means that we see beyond ourselves, first to other people and then to nature as spirit and as spiritual. Many philosophers have insisted that we should not view others as mere means to our ends, but this is not just an ethical maxim, a matter of duty. Appreciating people for their own sake is also the key to our own well-being, as Adam Smith, in the popular mind the advocate of selfishness, strongly suggested in his less well-known moral theory. It also means that we should not view nature as just a resource, or an obstacle to human ambitions, or an object of scientific study. Indeed, science at its best exhibits a spiritual dimension.

Nor should nature be viewed through the cold lenses of materialism and so-called reductive naturalism, which is a very different thesis than what I am defending here. A larger sense of life also includes a keen appreciation of the details of our lives, as sweating, sensual, sexual, hungry, living creatures with the special capacity of reflection, contemplation, and appreciation of ourselves as such and as part of the larger natural world. It also means appreciating art and all creative human productions as something more than artifice and novelty and much more than mere commodity or even creativity, but rather, as Hegel and Nietzsche viewed them, as a concrete embodiment of human expression and spirituality. It means thinking of one's life itself as an ongoing work of art, and loving it accordingly.

Not *any* larger view of life will count as spirituality. Pettiness and envy are enemies of spirituality. Patriotism is a larger view of life, and, indeed, patriotism undoubtedly has—or can have—a spiritual dimension. Unfortunately this is ruthlessly exploited by the worst kinds of demagogues and tyrants, from the conquerors of the Old Testament to Mussolini and Milosovic. What begins as Spirit ends up as fascism (which, not coincidentally, was defined by Mussolini—a failed philosopher—in precisely these Hegelian terms). Insofar as patriotism embraces all of humanity, as a concrete form of humanism, it may indeed coincide with the spiritual. Indeed, politics at its best represents spirituality, not perhaps in its nitty-gritty down-to-earthness, but in its social sensibility, the idea that we are all in this together and that in order to live well together we need to think of ourselves as doing something more than merely living together. Politics, like religion, becomes spiritual just to the extent that it embraces this nonsectarian vision of the world.

One might argue that sectarianism by its very nature embraces a larger sense of "us," except that the "us" is always defined in contrast and often in conflict with a "them," and this exclusivity is what makes it not spiritual. Spirituality has no boundaries. It is not exclusive (except in the sense that it may take hard work and many years to accomplish). It does not allow for an "us versus them." It defies comparison. (Some of my Buddhist friends delight in regaling me with stories about the "more spiritual than thou" politics of their peers, which resemble nothing so much as the mutually defensive ego-grand-standing of an academic department meeting.) So let me say it again, sectarianism is the antithesis of spirituality, but spirituality nevertheless embraces a larger sense of "us," not only all of humanity but ultimately the world as well.

Liberating the Soul of Philosophy

Philosophy is an attempt to come to grips with the perennial, personal, and universal human problems of meaning. This is not to deny, as Nietzsche suggested, that there is also a curious "will to truth," a fascination for puzzles and paradoxes that, once stimulated, may keep buzzing along for years. But philosophy is not this. It is an engaged wrestling with the perennial problems of life. Philosophy is not a specialty, a profession, an exclusive club with its own rules and passwords. Philosophy is nothing but coming to grips with our passions and thinking about matters such as the meaning of life, tragedy, death, our sense of ourselves, and, of course, philosophy itself, which is by no means the province or the privilege of any small number of university-trained professionals. As Maurice Riseling has commented, "Sooner or later, life makes philosophers of us all."

Philosophy and spirituality were once kin. There were no sharp divisions between philosophy and religion, or religion and mythology, or theology and religious practice and ritual, or a rational view of the world and a passionate one. (Socrates was but one of the most famous philosophers who exemplified both reason and *eros*.) Now, spirituality has been kidnapped by religion. Indeed, more than a few religious sects and cults define spirituality as exclusively particular to themselves. "To be spiritual is to believe in God, *in exactly this way!*" At the same time, spirituality has been exiled from philosophy—

although many philosophers are devout in their personal lives and more than a few try to defend their religion in their philosophy. As philosophy has become increasingly and self-consciously scientific, it has become divorced from the anguish and wonder that is the soul of human life and once provided the soul of philosophy too. Religion and myth have also been severed. As myth has been reduced to charming falsehood, theology has become as emaciated and impoverished as philosophy. Without spirituality, philosophy is nothing but puzzles, tantalizing puzzles, to be sure, but mere puzzles nonetheless, alienated from its larger audience and devoid of personal feeling. Philosophy like theology needs to reclaim some of the personal charm of myth and mythology.

One of the themes that I want to pursue in this book is the idea that spirituality is neither rational nor emotional but both at once, both Apollonian and Dionysian, as Nietzsche would say. Spirituality is living beyond oneself, discovering a larger self or, what amounts to almost the same thing, achieving what the Buddhists and Taoists refer to as "no self." Believing in God, not as an abstract proposition but as a personally enriching experience, is one way of being spiritual. But being in love, losing oneself in great music, feeling oneself at one with nature, these are others. Hegel, raised a Lutheran but arguably a closet atheist, defined spirituality as the recognition of the world and ourselves as Spirit, and using this cosmic personification he found spirituality everywhere. Nietzsche, also raised a Lutheran but a militant atheist, expressed far more spirituality in his warrior philosophy than did the sham Christians he criticized. What made Nietzsche an archetype of spiritual self-realization was his celebration of his own life (though it was not a happy one) with irony and humor, accepting and even loving his fate (what he called "*amor fati*"). What opposes spirituality is not naturalism, or secularism, or even materialism, but petty egoism, vanity, and vulgarity.

Finally, philosophy becomes spirituality when it learns how to *listen* (a hard lesson for those of us who have made our livings and reputations through lectures and monologues). It is to ask and attempt to answer for ourselves the most perennial philosophical questions, about the meaning of life, the inevitability of death, and the place each and all of us in an increasingly (perhaps tragically) human world. It is also to reach out to humanity with the humble sense that we might not be so smart after all and the answers we seek may be better conceived somewhere else and in a very different way. The antitheses of this view of philosophy are both the clever paradox and puzzle-solving of contemporary analytic philosophy and the often cynical obscurantism of much contemporary "Continental" philosophy. Philosophy, as Plato clearly saw, is a spiritual practice.

2

SPIRITUALITY AS PASSION

Destroying the passions and cravings, merely as a preventive measure against their stupidity and unpleasant consequences of this stupidity—today this strikes us as merely another acute form of stupidity.

—Nietzsche, *Twilight of the Idols*

Whatever else it may be, spirituality is passion. The spiritual life is a passionate life. This may not fit well with a long tradition in philosophy and religious thought since at least the early Stoics and in those strains of Buddhism that downplay the passions. They offer freedom from emotional turmoil, "tranquility," and "peace of mind." But one should weigh this tradition against an equally long if not always equally respectable tradition that recognizes the passions as the very essence of both spirituality and philosophy. Socrates and Plato, for example, those ancient paragons of reason and rationality, were passionate about philosophy and downright erotic about the Truth. In the *Symposium*, Socrates (Plato) makes evident that philosophy (from *philia*) is a kind of love, even a kind of lust (*eros*). The fact that the passion that thus defines Socrates's (Plato's) grasping after Beauty is not mild-mannered, gentlemanly *philia* but *eros*, sexual (erotic) desire, is therefore all the more striking. Saint Augustine may have despised the passions that moved his lower parts, but he praised to the heavens the passions that moved him toward God. Christian saints such as Saint Teresa were moved to ecstasy by their religious passion, and even the latter day Stoic and rationalist Baruch Spinoza praised above all the singular spiritual passion of bliss.

To defend a passion-based conception of the spiritual life is not to say that spirituality is irrational. Nor are the passions irrational. I will argue that some passions are *definitive* of rationality, but the heart of my thesis here is that the spiritual life is a passionate life and that neither spirituality nor passion is as such irrational. Foremost among these spiritual passions are love (predictably), reverence, and trust. I will not explore faith as such for the reasons I have suggested, because it is a term too exclusively wedded to a small number of religious traditions and, even there, it suffers from some deep philosophical ambiguities and equivocations. It is treated (e.g., by Kant) as a species of rationality. It is treated (e.g., by Kierkegaard) as a species of irrationality. It is treated by some philosophers and theologians as an emotion, but by others as a virtue or attitude very different from emotion. But I think that faith can best be understood as a kind of reverence and a variety of trust (as well as a variant of love). Reverence, trust, and love, I want to suggest, are the very essence of spirituality.

What I am calling the passionate life is neither exotic nor unfamiliar.[1] It is a life defined by emotions, by impassioned engagements and quests, by embracing affections. It has also been characterized by Goethe (in his *Faust*), Hegel, Kierkegaard, and Nietzsche as constant striving, even frenzy, typified by insatiability and impossible passions. This is, perhaps, pushing the notion a bit too far, particularly since critics often like to parody the passionate life as some sort of irrational out-of-control insanity, an almost Daffy (or Donald) Duck sort of imagery. Not all passions are irrational nor are they out of control. Not all passions are violent either. Some are calm, and may paradoxically be characterized in terms of being unemotional. (The use of "emotional" as an insult, together with such put downs as "sentimental," is worth a discussion in itself.[2]) But a life without passion would be a life barely worth living, the life of a zombie, an automaton, or even more unappealing versions of *Star Trek*'s Mr. Spock or Data.

Passion as religious ecstasy has been a part of human spirituality from the most ancient religions of the Middle East and the earliest religions of the Mediterranean and South Asia. The "bacchanalian revel" was an essential feature of religious experience long before theology, for example, in the Orphic or Dionysian religions of ancient Greece. Kierkegaard summed up the modern version of this view when he insisted that religion (Christianity) is "subjectivity," and "passionate inwardness," defined by its emotional commitment rather than its beliefs. Nevertheless, beliefs give shape and structure to emotion, so one should be cautious about emphasizing passion to the exclusion of belief. But Kierkegaard made an important point against the rationalizing of religion in his own day, which rendered religion *nothing but* belief coupled with a bourgeois sense of belonging. Faith, however rational it may be, must also be a passion. It can only be to a limited extent a mode of understanding. But this does not mean that it is limited to objective uncertainties or that it fills in for ignorance. What distinguishes the emotions from understanding is their motivational and personal nature, not the lack of (emotional) intelligence. The emotions of spirituality constitute a passionate awareness of the existential uncertainty of one's own trajectory in life.

Love in one form or another has been rightly considered the essence of the good life—sexual love, love of one's family and friends, love of one's country or community, love of one's work, love of one's life. The New Testament built on the old one in its opening up of spirituality to the "Gentiles" and its rejection (soon forgotten) of an us versus them mentality, as well as its celebration of love as the core of all ethics. One can complain that the love commanded in the *Scriptures* is too devoid of passion (indeed, Kant even celebrated the fact that the love commanded by the *Scriptures* was "practical, and not pathological"), but that, too, is a matter of considerable controversy. What is clear and welcome is the idea that love is one of the virtues, if not *the* virtue, a position that had been staked out several hundred years before by Socrates and Plato, in the *Symposium*. It is one of the passions that makes life worthwhile, and it is above all the passion that enlarges the self and gets us in touch with a larger, more luminous cosmos, as evidenced by any number of love songs as well as some of the great philosophers of ancient times. Nietzsche refers to such passion as "overflowing" and warns us against our tendency to identify the "eviscerated man" with the good man. Thus he defends a powerful sense of spirituality that comes only with a passionate enthusiasm toward the world.

Many philosophers, including Socrates, Spinoza, Schopenhauer and the Stoics, as well as Buddha, Confucius, and Chuang Tze, even Adam Smith, have defended some variation of "peace of mind" or "tranquility" as the highest good in life and the hallmark of spirituality. It is not as if these thinkers and their traditions have encouraged or defended the complete absence of emotion, to be sure. (Adam Smith was a firm defender of the moral sentiments, for example, and varieties of compassion, even bliss, are common to several Asian traditions.) But they have all been more or less staunch in their insistence that strong, violent emotion—the sort that is said to sweep us away—is at best untoward and often disastrous, even fatal. By contrast, I would like to promote the legitimacy of that Dionysian temper of life suggested by dynamic rather than static metaphors, notions of energy, enthusiasm, charisma, even mania.[3] Why should spirituality always be considered quiet, calm, solemn? Spirituality is also that erotic conception of life suggested by such poets as Homer, Byron, and (Allen) Ginsberg, occasionally weighted down with despair and *Weltschmertz*, perhaps, but part and parcel of an erotic spirituality that goes back to Plato, the Orphic religions, Hebrew mysticism, and the early Christians. Spirituality is passion, even "fear and trembling" (in Kierkegaard's phrase), but buoyed by joy and exuberance.

As part of the charge of irrationality, the passions are often depicted as flighty, frivolous, merely transient flotsam in the stream of consciousness. But, of course, a passion can go on for a very long time, even a lifetime, and it may implicate and include any number of other emotions. (I have often heard it argued, on these grounds, that love is not an emotion but rather a disposition to have emotions.[4] This, like so many arguments in this area, seems to me to oversimplify what it is to have an emotion—as well as to get very wrong what it is to be in love, confusing infatuation and crushes for the real thing.) Moreover, a passion can be "out of character" and quite contrary to anything that one might usually expect of a person.[5] "Falling in love" and stress-induced acts of heroism often exemplify such "lapses," but in fact such spontaneous passions make us seriously rethink who a person really is (or who we really are). Spirituality, in particular, is a passion with the power to transform our lives. In this sense it is self-deceptive or at any rate misleading to insist that some people are "naturally" more spiritual than others, as if to excuse our own lack of effort. Spirituality, contrary to being flighty, frivolous, or merely transient, is by its very nature persistent and enduring, first, perhaps, with great effort, then later, like all cultivated habits, the most "natural" seeming thing in the world.

When I say that I am defending the passionate life as spiritual, let me make it quite clear from the outset that not any passion or any emotion will do. Envy and resentment, for instance, no matter how strong, are not candidates for spirituality and, indeed, are among the greatest obstacles to spirituality. Certain collective emotions, despite the fact that they bring people together, nevertheless remain violently opposed to spirituality. I am thinking of the war hysteria, racism, and passionate hatred that lead to genocide, often provoked by demagogues and many of the monsters of history. I am also wary of those supposedly more innocent passions so prevalent in sports arenas, despite their manifestation as spirit of a rather limited kind. It is often argued that they are sublimated or displaced versions of otherwise more violent passions, but I would note that this amounts to an admission that they are, in altered form, perhaps, the same passions. Despite my Texas citizenship (or perhaps because of it), I continue to be unfashionably disturbed by the unconstrained joy of sports fans. I have no argument against those who simply enjoy the skill of the game or the festive camaraderie. But I am deeply suspicious of those who celebrate the same us versus them mentality that becomes so murderous outside the arena (and occasionally in the stands).

Emotions, even the best of them, may not *always* be virtues.[6] There are degrees or intensities of emotion (although I would challenge this quantitative characterization) that are by no means virtuous. In love, for example, there is a delicate line between passion and obsession (though ignored by *parfumiers*), and I am not defending obsession by any means (although the difference may have more to do with reciprocity than with the passion itself). Moreover, there are misplaced love, foolish love, and overly possessive love (better characterized as jealousy) that are not virtues or virtuous, though a foolish love may display more virtue than no love at all. It is particularly important to note the affinity of passionate love and obsessive love as well as the distinction between them. Passionate love is devoted. Obsessive love is compelled. And yet, the most powerful love is both devoted and compelled; it is both a willful commitment and an emotional investment that cannot easily (or without enormous pain) be withdrawn.

This dialectic between the willful and the seeming involuntary is the hallmark of all of the passions. It is often said that passion is what sweeps us away or grips us, but passions can also be cultivated and very much within our control. Being out of control is the very antithesis of virtuousness. (Consider the very term, "virtuosity."[7]) But it is the very essence of love that it is not, or is not wholly, within our control. It is firmly tied to fate as well as to the whims and well-being of the other person. We find that passion and desire wax and wane, quite indifferent to our hopes and commitments. What is called an obsession may just be the firm devotion that is called for in the churning seas of a changing life together, and what is called passion is in part due to the uncertainty that goes along with that devotion. What I want to suggest is that it is that passion, that devotion and enthusiasm in the face of uncertainty, the acceptance of a certain lack of control coupled with a responsibility for one's passions, that constitutes the virtue of love and the heart of spirituality.

I said that the emotions I will specifically single out for attention with regard to spirituality are love, reverence, and trust. One might note that all three are forms of *acceptance*. But erotic love is grasping, longing, almost lusting, and in its usual interpersonal form it presumes a kind of equality. (Stendhal says, "Where love does not find equals, it creates them.") Reverence, by contrast, presumes something greater than yourself, something awesome, wondrous, marvelous. Reverence is something less than worship but considerably more than either affection, respect, or admiration. Trust, in contrast again, is hardly a passion, it is more of an existential attitude. But trust, as opposed to reverence, presumes a vital interest, a vulnerability (as opposed to mere fascination).

There are many other emotions that enter into spirituality, to be sure, but my aim here is to triangulate a spiritual perspective and not rigidly define it in terms of its necessary and sufficient emotional conditions. Many people would also include hope and faith, for instance, but hope and faith are more specialized and focussed emotions (than reverence, for instance) and, seem to be particular to certain sorts of religions, especially those that insist on metaphysical and ethical *closure*. The entire Christian cosmology is established on the metaphysical presumption that time has a beginning and, even more pointedly, an end. Some of the most sophisticated cultures of the world, the Chinese, for instance, do not have a creation myth. They cannot make sense of the cosmos beginning in time (for then what would have come before it?). More importantly, not all of the world's cultures believe that the world will come to an end, that there will ever be anything like an apocalypse, or that good will ever triumph over evil once and for all. Hope might thus be construed as a degenerate emotion insofar as it encourages us to neglect or deny the here and now in favor of the merely possible.[8] Perhaps it is as Camus tells us, that we should live "without appeal." To live without hope, in this sense, does not mean living without meaning, nor does it imply living in despair or without a sense of the future—even an optimistic sense of the future. Insofar as faith implies that there is some supreme agent of whom we should expect something (for instance, an answer to our prayers, even our daily bread), the aim of a naturalized spirituality is precisely to get beyond such expectations. Nevertheless, I would not want to live without love, reverence, and trust, although, I admit, I have sometimes tried to do so.

Spirituality and Erotic Love

Love is the name for our pursuit of wholeness, for our desire to be complete.
—"Aristophanes," in Plato, *The Symposium*

No emotion is more central to the passionate life and a naturalized notion of spirituality than *love*. This promiscuously broad term might include everything from filial affection to saintly devotion, but only some of these would count as *passionate*. Among these would surely be the love that we call romantic, the love that "burns" (as Jane Austen's Marianne describes it in *Sense and Sensibility*). Millennia ago, Plato defended the passion of *eros* as such a virtue. But Plato ultimately defended *eros* not as the sexual passion for another human being, but as an erotic longing for the good, the true, and the beautiful. Erotic love has as its most obvious manifestation sexual desire, even lust. But without in any way implying that sexual desire is vulgar and without endorsing the notion that lust is a deadly sin, I want to expand the notion of the erotic to include passionate desires that are much more than physical (without denying for a moment that they are *also* physical). *Eros* transcends sexual passion, even in the straightforward sense that we sometimes want to passionately embrace a dear friend or comrade in whom we have no *sexual* interest whatever.

This larger sense of longing is especially evident in true love, which is often identified as spiritual experience (even without the pandering suggestion that sexual orgasm is the ultimate spiritual experience, in which "we are One with the world"[9]). We are all familiar with such an "overflowing" engagement with the world, enraptured by its beauty or sublimity, caught up in its magnificent sweep, if only for a rare moment or so. Or, on an interpersonal level, one can have such experience dealing in depth with any number of people in what we call intimacy (that is ill conceived as mere mutual vulnerability or candor). Again, at least for a moment, we recognize in that experience an expansion of ourselves, not only as reaching out but as a fusion, a merging with others in a world no longer merely "social". I take all such erotic love—with a lover, with the world at large, with other people more generally—as exemplary of spirituality. The erotic enthusiasm born of love's attachments is the most obvious and familiar example of spiritual eroticism, but eroticism in its larger more all-embracing manifestations.

There is a long tradition of what is sometimes called Platonic love, the idea that a loving relationship with even just one other person may provide a powerful glimpse into the nature and feelings of spirituality. [10] This is quite apart from any religious beliefs or commitments that one might have, although obviously such beliefs may mediate and facilitate such experiences. We may also have an erotic attachment to any number of people, or a large group of people, without any salacious suggestions of group sex and Orphean orgies. Indeed, the supreme Christian virtue of *agapé* (love of humanity, sometimes relegated only to God) might much better be reconsidered in terms of naturalized *eros*, not as divine, but as straightforwardly interpersonal or communal and none the less spiritually significant for that. The well-confirmed eroticism of fascism should horrify us, but we need not condemn eroticism along with fascism. Eroticism properly conceived is not necessarily sexual (but neither, of course, is it sexless). It is, at its best, enthusiastic, intimate, and spiritual.

It is tempting for philosophers (with an ax to grind) to say that what makes love and other feelings admirable is their consequences, the fact that they tend to result in morally good actions. It may or may not be true that love results in praiseworthy actions, but the worth of our feelings does not just depend on the desirability of any resultant actions or their consequences. [11] In love, on the contrary, the worthiness of our actions depends on the feelings they express. Generous and even heroic actions may follow from love, but the virtue of love stands quite on its own. (Socrates criticizes Phaedrus in the *Symposium* for just this reason. Phaedrus praises the consequences of love [good behavior] rather than the virtues of love itself.) We may think Jane Austen's Marianne foolish, but one can still admire her passion; while Edwardian literature is filled with Kantian gentlemen acting on their principles who are utterly repulsive precisely because they are cold and without compassion.

Not only is it desirable to love, but those who have not loved (whether or not they've also lost), or fear they cannot love, rightly worry not only about their characters but about their completeness as human beings—quite apart from any questions about action or performance. We (their friends) worry about them too. Love is admirable in itself, quite apart from its effects and consequences. [12] So, too, the passions of spirituality may prompt us to do good deeds, to be kind or at least tolerant, in short, to be a better person. But the virtues of spirituality do not depend on their consequences. Spirituality, like love, may be good in itself (without thereby denying that it may sometimes be inappropriate).

Emotions in general and love in particular are often said to be irrational (and therefore cannot be virtues) because they are capricious.[13] They simply come and go. They are all contingency without rational necessity and the constancy of reason. But consider, in the same light, the accusation of intractability.[14] It is notoriously difficult, when one has been in love, to purge that emotion, even when it becomes an intolerable source of pain. More positively, love tends to build on itself, to amplify with time, to find—through love—ever more reasons to love.[15] This is not, I would argue, an argument against the emotions but rather an aspect of their virtue. It is passing fancy that we criticize, not unmovable devotion. It is sudden anger that we call irrational, not long-motivated and well-reasoned animosity. (That is not to say that sudden anger is always improper or inappropriate, or to deny that long-term outrage is sometimes irrational and even insane.)

It is true that the emotions are stubborn and intractable, but this—as opposed to ultimately less dependable action in accordance with principle—is what makes them so essential to ethics. A person fighting with passion may be better depended upon than one fighting for an abstract principle. Intractability is a virtue of the emotions as rationalization is a vice of reason. It is thus that it is a virtue of emotions that they are intractable and resistant to change. This is nowhere more true than with spirituality, where durability and resistance to change are considered not only desirable but essential. Even brief moments of spirituality lay a claim to continuance (typically misdescribed as a desire for eternity). But demands for continuance, even intractability, are by no means tantamount to irrationality.

We think less not more of a lover if his or her love "alters when it alteration finds," or if he or she bends to the opinion of friends. We think more not less of people if their spirituality refuses to waver when the world turns against them. Just as many people think it admirable even if foolish to continue to love someone who has proven him- or herself utterly undeserving, most of us find something praiseworthy in the fact that spirituality does not bend to misfortune. Objectively, all of this may seem like nonsense, but aesthetically, in terms of the well-lived life instead of some cold notion of truth, isn't there quite sufficient reason to prefer such "irrationality"? Why, then, consider it irrationality at all, why not a more appropriate and better sense of rationality?

It is also said that love and other emotions confuse or distort our experience and are therefore irrational. But consider a homely lover who looks longingly at his equally plain love and declares, "You are the most beautiful woman in the world." How are we to understand this? Self-deception? Insanity? Surely not "blindness," for the problem is not that he cannot see. Indeed, he might well claim to see much *more* than we do, or more deeply. Impolitely pressed, our enraptured lover may resentfully concede the point, perhaps making a phenomenological retreat to, "Well, she's the most beautiful woman in the world *to me.*" But we know how such qualifications are treated in philosophy—with proper epistemological disdain. Wouldn't we do better to consider such privileged vision part of the virtue rather than a vice of love? Erotic love improves and intensifies, it does not distort, our perceptions.

Spirituality involves just such subjective and selective vision. In spirituality, one chooses to see the world as beautiful or sublime instead of as an industrial resource or a scientific challenge or a merely contingent set of facts. ("The world is everything that is the case," wrote Wittgenstein at the start of his *Tractatus Logico-Philosophicus.* But his intent was to save spirituality from science.) Why should we insist that a view of the world as beautiful or sublime is less defensible because less objective? Or why should we insist on the priority of just one of those views rather than all of them, each in its proper perspective? With regard to romantic love, Erich Fromm argues (in *The Art of Loving*) that what is essential to love is not to be loved but to be a loving person. Perhaps he overstates what is surely a valuable truth and insight. How much talk about spirituality has been misspent on the importance of *being* loved, for example, by God or gods, instead of the active emphasis on the importance of loving? Fromm's emphasis on being a loving person suggests a renewed variation on one of the oldest of Christian teachings: One loves one's neighbors—only if one learns or teaches oneself to look at others from an enchanted perspective, enjoying personal stories, idiosyncrasies, and the richness of human intimacy. It is all too easy to view the world as a mundane source of pleasures, problems, and frustrations rather than as an object of love and fascination.

Objectively, both love and spirituality are said to be contrary to everything that philosophy and science like to emphasize—objectivity, impersonality, disinterestedness, universality, respect for evidence and arguments, and so on. Yet, it seems to me that such so-called irrationality constitutes some of our most important *moral* virtues. We care about each other prior to and sometimes independent of any evidence or arguments that we ought to. We find each other beautiful, charming, and desirable, seemingly without reference to common standards. We find nature awesome even while our science friends insist that it can, with a lot of hard work, be totally comprehended. I don't mind the work, but comprehension alone is not sufficient. Aesthetic appreciation, for instance, is at least as important. Kant was right locating beauty somewhere between the objective and the subjective and realizing that it was, in some sense, a larger synthetic vision that embraced, gave meaning to, and ultimately justified both knowledge and morality.

Erotic love is so central to spirituality (although this is precisely what is rejected by some familiar religious traditions) because it is so *exciting*. Spirituality is not merely peace of mind, tranquility, contentment. It is a passion, the passion for life and for the world. It is a movement, not a state. Unlike many of the virtues (amiability, trustworthiness, fairness, modesty, temperance), erotic love has its violent aspects. Spiritual passion is not complacency. But the sense in which erotic love is exciting should not be reduced or restricted to what is commonly (and ambiguously) referred to as arousal. Physical arousal, like sex, is morally and hedonically neutral; its role in our lives depends on context, and, in particular, on the emotions that accompany it and the relationships in which it comes to count as expression. Much of the excitement of sex might better be understood in terms of our vulnerability, our openness to others, and ultimately our openness to the world and to our own natural being. In this excitement, too, we recognize the passions of spirituality.

Kierkegaard described the openness of love in general (although he was cynical about sexual love) as "a leap of faith," as "subjective truth," as "commitment in the face of objective uncertainty." Most noticeably erotic love involves the question of *choice* (however much it might also seem a matter of fate), and choice—continuous choice—readily leads to existential angst. All too often, we confuse the excitement of newness with love, thus endangering the very idea of love's lasting or desperately adopting the implausible aim of keeping it new.[16] Nevertheless, some of the excitement of erotic love is the uncertainty, whether at the beginning of a relationship or in the face of a situation beyond our control. What we think of as the excitement of love is only minimally the excitement of sex and much more the anticipation of the unknown. The passions of spirituality are not sublimated sexuality so much as an erotic engagement with existence itself, the passion for life.

Spirituality is often said to be (or to be about) the *mystery* of existence, but this, I think, overdramatizes and obscures the matter. Yet there is a familiar sense that bears this out. In a relationship, one has the experience of finding oneself not only wondering but even mystified by the question, *Who is this person* who has shared my bed and my life for 2, 10, 20, or even 50 years? The mystery is not the product of inattention or psychological obtuseness. It rather comes from deeply caring and feeling the impossible *need* to plumb the depths of the other's consciousness (and the unconscious too). It is here that the philosophical "problem of other minds" gets its poignancy, but no longer as a mere skeptical conundrum about possible hominoids but rather as a deep, even paranoid worry about one's closest loved ones. It is one of the more familiar paradoxes of everyday life that sometimes the better one gets to know someone the more one realizes how difficult it is to really know another person. To experience another as a tantalizing mystery, never to be fully understood, is what Kierkegaard was talking about with his leap of faith. But in our protracted dealings with other people, unlike Kierkegaard's anxious commitment to his objectively uncertain God, there is not only a leap of faith, but also the palpable presence of the other person, not to mention the reward of reciprocity. The best scientists know this sense of mystery about the world. However they may unlock nature's secrets, they know that there will always be more questions, larger questions, always more to know. Thus it is said that true knowledge begins with the appreciation of how ignorant we really are, which is not an excuse for resignation but rather a spur to enthusiasm and engagement with the world.

The ultimate reason for the excitement of erotic love, however, might best be put in the philosophical terms of self-identity. Passions are often distinguished from ordinary emotions and emotions from dispassionate beliefs or judgments in terms of their intensity,[17] but I think a better explanation might be put in economic terms, what one might call emotional investment. Passions define the self, they are the heavy investments of the self, in a way that most emotions are not. Love, notably, might be defined (in part) as *defining yourself in and through another person*. This is, I suggest, rather an updated version of Plato's original "Aristophanic" language of love as the completion and merging of two halved souls.[18] This suggests that the intensity of love (and other passions and emotions) is something much more profound than mere neurological and hormonal agitation. Love is by its very nature an expansion of the self, embracing another person not only physically but, we might say, metaphysically, in terms of a redefined concept of self as a *we*, ultimately embracing life itself. The refusal to do this, the refusal to invest in life, is all too familiar to us. It is called cynicism, and it is the diametrical opposite of spirituality and erotic love alike.

Erotic love is not, like romantic love, exclusive. Spirituality includes a generalized erotic love of other people, a love that has learned to appreciate their depth and mystery, a love that has learned to listen, probe, and share. Love consists essentially of desire, and in particular the desire for intimacy. But intimacy here should not be conflated with sexual intimacy nor with exclusivity. Indeed, the desire to "be with" is not limited to (and it is by no means assured by) sexual intimacy, and it becomes enriched not threatened as more and more people are included. That is why Nietzsche, following the ancient Greeks, celebrates the Dionysian as the transcending of individuation, our ordinary tendency to distinguish ourselves as individuals, and instead appreciate ourselves collectively in the exhilarating flow of the world. Thus it would be a shame to limit spiritual love to just one other person, although I should admit that I have a great deal of trouble believing that it can or should be extended to *all* others without distinction. Perhaps such an attitude is possible by God (although the evidence of the Scriptures strongly suggests otherwise). That would put love beyond our reach, or turn it to banal hypocrisy.

We do not want to insist on a love so broad that it is nothing more than bland. What is most desirable is that no one should be excluded, and that intimacy with some should not necessarily come at the expense of others. But this too is probably asking too much of us. Time and patience as well as good old prudence dictate that we not try to become intimate with everyone, but the more we can expand our erotic world the more fascinating and exciting our spiritual life becomes.

Spirituality as Reverence[19]

> Reverence survives among us in half forgotten patterns of civility, in moments of inarticulate awe, and in nostalgia for the lost ways of traditional cultures.
>
> —Paul Woodruff

Erotic love alone, needless to say, falls short of spirituality. It can be too exclusive, or it can be too physical (not just physical, of course, for that is not love). Erotic love can be desire devoid of respect, or narcissistic desire. It can be desperate, jealous, or defensive. Erotic love can be a mere façade for that conquest-and-challenge mentality that is so often mistaken for falling in love. In addition to the erotic love of life, no matter how passionate, spirituality requires reverence. Reverence is a passion that complements love. Whereas (erotic) love is first of all desire, reverence is a passionate sense of one's limits and limitations. Thus it is often conflated with humility, for it, too, is the recognition that one is not the master or legislator of the world (Freud's "primary process"), but subject to powers far greater and more significant than oneself and one's desires. Reverence is the recognition that one must respectfully *obey*, whether the laws of God, the laws of the land, or the laws of nature. But being bound by the laws of nature is not the same thing as having reverence for them. Without reverence, love too easily tends to degenerate into possessiveness and life itself becomes brutish and selfish ("nasty, brutish, and short," in the memorable words of Thomas Hobbes). Indeed, what is called a passion for life is sometimes just such a desperate grasping. Reverence (again according to Mr. Hobbes) is the recognition of a *sovereign* to whom we pledge our fidelity, and the sovereign remains above us even if we ourselves (collectively) constitute this sovereignty. With reverence, the perspective of love loses any sense of self-centered indulgence and opens us up to the suprapersonal world of spirituality.

All too often, reverence (like spirituality) is conceived as a kind of enlightened spectatorship, in terms of passivity rather than activity. Thus one familiar way of construing reverence is in terms of the humility that one ought to feel before an all-powerful God. But to limit reverence to an attitude before God too readily eliminates the rest of the world and other people as objects of reverence. It also compromises our sense of responsibility. To employ humility before God in the guise of reverence as an excuse for one's shortcomings and one's passivity is truly to take the Lord's name in vain. Moreover, reverence does not have to be humble, nor need it be a religious notion, and the recognition of one's own limitations by no means requires a humiliating comparison with the Almighty. One notoriously belligerent theist I know is fond of being quoted, "I learned to be terrified of God, and compared to that I knew I never had to be afraid of anyone." But this is the very opposite of reverence. While being reverential before God, some of the most arrogant and self-righteous politicians, corporate bosses, and even ruthless dictators cause great suffering and perpetrate great cruelties on the world. Being reverent means recognizing one's limits even with regard to the weakest people and the most feeble creatures in the world. This, again, implies responsibility, not mere humility. Being reverential—being spiritual—means being reverential before the world, before nature, before other people, before the law and other social institutions worthy of reverence.

Reverence is not the same as awe. Awe is often cited as one of the hallmarks of spirituality, when it is not simply identified with spirituality all by itself. But awe is too passive, too overly receptive, too close to being *dumbstruck*. Reverence is active and responsible. One can be in awe of the sublime—a magnificent waterfall or the beauty of a tropical sunset. One might be in awe of what one fears—a wild animal or a huge bouncer in a bar. Or, one might be in awe of what one most admires—a remarkable musician or a courageous politician. But all of these awesome spectacles are just that—spectacles, in which we observe rather than participate (except, in the case of fear, as victims).

An acquaintance of mine was in Salt Lake City a few years ago, when the city was struck by a freak tornado. He thought he would drive up to one of the nearby foothills, to admire the storm in all of its glory. But the twister was faster than his sedan, and he soon found himself caught in the ferocious winds with boards and branches smashing against his windshield. His aesthetic intentions turned into terror, and terror is emphatically *not* the same as reverence. I would not for a moment deny that the sight of a tornado inspires us with awe, but mere spectatorhood, like pure terror, fails to capture the essence of reverence. Reverence requires an active role, an engagement, not merely the experience of awe. In human affairs, reverence means taking a stand, in active and full participation. Reverence means taking responsibility, recognizing and accepting one's limitations, but not shirking from responsibility. Confucius says, "The loss of virtuous action leads to a tendency to sham spiritualism." To be awe-struck is to be paralyzed. To be reverent is to be moved to action. Thus reverence is not an awareness of one's insignificance but its contrary. To be responsible is to be significant.

Consider the attitude of the Greek heroes with respect to the gods, especially to Zeus, in the *Iliad*. (Consider, too, the attitude of all but the greatest Greek gods and goddesses with respect to Zeus.) To be sure, it was an attitude defined largely by fear and uncertainty, given the gods' habit of intervening in human affairs and often causing great misery (the Trojan War being one of the more notable examples). But it was also an attitude of reverence and responsibility, the recognition of obligations and duties borne not only from terror but also of gratitude for favors received as well as in anticipation. It would be a mistake to think of the Greeks and the gods as engaging merely in a quasi-commercial transaction of favors, bribes, and hedging bets. The reverence of the Greeks was both a deep respect for the power and divinity of the gods and an expression of their own sense of power and mastery. Coupling the two was the Greek sense of reverence (the opposite of which was *hubris*) and the kinship between the gods and men. The fact that divine power could sometimes be summoned (or enjoyed unsummoned) was secondary to their primary relationship.

This notion of reverence developed more or less contemporaneously in ancient China, in the writings of Confucius in particular. The *Tao* has much in common with what we are calling naturalized spirituality (as opposed to that sham spirituality obsessed with the spirits that Confucius rejected). The Way is a very Chinese way of describing spiritual movement towards a larger appreciation of our roles and fate in the world without the need for transcendence that defines so many otherworldly religions. Confucian virtues resonate with reverence, especially reverence for one's parents (*xiao*), humanity (*jen*), the sense of appropriateness (*yi*), and most of all, ritual (*li*), not just a set of regulated movements much less going through the motions, but a heartfelt engagement with one's traditions and community. The Taoists, thinking Confucius put too much emphasis on society and the social, reconceived the Confucian virtues as virtues aimed at nature (after which the Confucians, partly out of recognition of the validity of the extension, partly out of sectarian politics, so extended the virtues themselves). What kept Confucianism and Taoism together as two sides of the same coin was their shared sense of reverence for the Tao—the Way—and their sense that the daily rituals of life both expressed and reinforced the Tao.

We should not conflate reverence with mere politeness, its familiar domesticated translation, nor should we confuse reverence with hyperseriousness, or with lack of humor. Reverence is not so easily domesticated, nor need it be humorless. The phrase "irreverent humor" has done a great deal of damage in its apparent juxtaposition of reverence and laughter. No one raised in the somber mainstreams of the big three Western religions can fail to be struck by the exuberant joy and laughter in a great many tribal and Asian religions, including the most delightful versions of Taoism and Buddhism (notably Zen). In the name of spirituality, we need to promote what might be called reverent humor, no less humor (and not necessarily any less critical either), but humor in the service of a larger vision.

Although reverence is the recognition of our own moral limits, acknowledging that there are concerns that transcend our own self-interest, it is nevertheless (as the Greeks said of all of the virtues) a matter of self-realization, even self-perfection, as well. Reverence is ultimately a kind of confidence, a confidence not just in our limited powers but in our ability to use them wisely. That in turn presupposes a commitment to the goodness of the world, a goodness that may be infinitely multifaceted and pluralistic, but that we nevertheless recognize as being much greater and more powerful than we are.

The Passions of Spirituality: Nietzsche on Overflowing

> You force all things to and into yourself that they may flow back out of your well as the gifts of your love.
>
> —Nietzsche, *Thus Spoke Zarathustra,* *"The Gift-Giving Virtue"*

Again I want to draw Nietzsche to my side. He was a deeply spiritual thinker and a passionate advocate for worldly or naturalized spirituality. What Nietzsche opposes is a kind of bogus spirituality, edifying discourses for the weak and poor in spirit, rationalization for mediocrity, escapist philosophies that prefer a dim fantasized future to the robustness of this life. What he defends is a robust, this-worldly spirituality, a philosophy of the earth, a philosophy that prizes instead of denigrates the passions and the passionate life. This is what his Zarathustra, Nietzsche's alter ego, proposes in the book that bears his name. It is also what Nietzsche has in mind in one of his most striking and controversial coinages, the Will to Power.[20]

Nietzsche quite clearly rejects the idea of power as power over other people (including political power, or *Reich*), and although he certainly approves of competition he is adamant about the primacy of power as *self*-mastery. Nietzsche explicitly equates power and spiritualization, although always with the warning that much of what passes for spirit in both religion and philosophy is unworthy of the name. What Nietzsche mainly has in mind is *creative* power, the power of the artist, the poet, the occasional philosopher. It is not, as it is too often interpreted, irrational power. "When the degree of *worthiness of being honored* is to be determined, only *the degree of reason in strength* is decisive; one must measure how far strength has been overcome by something higher and now serves that as its tool and means!"[21]

The guiding metaphor of Nietzsche's spirituality is *overflowing*. Nietzsche talks about courage, for instance, as a kind of overflowing. What he has in mind, of course, is the sort of personal courage that it takes to face a lonely life wracked by illness, and nevertheless overflow with works of genius, as he did. Consider generosity (in *Zarathustra*, "the gift-giving virtue"), an important manifestation if not an essential ingredient in spirituality. Generosity is not mere giving, nor the habit of giving. A current charity insists, "give 'til it hurts!" One can imagine the donor, struggling against the pain of his or her own miserliness, weighing the burden of conscience against that bottle of Cabernet Sauvignon that is on sale at the wine store down the street. Finally, generosity overcomes resistance, and the virtue is admirably displayed. *But,* notice that the more one has to struggle to give, the less virtuous one is. Aristotle insists that, with all virtues, their performance is actually pleasurable, not painful; this itself is a test of one's virtuousness. Suppose, however, that one's generosity consisted of what one might simply call one's overflowing nature. This abandon and lack of concern, one might argue, is true generosity, not the struggle against personal deprivation but a sensibility that can only come with great wealth or saintliness. What constitutes Nietzschean spirituality, in other words, is first a kind of fullness, an expansive sense of self.

So, too, Nietzsche describes forgiveness as a kind of overflowing, indeed, as a kind of generosity. Too often, we conceive of forgiveness in terms of a great personal sacrifice, something achieved only with great resistance. But the images of overflowing and abundance give us a very different picture. We too easily think of ourselves as selfish and meanspirited—and not surprisingly we then behave selfishly and meanspirited. But the ideal should rather be a kind of fullness, a sense of spirituality that is more like love than it is like obligation. For Nietzsche, the good life consists not of humility (satisfaction in the minimal sense, having all that you need), but of exuberance, passion, *eros,* or what Nietzsche often, in the philosophical style of the century, calls simply *life*. With ample resources, ideally all of them spiritual, one can develop *style* (i.e., self discipline and character, not fashion) and *depth*, which, as in the American phrase "having soul," means complex, conflicted, agonistic, Dionysian. When Nietzsche insists, "I am dynamite" (in his last book, *Ecce Homo*), he wasn't simply displaying the signs of incipient insanity or merely being ironic. Nor was he immodestly announcing the potentially devastating effects of his philosophy. He was summarizing a new and exciting conception of spirituality, the overflowing spirituality of a passionate life.

3

SPIRITUALITY AS COSMIC TRUST[1]

What he did not know was that Sabina was charmed more by betrayal than by fidelity. The word "fidelity" reminded her of her father, a small-town puritan, . . . Betrayal, From tender youth we are told by father and teacher that betrayal is the most heinous offense imaginable. But what is betrayal? Betrayal means breaking ranks, going off into the unknown. Sabina knew of nothing more magnificent than going off into the unknown.

—Milan Kundera, *Unbearable Lightness of Being*

Trust and betrayal. How easily we confuse those two for innocence and malevolence! But trust is not necessarily innocent or naïve, and betrayal, like beauty, may be very much in the eye of the beholder. Trust is a kind of confidence, both in oneself and in the world. But there is sophisticated, knowing confidence as well as unthinking dependency. And whether or not our trust is betrayed depends, in part, on what we have a right to expect, of the other person, of people in general, or of life itself. Disappointment is not betrayal, and a sense of entitlement is not the same as trust. If we believe that the world owes us, that we should be treated as something special, then (as the Stoics wisely insisted), we may feel betrayed by the world but we are rather tripped up by our own uncritical beliefs. Insofar as our trust in the world is based on a sense of entitlement, it is the very opposite of the trust that is involved in spirituality.

Trust, together with love and reverence, provides the foundation of both spirituality and our emotional well-being. But trust, unlike love, is relatively passionless. It is not a form of intimate attachment (although intimate attachment almost always involves trust.) Trust is more like an attitude or, I will suggest, a determined stance toward the world. And trust, unlike reverence, implies dependency and vulnerability. Trust entails risk and a certain lack of control. We trust, in part, because we have to. We cannot control the world or our fate. But, at the same time, trust also entails responsibility, if not for the fate of the world then for our engagements in it. Trust also includes being prepared to accept life's many possibilities, or as Nietzsche expressed it, *amor fati* (the love of fate).

This is not to say that we are prepared to accept anything. Spirituality does not require this, and it strikes me as at least foolish if not humanly impossible to expect this of ourselves. (Thus I take Nietzsche's bold pronouncement in *Ecce Homo*, "that one wants nothing to be different, not forward, not backward, not in all eternity. Not merely to bear what is necessary . . . but to *love* it,"[2] as no more than a momentary burst of enthusiasm.) We cannot accept everything, but wisdom consists in separating out what we should accept and what we should not. It also consists of separating out what we should trust and what we should not.

The contrast to trust and acceptance is distrust and alienation. We do not like to think of life, much less love, without trust. Distrust breeds disharmony and alienation, and extreme distrust—paranoia—makes life unbearable. Our concern about trust usually has to do with our immediate relationships—trusting or otherwise—with our fellow human beings, with friends and family, with business partners and colleagues, with the many people and enterprises we casually deal with over the course of a day, or years, or our lives. But there is also that general sense of trust that has to do with our very being in the world, that sense of what Eric Erickson called basic trust, and that is what concerns us here as an essential ingredient in spirituality.

Basic trust concerns not only our physical security and the fulfillment of our basic needs, but also what R.D. Laing some years ago called "ontological security," security in one's own existence and confidence in one's place in the world. Basic trust gets established—or destroyed—very early in life. As infants and young children, trust is inarticulate and unreflective. But as we become articulate and learn our way around the world, this basic sense of trust becomes philosophical. Above and beyond our particular concerns with trust, there is that sense of *cosmic* trust, our overarching emotional sense of being secure in the world.

What is trust? It is not a feeling and certainly not a passion, although it clearly has feelings associated with it and its betrayal may prompt vehement passions indeed. Trust is not a set of beliefs or predictions, though beliefs, are certainly necessary to trust. Trust is *a way of being in the world*. What this means is that trust is neither an attitude, nor a feeling, nor a set of beliefs, but first of all a stance, the taking of a position, the resolution to conceive of the world or some aspect of it as trustworthy. Its opposite, distrust, encompasses both personal character and global perspectives, world-views governing virtually every situation. We talk quite freely of people as trusting or distrustful, and so, too, we perceive the world as more or less trustworthy. We distinguish between optimists and pessimists, and there are whole philosophies that spell out and support these basic attitudes towards life.

Among those philosophers who emphasize the trustworthiness of the world, the tendency for things to come out right, the most famous example is Gottfried Wilhelm von Leibniz. Answering an age-old theological problem—how evil could exist in a world overseen by an all-powerful, beneficent God—this champion of philosophical optimism came to the conclusion that "this is the best of all possible worlds." Leibniz's thesis was the most uncompromising statement of cosmic trust imaginable.

Nevertheless, it is telling that Leibniz's thesis is probably best known by way of its refutation, Voltaire's great parody, *Candide*. The story of *Candide* is one horror after another, all commented upon by the Leibnizian philosopher Dr. Pangloss, who asserts, with each new tragedy, that "this is, indeed, the best of all possible worlds." Voltaire, one of the most active social reformers in one of the most corrupt regimes of the eighteenth century, was not a man who appreciated cosmic trust. He was unwilling to accept injustice and instead aspired to what I will call authentic trust, trust not as God-given assurance, but as a challenge and a human accomplishment.

Trust is not a given. Basic trust may be considered something of a blessing—good parents, an untraumatic upbringing, a safe childhood—but authentic trust can and must be cultivated. Cultivated trust in the world is an essential part of spirituality. But spirituality should not be confused with self-confidence that is limited to confidence in one's own abilities and skills for making one's way in the world. Trust in the world includes the acceptance of a *lack* of control and the recognition of one's own vulnerability. The concept of trust I want to endorse here is an existential concept of trust, trust as something not given (by God, by the world, by a happy childhood), but something earned, and cultivated, and worked at. This is *not* the best of all possible worlds, nor is it conceivable that we could make it so. But what is both possible and necessary is that we cultivate trust even in the face of our recognition that a perfect or even a "best possible" world is impossible.

On the other hand, the nineteenth-century cosmic pessimist Arthur Schopenhauer represents in an ingenious way the utter untrustworthiness of the world. The world, he argued, is essentially Will—not my will, or your will, or any particular personal will, but a cosmic force, an insatiable, irrational, always demanding craving that manifests itself in everything and in all of us. There is, accordingly, no reason to trust the world because there is no underlying rationality, no purpose, no God. It is a well-known fact that Schopenhauer's profound distrust of the world did not keep him from enjoying it, though he was always defensively steeled against betrayal and disappointment.[3] But pessimism, even as a global philosophy, tends to close off the world (even if, as Schopenhauer argued, it stimulates compassion, the recognition that everyone is in the same meaningless position). For all of its cosmic import, his philosophy was not at all spiritual, since neither love, nor trust, nor reverence was part of it. Nietzsche, in contrast to both Leibniz's optimism and Schopenhauer's pessimism, insisted on philosophical "cheerfulness." But even he embraced the world not out of trust, but out of a kind of desperation, "*amor fati.*" That, in a nutshell, is the problem. How do we get past the cynical (aka "realist") position that sees the utter contingency of life without falling into the naivete of philosophical optimism?

To see how distrust closes off the world, consider the paranoid, who instinctively suspects everyone of ulterior motives, malevolent aims, or sinister opportunism. Of course, most paranoids are paranoid only in certain sorts of contexts, and most of us would admit to being paranoid on at least some occasions. (After all, we sometimes have good reason to believe—for example, visiting the tax office—that they really are out to get us.) But paranoia need be neither a falsification nor the imposition of an implausible interpretative scheme. It may be a plausible but tragically self-destructive perspective on the way things really are. It is locking oneself into a vision that, even if true, makes a good life and flourishing human relationships impossible. (It is well-confirmed in the social science literature that people who have a more accurate estimate of the likelihood of failure and betrayal do far worse than people who are overly optimistic.[4]) When every face is malicious and threatening and every situation, no matter how ordinary, seems menacing and portending evil, spirituality is unimaginable. To a paranoid, the trust required for opening up to the world seems like utter foolishness and fatal vulnerability. If total trust presupposes a perfect world, total distrust presumes a terrible world, a world in which one should never, ever, let down his or her guard and in which the possibility of some larger, spiritual vision is all but foreclosed.

Spirituality and Authentic Trust

> To thine own self be true, and it must follow, as the night the day, thou canst not then be false to any man.
>
> —Shakepeare, *Hamlet*

Spirituality is a synthesis of uncertainty and confidence, a sense of powerlessness combined with resoluteness and responsibility. Either half of these antitheses, uncertainty without confidence or confidence without uncertainty, a sense of powerlessness without resoluteness and responsibility or resoluteness and responsibility without a humbling sense of powerlessness, makes spirituality impossible. With this in mind, we can see what is wrong with the common view that trust is a kind of knowledge. Trust is not to be confused with reliability and predictability, the more or less mechanical behavior of *things* (cars, computers, the seasons, the weather). If we *know* that such and such will happen, it hardly makes sense to talk about trusting that it will happen. (In Elmore Leonard's *Jackie Brown*, the character played by Samuel Jackson says of his girlfriend, "I don't need to trust Melanie. I *know* her.") Trust, like love, confronts uncertainty with a special kind of confidence. The heart of trust is *trusting*, not knowledge. Nor is trust a sense of control. To trust in the face of uncertainty and lack of control, to accept (though not necessarily happily) whatever happens, is *authentic* trust. To insist on certainty and control—let's be honest here—is to refuse to trust. A control freak is precisely someone who refuses to trust anyone or anything else.

Authentic trust is something more than the *basic trust* that consists of the sense of physical and emotional security that many of us routinely and happily take for granted. Authentic trust is trust born of experience—including bad experience and betrayal—although basic trust may well provide the psychological foundation on which authentic trust is possible. Authentic trust should thus be contrasted with *simple trust*, naïve trust, trust as yet unchallenged, unquestioned (i.e., the faith of a well-brought-up child). It should also be contrasted with *blind trust*, which is not naïve but stubborn, obstinate, possibly even self-deluding. Authentic trust is trust reflected upon, its risks and vulnerabilities understood, distrust held in balance. Authentic trust, as opposed to simple trust, does not exclude or deny distrust, but rather accepts and even embraces it, transcends, absorbs, and overcomes it. With simple trust, one can always be surprised. (In blind trust, one refuses to be surprised.) In simple trust and blind trust, reasons for distrust are not even considered, much less taken seriously. All too often, spirituality is identified with simple or blind trust, the trust of a child or a fanatic. But I want to suggest instead that it should be construed as a mode of authentic trust, a wizened confidence in the world and one's role in it, trust with its eyes wide open.

Trust, like love, is often misconstrued as an attitude we take *toward* another person (or persons, or even people in general). Having trust in the world is thus construed as a certain sort of attitude. But when I say that trust is a kind of confidence I am not speaking of a mere state of mind towards others. Confidence is a function of a *relationship*, a dimension of interpersonal and social interplay rather than an individual attitude. (The current use of the word "attitude" to refer to a particularly aggressive way of relating to other people simultaneously reinforces and complicates this point.) When trust involves another person, perhaps the most important but neglected point to make is that *trusting changes the person who trusts*. In fact, when trust involves the concrete trust of another person, I would also argue that trusting changes *both* the person trusted and the person who trusts. With cosmic trust, the same point holds, although it is both more complicated and more simple. Cosmic trust is more complicated because it involves not just a particular relationship, but our relationship with the world. It is more simple because our relations with people are complicated, the more so the more we trust them. But in cosmic trust too, trusting changes *both* the world as trusted and the person who trusts the world. It is what Sartre called a "magical transformation of the world."

In basic trust, we learn to grow up trusting. In authentic trust, we *decide* to trust. Trusting is a choice, and authentic trusting takes into primary account the way the relationship will change as the result of that choice. A father trusts his young son to carry out a task for the first time. There is no evidence that the son is competent or mature enough to do so, but by being trusted, he comes to acquire both competence and maturity. Hence, the relationship between father and son obviously changes. The father comes to respect his son, which is different from simply loving him or having affection for him. The son gains a modicum of independence from his father, but, more importantly, he comes to understand his own desire to please his father, to solidify the relationship on a new basis. Thus, authentic trust necessarily involves *both giving and taking responsibility*. It is not just a passive attitude toward the world, and it is not a matter of taking control. To trust the world is to take responsibility for one's role and actions, in part by acknowledging that the outcome is never wholly in one's hands.

Trust presumes that matters are *not* entirely in one's own hands. But one should not leap to the opposite view, that matters are totally out of our hands. Trust (as authentic trust) and trusting in spirituality is something we *do*, and thus something for which we must take responsibility. We take responsibility not just for the trusting but for all of the obligations and responsibilities that come with the sense of shared or enlarged identity that is as crucial to trust as it is to love. Thus spirituality is not just acceptance. It is a willful stance toward the universe in which we take responsibility for our own actions, thoughts, and feelings, and to some extent for the actions, thoughts, and feelings of others as well.

Spirituality as authentic trust includes the trust of one's fellow human beings, but extends much further to the world as a whole. Of course, to trust nature is not to be stupid. It is not fooling yourself into thinking that the bear in the woods is as affectionate as your German shepherd or Chow Chow puppy at home, and it is not trusting that all will be for the best when what happens is largely in your own hands. Spirituality resembles basic trust in its comfort with the world, but it is authentic in the sense that it is neither simple nor naïve. It acknowledges the dangers and disappointments of life, yet affirms the individual's responsibility for dealing and coping with them. In this it resembles nothing so much as Nietzsche's *amor fati* (the love of fate), not as blind destiny but as open-eyed affirmation of the world and whatever we can do, whatever life holds in store for us.

Faith as Trust

> What I really lack is to be clear in my mind what I am to do, not what I am to know, except insofar as a certain understanding must precede every action . . . what good would it do for me to be able to explain the meaning of Christianity if it had no deeper significance for me and my life?
>
> —Søren Kierkegaard, *The Journals*

I have avoided talking about faith even though many people would insist that what I have been saying about trust is really about faith and that it is faith rather than trust that is essential to spirituality. But I have noted that faith is too limited. It is too often restricted to the monotheistic context of trusting (and loving) God, and in particular trusting God to do such and such (smite our enemies, make us rich, take us to Heaven). Spirituality is a much more general attitude toward the world. It does not involve anything being done for us. It rather involves acceptance, not by way of last minute desperation after all hopes have been dashed ("It's God's will"), but in its very essence. Faith, too, is best conceived as authentic trust.

Faith as authentic trust is constituted as much by doubt and uncertainty as by confidence and optimism. Saint Augustine, Kierkegaard, and Dostoyevsky all experienced intense periods of doubt and despair, but all three came to see this not as antithetical to faith but as essential to it. Faith, in other words, is not simple, but is, like trust, also a matter of authenticity. Put in a different way, authentic trust, like true love and genuine faith, may be possible only in the light of a *breakdown* of trust (or love or faith). One cannot authentically trust unless one has experienced, if only vicariously, disappointment, loss, or betrayal. What makes simple faith simple is the fact that nothing has challenged it. What makes blind faith blind is that it refuses to associate *this* instance of trust with any previous experiences of disappointment, loss, or betrayal. Of course, one need not actually suffer from a breakdown in a relationship in order for trust to be authentic. Just as the very thought of losing or disappointing one's beloved may be enough to spur true love, the thought of betrayal is essential to faith as authentic trust. The Old Testament is full of such seeming betrayals, and the story of Jesus, stripped of its larger implications, is first and foremost a story of betrayal, and not only by Judas. ("Father, why have you forsaken me?")

Consider, too, the phrase "In God We Trust." To believe in God, most people would argue, is to trust in God. Nevertheless, it is not at all difficult to imagine a true believer who nevertheless thinks of God as mischievous, undependable, even malicious. The entire Hebrew Bible is filled with stories of just such a God and the difficulties of those who try to believe in him. The Old Testament Jehovah is by his own admission jealous and wrathful. He tests his own people, over and over again. The story of Abraham and Isaac is an account of one such test, in which God commands a man to do the most horrible thing imaginable, kill his own son. (And this after God had *promised* him that son.) Of course, God countermands the sacrifice, but only after Abraham (and presumably Isaac and Sarah) have been put through an excruciating ordeal. The enormity of the trust involved in such a situation is such that it prompted the early existentialist philosopher Søren Kierkegaard to write a whole book about the ordeal of trusting in such a God. Kierkegaard's conclusion is perhaps the most eloquent statement we have of authentic trust. One knows and accepts the counter-evidence but nevertheless chooses—passionately—to trust. Of course, trust in God may be unique in that it requires an unconditional trust unlike any other, a trust that may remain firm and consistent through any number of seeming betrayals (which, of course, we refuse to consider betrayals). Our trust in the world may also be like this. Terrible things happen. There are no answers to life's biggest questions. Nevertheless, spirituality is the continuing trust and insistence that the world is benign and life is meaningful, that the world is not out to get you and that the defensive measures of distrust and paranoia are unnecessary and self-destructive.

The most upsetting text that expounds on the unconditional trust that supposedly constitutes faith is the Book of Job, in which a good man is punished repeatedly and severely in order to satisfy a wager between God and Satan. Job maintains his trust (against the advice of his friends), and, in the end, God makes Job whole. One might well continue to doubt that there can be *any* just compensation for such an ordeal and whether such a God can in any sense be deemed trustworthy. It is at this juncture that faith and trust tend to part company on the grounds that trust is always in some way conditional (for example on the good intentions of the one trusted[5]). The calamities depicted in the Old Testament are so extreme (whether or not they are based on historical facts) that they make it quite clear that the Hebrews' faith in God was unlike any other kind of trust. It was this that assured the religion's long and continuing success. But the calamities described in the Bible can be found in modern times too, notably in the Nazi Holocaust and, on a more personal scale, in the difficult and tragic lives of many millions of faithful believers. The New Testament reaffirms the Hebrews' faith, but makes it quite clear that there are no Chosen people as such and that trust in God and God's grace are not automatically correlated.[6] Thus, being a believer and a good person is no guarantee of salvation (nor, to be consistent, is being a nonbeliever and a bad person any guarantee of damnation). If one wants to believe in God's grace, what is required is trust, and given the inevitable calamities in life, a kind of unconditional but nevertheless authentic trust as well.

Although authentic trust is not strategic, it is almost always optimal in terms of long-term results. This is a familiar paradox in discussions of the virtues: We trust without regard for our long-term advantage in order to gain a long-term advantage. A person is generous because she is so moved by the plight of another, or because she feels an obligation to help out. But if she thinks too much (this is what philosopher Bernard Williams calls "one thought too many") about how this will enhance her reputation or how this will make the recipient grateful and indebted, then it is no longer generosity. This paradox has wreaked special havoc in the realm of religion. On the one hand, believers are told to have faith in God in order to reap the benefits of salvation and, sometimes, other more worldly advantages as well. But if one has faith in God just *in order to* reap the benefits, that is considered something less than faith. On the other hand, it is perhaps asking too much to require believers to have faith without the promise of such benefits. (Kant, a pious believer, insists that such faith would be *irrational*.)

Trust in the world is not motivated by our hopes and expectations. It is a degenerate notion of faith (and trust) that says that we have faith in God because we expect something back (even if one also insists that his grace is by no means automatic or simply to be had for the asking). We do not trust in order to get something back. Nevertheless, we do get something back, and we certainly know or at least hope that whenever we trust, we reap the benefits of a self-willed comfort in the world, more congenial relationships with others, and the opening up of all sorts of possibilities that distrust or the lack of trust keeps closed. Paradoxically, we trust because it is right to trust, not because we are pursuing our own advantages, but there is no better way to secure our own advantage than through trust. To put the paradox in a nonparadoxical way, authentic trust is *primarily concerned with the integrity of relationships* (including our relationship with the world), not with personal advantage, whether in the short or even the very long term.

Nothing is more relevant to our overall well-being than the integrity of our relationships, in particular our relationship to the world as a whole. Insofar as faith is a concern for the integrity of one's relationship to God (as it was for Kierkegaard), it fits our model of authentic trust. But faith can also have such a relationship with the world itself, and in the scope of our naturalized spirituality this is much more appropriately called trust than faith.

Emotional Poisons: Paranoia, Envy, and Resentment

While the noble man lives in trust and openness with himself, . . . the man of *ressentiment* is neither upright nor naïve nor honest and straightforward with himself. His soul squints . . .

—Nietzsche, *On the Genealogy of Morals*

If spirituality is love, reverence, and trust, what would be the opposite of spirituality, as we are construing it? There seem to be many candidates, not only cold, calculating, merely utilitarian rationality, but a good many of those emotions that fall into that ill-conceived category of negative emotions. (I say "ill-conceived" as there is rampant confusion between painful emotions, wrongful emotions, vicious emotions, enervating emotions, misery-making emotions, disapproving emotions, etc.) Nevertheless, negative emotion does serve to designate a certain class of anti- and nonspiritual emotions (perhaps because the category comes down to us from Christian and also Buddhist psychology). Hostility, vengefulness, anger, hatred, contempt, and what the Buddhists call "agitations" (*klesas*) are plainly opposed to the open-minded acceptance that is essential to spirituality. Other plausible candidates would be embarrassment, shame, and (perhaps) guilt.[7] But among the lot, two stand out with particular notoriety—envy and resentment.

Resentment and envy are emotions that are all too familiar. Resentment is usually aimed at other people, groups or institutions, but it can just as well be directed at divine or inanimate objects and even at the world as a whole. Camus's Sisyphus, in his mock-heroic role, shakes his fists at the gods, "in scorn and defiance." So, too, Camus says, we all are caught in the sensibility of the Absurd, in which our rational minds confront and rebel against the oppressive "indifference of the world" (*Myth of Sisyphus*). Envy, by contrast, is usually restricted to other people. Envy, one might note, is a recognition of our own limitations, but it is the very antithesis of acceptance and thus the very antithesis of reverence and spirituality. (It is also the most destructive antithesis of love, as anyone in a green-eyed marriage knows all too painfully.)

Resentment is opposed to spirituality because, among other things, it is a refusal to trust. Nietzsche writes, "This *need* to direct one's view outward instead of back to oneself—is of the essence of *ressentiment*: in order to exist, slave morality always first needs a hostile external world."[8] It may also involve the falsification of other people and their intentions and the mischaracterization of one's own life. As a very sophisticated and cognitively complex emotion, resentment is keenly aware of injustice and victimization, at least when it is directed at oneself or one's people. Of course, injustice and victimization are real enough in this world, but it is worse than ironic that many of the folks most prone to such a view of the oppressiveness of the world are those who are by any measure least oppressed.

A student of ours who was beaten up in Tianamen Square in the infamous democracy crackdown says of the government there, "they were just doing what they had to do." He expressed no blame. He didn't feel sorry for himself. But here in Texas there was a virtual sandstorm of protests at the very suggestion that Texas was about to pass a seatbelt law, a clear conspiracy of Communists and Big Brother government telling us how to live our lives. This is neither to condone the actions of the Chinese government nor to offend my fellow Texans, of course, but it is all too often our own expectations and demands that are in error, not the world. Thus Camus insists that the Absurd is a confrontation between our expectations and an "indifferent world," but he too easily turns to scorn and defiance and slides from happy existentialism into impotent and resentful rebellion, shaking his fists (through his hero Sisyphus) at the gods.

Resentment, like spirituality, is an emotion that is concerned with power in its awareness of the fact that there are forces in and surrounding one's life that are clearly beyond one's control. Unlike spirituality, this awareness is the very antithesis of acceptance and full of indignation and annoyance. It is painfully aware of (and may to some extent cause) its own impotence. Thus resentment is typically obsessive. "Nothing on earth consumes a man more quickly" Nietzsche tells us, and its description often embodies such metaphors of duration and consumption as smoldering, simmering, seething, and fuming—rather than raging, which would quickly burn itself out. Resentment thus reduces the world to our own impotence, and a fury against those whom we blame for our own oppression. Within such a limited vision of the world, there is little room for the expansiveness and acceptance of spirituality.

Envy, by contrast, is all about frustrated desire. Envy wants, even if it cannot and has no right to obtain. If resentment has a desire, it is the desire for revenge. But even this is rarely very specific, for example, as the abstract desire for the total annihilation, prefaced by utter humiliation, of its target (though the vindictive imagination of resentment is such that even that would probably not be sufficient). But envy remains so focussed on specific wants—even if there are many of them—that it fails (or refuses) to entertain any larger view of the world. The focus is always *her* hair, *his* car, or *their* talent, *their* success. It is not at all far-fetched to construe our entire consumer society as the embodiment of envy, whether or not the competition it inspires is good-natured or cutthroat, and whether or not the once-envied goods do or do not give some sort of temporary satisfaction. Thus envy gets listed among the seven deadly sins," not only because of its self-centeredness and divisiveness but because of its narrowness of vision. Envy closes off any possibility of appreciating ourselves *for ourselves* or getting along with those we envy (although shared envy, like shared misery, makes welcome company). More to the point, it closes off that larger view that allows us to be thankful for what we've got, accepting of what we do not have, and grateful for the very chance to be so alive at all.

Nietzsche famously tells us that certain emotions "drag us down with their stupidity." However clever resentment may be (and there is no emotion more clever), it is, from the point of view of living well, a stupid emotion. The same can be said for envy. These emotions shut us down and focus us in the worst possible way. Envy and resentment may prompt ambition and hard work, as Helmut Schoeck once argued,[9] but they remain the most common roadblocks for most of us—and I certainly include myself—to spirituality. "Let it go" is profound advice, even if it is often over-extended and overused. Let it go, when it refers to envy and resentment as well as to petty anger and indignation, is something I find worth saying to myself over and over again. It is not, to be sure, always easy. But that is why spirituality is such a challenge for me and not just a natural way of being in the world.

Beyond Envy and Resentment: Contentment and Forgiveness

Envy stops with contentment. "The wise man is one who is content with what he has," says the Talmud. But contentment doesn't mean the end of striving. It only signifies the absence of strife. We can still pursue our projects, including our desire for a new sports car or a larger house, but this does not mean that we should lose our identity by defining ourselves in terms of what we have (or, the flip side, what we do not have). Nor does this mean that we should turn our backs on our desires, in essence converting our envy into resentment. This is what Nietzsche suspected when he pursued the ideals of the ascetic life, the life of self-denial. Envy is not thereby subdued. It is only suppressed in favor of a more prudential and powerful sensibility that adjusts to the fact that what is envied is probably not attainable and seeks instead a different kind of satisfaction, the satisfaction of self-righteousness. This is often done in the name of spirituality. But spirituality could not be further from this subverted envy turned to bitterness.

It is ancient wisdom, but by no means so evident throughout history, that forgiveness is the way beyond resentment. Forgiveness ranges from the petty ("you stepped on my shoe, but don't worry about it"), to the extraordinary (South Africa's remarkable Reconciliation policy), to divine Grace and absolution. But the sort of forgiveness I have in mind is limited to the range of *natural* transgressions (that is, offenses against us by our fellow human beings, and tragedies inflicted upon us by nature). To refer forgiveness to God is not to forgive, which is something one *does* and not something one simply alludes to. (To forgive with the understanding that God will take care of the punishment is doubly not to forgive. It is rather like hiring a hit man as a means to keep one's own hands clean.) One might argue that forgiveness is not itself a matter of spirituality, although it *follows from* spirituality. That is, if one is spiritual then one will tend to forgive one's enemies. I would argue just the opposite, that forgiveness might best be conceived as *instrumental* for spirituality, that is, by forgiving one opens oneself up and overcome such drag-down emotions as resentment, anger, and vengefulness in order to allow for a more expansive vision of spirituality.

Forgiveness plays a particularly dramatic role in spirituality. Forgiveness is the most effective instrument for overcoming the most hostile emotions. Forgiveness may be a direct response to betrayal, a way of getting beyond the "natural" reactions of resentment and vengefulness. But forgiveness is not itself an emotion (although it may be tied to a remarkable complex of emotions). Forgiveness is an action—or a sequence of actions. It is not simply a state of mind. It is, by its very nature, a reaching out to the world. This is most evident when the offender is another person. When one person betrays another, forgiveness is a way of reaching out to the betrayer. It involves a ritualized undoing of the act or acts of betrayal. Given the wariness aroused on both sides by the betrayal, the explicit act of saying "I forgive you" or "forget it" is particularly desirable. Of course, one could undo the act or acts in his or her own mind by simply acting toward the betrayer as if there is nothing wrong. Unfortunately, this carries with it the obvious liability that such behavior may be interpreted as mere stage setting, tricking the betrayer into lowering his or her defenses in order to get even in some equally hurtful way. Or, the absence of explicit forgiveness may indicate that the person betrayed simply does not take this particular betrayal—or the betrayer—very seriously, which may constitute an offense in its own right. For such reasons, an explicit verbal act, meant sincerely and backed up with subsequent action, works wonders.

This is also true when the betrayer is not another person but life itself, when our hopes and expectations have been thwarted. Here it is not a question of convincing the betrayer (i.e., life) of anything, but rather working on our own expectations and reminding ourselves of the liabilities contained in hoping. It means, through our actions and feelings as well as through our thoughts, *forgiving the world*. Odd as it may seem, "I forgive you, world" is a surprisingly effective ritual, the implicit animism supporting rather than undermining the gesture. The point here is that even the most hard-headed materialists tend, in their personal dealings with the world, to be animists. Thus Camus has his Sisyphus shake his fists at the gods who condemned him although he (Camus) was an atheist. Camus was a delightful human being and a true humanitarian, but he nevertheless could not surrender his unforgiving view of the world.

Even if one conceives of a cold, cruel world, such a conception is already bound up with an animated world that can be cursed. But a world that can be cursed can also be thanked, and one impoverishes his or her life by restricting gratitude and forgiveness to other people or, more to the point, to a personal God. Of course, most of us realize that personifying the world is an intellectually suspicious even if poetic endeavor. Nevertheless, the urge is there, so most people prefer gestures that are properly wrapped in a complex submission to a personal God (e.g., It's God's will) rather than appear to be conversing with a godless and therefore (so the fallacious reasoning goes) meaningless world. As spirituality and forgiveness are concerned, it is the gesture and not the recipient that is critical. Whether one forgives the world or appeals to God's mysterious ways is ultimately not the important point. In either case, one adopts an attitude of trust and acceptance that brings an end to resentment and bitterness. Forgiveness is the revision of one's relationship (whether with the world or other people) by way of philosophical acceptance, getting over it so that the relationship can continue.

Forgiving is not the same as forgetting. Forgive and forget make up a familiar duo, but we should ask why one needs to do both. Isn't forgetting alone sufficient? If one doesn't even remember the betrayal, what is there to forgive? One might argue that to forgive and not forget is to keep the betrayal alive, to leave it in a latent mode ready-to-hand should future breaches of trust call for its use. True, but why should we take forgetting—that in such cases is often a species of denial or self-deception where it is not simple human frailty—as a virtue? Betrayal and tragedy are essential parts of life, and forgiveness *without forgetting* is very different from becoming oblivious to the truth. What would reconciliation mean in South Africa's history, if everyone had simply forgotten about the years of horror and apartheid? Betrayal is not necessarily the end of a relationship. (In a nation of people living together for centuries, how could it be?) Betrayal becomes an essential part of the relationship and its history. Forgetting it is not likely, nor would it be particularly commendable. What is both a virtue and compatible with the living truth of the relationship is the act of forgiving—putting the betrayal behind us but not out of mind, and moving on. That's what spirituality is all about, moving on, forgiving the world for the misfortunes it (inevitably) inflicts upon us. Thus spirituality is also called *wisdom*.

4

SPIRITUALITY AS RATIONALITY

The heart has its reasons, of which reason does not know.

—Pascal

I can stand brute force, but brute reason is quite unreasonable. There is something unfair about its use. It is hitting below the intellect.

—Oscar Wilde, *Portrait of Dorian Gray*

Socrates, the great champion of reason, took as his motto the slogan at Delphi, "know thyself" and the rather extreme injunction that the unexamined life isn't worth living. The most important part of self-knowledge, surely, is our understanding and appreciation of our emotions, which are, after all, what make life worth living. A life without emotion, a life without passion, without *eros*, would be only a depressing shadow of life. So the examined life, whatever else it may be, is not just an abstract philosophical understanding but, as for Socrates, a kind of emotional translucency and self-mastery.

Nevertheless, Socrates insisted on treating the emotions as unworthy of serious philosophical reflection. According to this ancient tradition, the emotions are limited and notoriously undependable. They may tell us a great deal about our subjective psychological states, but they tell us very little about the true ways of the world. Even if (as in Plato) it is passion that moves us to seek such truth, there is very little truth in the passions themselves. Plato, following Pythagoras, saw very clearly that spirituality was incomprehensible and worthless if it did not tap into some deeper truth about the world. But whereas the passions are erratic and transient the truth, they thought, is eternal and unchanging. So the part of us that comprehends it, they thought, must be eternal and unchanging too.

58

Accordingly, philosophical accounts of human nature have tended to reduce all of the richness of spiritual life to a single feature, *rationality.* "Man [sic] is a rational animal," said Aristotle, twenty-five centuries ago and just one generation removed from Socrates. One would be hard put, reading much of philosophy, to remember that people also eat, sleep, have sex, feel as well as think, are proud and vain as well as (sometimes) thoughtful, that they get sick and suffer horrible accidents, fall in love, fear death, and die. Reason might comprehend and even help us to attend to these matters, but reason has higher aims. It is our instrument for ascertaining the ultimate truth about the world. Accordingly, all of those lesser concerns should be put aside, or at least put in their place as we exercise our higher powers, what Aristotle immodestly referred to as a spark of the divine. So say the philosophers.

To say that we are spiritual creatures has always been to say something about these higher powers and higher aims, our ability to seek and perhaps even discover the ultimate truth about the world. Spirituality has always been about knowledge, even when the attempt is made to force some distinction between ordinary or scientific knowledge on the one hand and some special spiritual or esoteric knowledge on the other. Critic Jamie James defends the fascinating thesis that the entirety of Western thought and the whole history of Western music, from Pythagoras and Plato through modern times, have been based on the search for the ultimate order of the universe, the music of the spheres.[1] Thus reason and spirituality go together, and one might note reason and music as well. They are not opposites or antagonists. Spirituality, whatever else it might be, is not know-nothing innocence. Reason, whatever else it may be, is not opposed to spirituality. Indeed, for most of Western history, they have gone hand in hand.

But reason, obviously, is not always so viewed. Reason and religion are too often set against one another, and reason and spirituality are deemed not only opposed but mutually incomprehensible. Thus Jamie James chastises both modern science and romanticism in music (beginning with Beethoven) as decadent movements that have given up the higher quest for ultimate understanding in favor of mere technology (in place of genuine science) and emotional expression, personal enjoyment, and crass commercialism (in the case of music). In science, this has meant a retreat from the pursuit of truth in favor of technology and gadgets. In music, it has meant a retreat from the quest for the music of the spheres in favor of audience entertainment. By way of contrast, Leibniz characterized music, and in particular the music of his great contemporary Johann Sebastian Bach, as "unconscious calculating," with a resultant joy in harmony, yielding insight into the "highest truth." Beethoven and Brahms, by contrast, mainly mirrored the pathetic passions of the individual human psyche.

The underlying assumption of this ingenious perspective would seem to be that emotional expression is considerably less than the rational search for ultimate truths. I would argue, contrarily, that the best of romanticism, by taking proper account of our emotions, satisfied the requirements of spirituality in a way that would have been impossible by way of pure calculation, conscious or unconscious. Harmony of the soul requires harmony of the parts, as Plato suggested, and reason alone cannot provide this—even reason expressed as beautiful music. But neither is reason to be dismissed in favor of unthinking music and the joys of mere sensuous feeling.

Reason Versus the Passions?

Religion itself has been sundered by two long-standing oppositions, between reason and the emotions, and between reason and faith. Spirituality has typically been taken as the faith and feeling side as opposed to the reason and thinking side. Thus spirituality has been rightly distinguished from merely *believing* in God or being tantalized by one or another ingenious "proof" of God's existence, devoid of any sense of reverence, or love, or passion of a distinctively religious nature. We find the opposition of faith and reason throughout the later Middle Ages (in Jewish and Islamic philosophers along with some Christians), throughout the Enlightenment and much of modern times, and in Kierkegaard, who notoriously rendered faith as "passionate inwardness" and "subjective truth," setting these off against reason with a great many sarcastic comments. But this has done great damage to the notion of spirituality. It is not my concern here to mend this split with regard to religion and faith, but I again want to confront the first opposition, between reason and the emotions, this time from the side of reason.

One of the oldest and most vicious oppositions in philosophy is the split between reason and the passions. In the Western philosophical tradition, beginning with Socrates, the very expression "getting emotional" is taken to indicate the very opposite of reason and rationality. Torn between reason and passion, what are we to make of spirituality? Plato introduces a tripartite model of the soul, with appetites, and reason, and "the spirited part."[2] But is that where spirituality fits, somewhere between the appetites and reason? Isn't it suggestive that even Plato did not have a proper name for it? "Be rational," in many circles, is tantamount to simply dismissing spirituality from the discussion. Starting with the view that spirituality is first of all a matter of emotion, we now need to develop a conception of spirituality that is rational as well.

The fabulist Aesop urged us to make sure that reason remained the master, controlling those dangerous passions. When David Hume insists that reason should be "the slave of the passions," he leaves that dangerous dichotomy in place.[3] I want to suggest that reason and the passions are not only complementary. They are ultimately one and the same. As Nietzsche puts it, "as if every passion does not contain its quantum of reason" and "reason is . . . a state of the relations between different passions and desires."[4] To contrast reason and the passions, to juxtapose the rationality of reason against the irrationality of the emotions, is to talk as if reason and emotion occupy two distinct realms of human existence and issue from two separate faculties of the human mind. But the passionate life, the spiritual life, is not irrational, without reasons or against reason. It is a poor excuse for spirituality that eschews reason in favor of an uncritical and indiscriminate emotionality. Indeed, not only do our passions and emotions provide us with reasons but, as I have suggested, the passionate life may itself be the rational way to live.

Rationality is not independent of the emotions and the passions, nor is it merely the logical structure around which the emotions and passions find their proper place. Reason is not a monolith and it is not, as Kant and many others say, autonomous. It is not as if emotions are to be judged in the all-mighty court of reason but rather reason itself that is subject to judgment, and not just—as in Kant and a number of other philosophers—in its own court of law. Reason and rationality are contingent on our human natures, and on our particular cultures as well. It is in the light of our emotions that reason is rational and that our actions have the justification (or the lack of it) that they do. Indeed, perhaps the question should be, how does rationality satisfy our passions, and, in particular, our passion for life? Reason enhances our lives, and that is ultimately the only justification for praising it. The fact that our rationality does not always make us happy (as Kant argued) is no reason to conclude (as Kant did) that reason and happiness (and all of our other "inclinations") are opposed, only the former being of distinctive "moral worth."

It is only at our peril that we so divorce rationality from our emotional lives and relegate emotions to the realm of the irrational. According to the legacy left to us by Hume, rationality is to be construed as a *means* only, as purely instrumental. But to take our ultimate goals and our emotional and spiritual needs in life out of the realm of rationality, to put them beyond criticism, evaluation, and appraisal, is absurd, as Hume himself clearly recognizes when he comments, "Tis not contrary to reason to prefer the destruction of the whole world to the scratching of my finger."[5] Though they are *also* instrumental, it is our emotions that are constitutive of our ultimate ends in life, the things we *really* do and should care about. Thus spirituality is and must be both rational and passionate at once (but this is not to deny that there are both irrational and dangerous forms of spirituality).

Rationality, like spirituality, involves the heart as well as the mind (two organs that the Chinese wisely refuse to distinguish and thus treat as a unity, *hsin*). But what is rationality? Rationality, at its core, suggests something rich and textured about our experience, not just our ability to criticize and argue, but also the perspicacity and vision to appreciate complexity, to find (or make) meaning in disorder and confusion. But this is what the emotions do, too. The emotions endow and bestow meaning to our experience. Without the right passions, without perspicacity and vision, criticism and the techniques of argument are empty. Outside of the philosophy seminar room, they threaten us with social catastrophe by promoting cynicism, the *ressentiment* of passions denied.

Rationality Relativized

I cannot see the top of Mount Fuji because I am standing on top of it.

—Chinese proverb

I am at a conference on Mount Abu, in India (1991), and a local philosopher is presenting. There is a slow wind up, a few casual words of praise, an expression of modesty, a tweak of humor, a thesis, then another one, a reference to a Hindu myth, another expression of modesty. He shifts from thesis to thesis, building as he goes, speeding up his delivery. I wonder, eager philosophy student that I still am, where he is going, and what, really, is the thesis, as he Nagarjuna-like gives thesis and counterthesis, a few quick arguments and a conclusion that always seems like "neither of these." The theses come faster and more furiously, though no theme as such has been stated. Rather, the theme is the stream (of dialogue, although only one voice is actually heard). The speaker has lost track of (or never bothered attending to) time. He is already twenty-five minutes over his preassigned slot. The speed increases to a controlled frenzy. Then, in a burst of cosmic *chutzpah*, it comes to an end. Thinking about it afterwards, I realize that I have just enjoyed a philosophical *raga*.

The contrast provided by the next speaker, a well-known American philosopher, could not have been more pronounced. In the first paragraph, he presented a problem, proposed a thesis, mentioned two famous (Western) philosophers who had written contrary views on the subject, and announced the method and the argument he would pursue. Indeed, he did just that, in four brief, equally apportioned sections: the first devoted to a study of the problem; the second dedicated to examining (and arguing against) the opposing views of his predecessors; the third a presentation of his own thesis and its argument; the last (and briefest) mentioning a few loose ends and suggesting a few modest implications. I considered the idea that I had just listened to a classical sonata, utterly predictable, perfect in form, and lasting precisely fifty minutes, the time allotted. But then I thought, no. This wasn't music. It was only form.

The analogy of philosophical reason and music is not far-fetched; it has been utilized many times before, all the way back to the Indic Vedas, and, of course, by Nietzsche. Confucius and the Greeks, particularly Pythagoras, who thought music, philosophy, and reason inseparable. It could be argued that their separation was an aberration, the product of impoverished science and a vulgar romanticism.[6] The Australian Aboriginals thought and think that the order of the world was created and is maintained through song. The Navajos and the Pawnees in this country held similar beliefs. As a way of illuminating rationality, the comparison of philosophy to music encourages us to think of what rationalists have always denied, the idea that rationality may be regional rather than universal, even if it is to be found everywhere.

Different musical styles have at their bases different senses of order, different rationalities, so to speak. My Western colleagues shared my confusion about the direction and nature of the Indian *raga*, and the Indians, not surprisingly, found the Western talks stiff, static, uncreative, and not very interesting. A famous Indian musician, Pandit Nikhil Banerjee, was once taken to a Mistoslav Rostrapovich concert, his first exposure to Western music. He sat in silence, aghast. Afterwards, he complained, "He played out of tune the whole time, he never developed any themes, and it sounded as if someone else had written the music for him."[7]

What counts as rationality depends on what one expects. In the Western industrialized world, we too often emphasize logic and rigor at the cost of creativity and passion, neither of which is known for its neatness. Or we ignore development and flow in favor of (static) soundness, truth, and validity. Looking further east, we might say that we ignore *Tao* in favor of *Logos*, insist on one kind of order while abandoning another, more natural order. As we know from visiting one another's desks and offices, one person's order is another's chaos. One people's rationality is to another lack of imagination, even a refusal to see what is right in front of their eyes. It is one thing to define an extremely "thin" nonnormative and arguably universal conception of rationality, such as the ability to manipulate symbols or the choice of the most efficient means to a specific end or the inference to the best explanation. It is something quite different to specify what a well-ordered life should be, or, in a different vein, a rich and all-embracing understanding of nature. We should not by any means assume that all of these will turn out to be the same.

Western philosophy, in particular, has elevated the claims of rationality to absurd heights, manifested most embarrassingly in philosophers' conceptions of themselves. Philosophers ever since Socrates have made philosophical reflection the hallmark of rationality, even a condition for a life worth living. Needless to say, this eliminates from candidacy a great many cultures in which self-reflection and self-criticism have not been encouraged or developed. In such cultures, myth and metaphor remain far more interesting than unimaginative, literal description. The theory of knowledge is not an interesting or an intelligible set of concerns, and justification is a matter of authority or tradition and not of intellectual autonomy. Nor would such a notion of rationality apply to virtually any species of higher animal, no matter how intelligent.[8]

Philosophers often exercise great ingenuity to establish what they in fact all began by acknowledging, that rationality is the virtue best exemplified by philosophers. Ideally, rationality might dispense with the philosopher altogether and become pure thought thinking itself. Short this divine purity, the Anglo-American philosopher, merely finite as he or she may be, becomes the very measure of reason. All other putatively rational creatures, from the squid to the dolphin and the ape, from "primitive" and "developing" societies to the most sophisticated cultures of the East, not to mention the French, the Italians, and the Finns, are more or less rational insofar as they are or are not capable of doing what philosophers in the (narrowly defined) Western tradition do so well, namely, argue logically with those who differ from them. Confucius and the Buddha, not to mention Jesus, would certainly not be welcomed into such a conversation.

Once we have given up the self-reflective overlay superimposed on the good life by such philosophers as Aristotle and Socrates, who insisted absurdly that the unexamined life is not worth living, and the equally chauvinistic but angstridden emphasis on "purifying" reflection and "absolute freedom" imposed on us by Jean-Paul Sartre, it becomes quite evident that a rational (and happy) life may be readily available to those who do not display any predilection or talent for philosophy or reflection or what is narrowly considered *reasoning*. Indeed, on the other side of the coin, we should remember that Dostoevsky, Kierkegaard, Camus, and Unamuno as well as a number of iconoclastic ancient Greek and Asian philosophers insisted that rationality *means* anxiety and suffering. Nietzsche remarked (in his *Gay Science*) that reflective consciousness becomes philosophically interesting only when we realize how dispensable it is, and much of Nietzsche's philosophy is an apologia for the more instinctual and the less reflective aspects of creative life.[9] Here, again, we are faced with the question how rational, and how reflective, spirituality must be. On the one hand, we do not want to put so much emphasis on critical reflection that we strangle spontaneity and reduce spirituality to skepticism. On the other hand, we do not want to turn spirituality against science and critical thinking, celebrating mere mindlessness. Spirituality, I want to argue, must be both rational and reflective. But this is not the same as insisting that we must all become professional philosophers, many of whom manage to be both rational and reflective without exhibiting even a hint of spirituality.

But what, then, is rationality? We can make considerable headway by noting that the word "rationality" is an honorific, an endorsement, a word of praise. To say that something is rational is to give it high marks indeed. So to say of human beings that they are rational is not just a piece of descriptive anthropology. It is also a bit of self-congratulation. But to then limit the notion of rationality to *reasoning* in philosophy, to merely instrumental rationality, is to thin it down to nothing and deprive it of its rich theological, philosophical, and scientific history.[10] Rationality, whether by way of reflection or insight, has long stood in an important relationship to God, to the ultimate truth, to the way the world really is. For Plato, rational insight was akin to erotic ecstasy. Thus rationality points to what is best in us, and spirituality is very much kin to rationality. But just as we should not assume that all rationality—or should we say rationali*ties*—are the same, so, too, not all spiritualities are the same, nor do they serve the same purposes in different forms of human life.

Science, Spirituality, and Rationality

Nature, to be commanded, must be obeyed.

—Francis Bacon

In reaction to the reduction of all legitimate thought and thinking to the supposedly universal and imperial demands of reason, many recent works on spirituality and much of recent Continental philosophy has exemplified a kind of "rage against reason," a rejection of not only rationality but, many would argue, intelligibility as well.[11] The prose styles of many recent philosophers violate not only canons of courtesy but the minimal requirements of comprehensibility. The real target for much of this rage is science, the reigning paradigm of rationality. Science, accordingly, has been reduced to "just another discourse" and thus it becomes fair game for "deconstruction" without the necessity, it seems, of any sympathy for or understanding of its claims and methods.[12] In addition to the long-standing complaints about science as cold and devoid of values, it is now accused of being merely rhetorical and deceitful as well. Even the Prince of Wales has taken up a royal soapbox to urge us to get beyond science and appreciate the wonder of the universe. But how did we forget that wonder has always been motivated by the urge to knowledge, whether of God's creative genius or of the intricacy of nature?

The very idea that ignorance might be the key to life's mysteries should cause us to shudder, and not only because of all the evils that have been done in the world due to ignorance, which is emphatically *not* bliss. Ignorance is crippling as well as dangerous. It should not be allowed to pass for wisdom. There are too many people, including some of the best-known writers on spirituality, who take their indifference to and ignorance of science as a kind of virtue, as if this means that they are uncontaminated by a dangerous and distorting set of beliefs. But science isn't just a body of knowledge or a method. It begins and remains in a healthy and aggressively active skeptical mood, taking no conclusion as fixed and ultimate and, ideally, no idea as beyond investigation. Indeed, it is hard to imagine spirituality without such an attitude of openness and self-doubt.

Spirituality that demands certainty is more properly identified as something else—dogma. The new know-nothingness presents itself as a perverse reversal of Bacon's notorious declaration, "knowledge is power." Whether it is medieval resistance to the theory of evolution or the tinker-bell mindlessness of the worst excesses of New Age thinking, pride in ignorance is a false road to spirituality or any higher knowledge.

Spirituality is supported and informed by science. The more we know about the world, the more we can appreciate it. This has been the view of virtually every great scientist and of all of the best science students, from the medieval scientists who saw themselves as comprehending God's plan to modern-day physicists who delve into the world of big bang and the very origins of the universe. Some of them believe in God and subscribe to one or another of the organized religions. Others do not. But the conclusion is not, as it is often presented, that science and spirituality lie in two different realms of human experience, a position articulated most radically by Kant, but continued in milder forms by many of those who (like Kant) want to hold onto both their religious beliefs and their scientific credibility.

There are several senses in which this may be true, particularly where it is religion rather than spirituality as such that is in question. But spirituality does not occupy a separate compartment or faculty from reason, and insofar as science is the shining paradigm of rationality it must also be considered as a component of spirituality as well. To be sure, there are problems in science that are small-minded and merely pragmatic, as are most of the questions of technology. But science like philosophy, as Aristotle wrote, is born of wonder, and the love of knowledge is as basic to spirituality as it is to science.

I do not distinguish the knowledge gleaned by science from some special sort of spiritual knowledge. It may be that the timidity or grant-seeking pragmatism of scientists prevents them from investigating or taking seriously many phenomena that might well worth be investigating. It might be too that much of what is called spiritual knowledge is so ill-conceived and poorly formulated that even the most sympathetic scientists cannot get a handle on it. Then, too, it may or may not be the case that there really are phenomena that escape the auspices of science altogether. This is surely a question that itself must be approached scientifically, that is, with a modicum of intellectual skepticism and humility, an open mind, and a careful eye for evidence. Take, for instance, the ubiquitous concept of energy (Chinese *ch'i*). It would be foolish just to deny any linkage with widely investigated and well-understood scientific notions of energy, the many varieties of electromagnetic energy in particular. It would also be foolish to simply assume that what we know about energy in science is all that we need to understand spiritual energy. Some phenomena—acupuncture being an obvious and tangible example—both defy current scientific explanation and are impossible to deny. This is reason to expand our scientific inquiries, not shut them down with an ad hoc distinction between what is scientific and what is not.

One might complain that those who reject science in the name of spirituality confuse science with *scientism*, which is really a kind of imperialism, insisting that science and the scientific method are the only rational standard in *every* field of human enterprise. But to defend science as a paradigm of rationality is not necessarily to defend science as the *only* kind of rationality. There is a social rationality—now popularly designated as people skills—that is not (despite the best efforts of management science) reducible to any set of scientific principles. Most human endeavors are social practices (yes, science is one of them) that might better be classified as art than as science. (Science is science, but the practice of science is nevertheless an art.) Such disciplines as law and medicine, before the rise of scientific medicine in the twentieth century, were arts. (Physicians still take the oath prescribed by Hippocrates, over two thousand years ago.) Practices are rational, or rather, they prescribe their own canons of rationality. The canons of rationality embedded in the scientific method are nevertheless products of human practices and these practices can vary in many ways.[13]

Then, there is art, the creative life, the beautiful, and the sublime. Artistic creation and appreciation is a human social practice, but it, too, is often deemed to be something more. Indeed, aesthetic truth is sometimes taken to be a competitor of scientific truth. Nietzsche sometimes talks this way, as do many of his postmodern followers. But one need not go nearly so far in order to recognize that art too has canons of rationality (whether or not it can claim a special kind of truth). Art has often been said to represent the ultimate truths of the cosmos (as Jamie James claims of music before Beethoven), and it has also been said to express something deep inside the human psyche (as Beethoven did). Art has also been reduced to commodities for wealthy patrons or the commercial art market. I do not want to comment on these claims here, except to insist again that art and aesthetic attitudes may be essential to spirituality, as reverence, whether or not they embody any bolder metaphysical or cosmic notions.

We should further note that aesthetic attitudes are essential to science at its best. Scientific experiments and mathematical proofs are celebrated because they are elegant and even beautiful. Any conception of science that rejects such values as unscientific and thus opposes itself to spirituality is not only contrary to the view of the very best scientists, but cold, corrupt, and self-defeating. But then, any form of spirituality that rejects science (as opposed to merely rejecting scientism) is, from our naturalistic standpoint, an impoverished quest.

Rationality Perverted: Smart Selfishness

> The madman is not the man who has lost his reason. The madman is the man who has lost everything except his reason.
>
> —G. K. Chesterton, *Orthodoxy*

Science is taken as a paradigm of rationality in part because of its rigorous disinterestedness. The scientific method is designed to eliminate personal and cultural differences and perspective biases from its studies. It does not matter who did an experiment. It is designed such that it can (one hopes) be duplicated by anyone. Ethical principles and codes also aim at eliminating prejudice and favoritism (especially favoring oneself) in ethics. This effort to remove ourselves from our knowledge claims and our ethical principles is surely praiseworthy. (The misguided defense of absolute ethical principles sometimes serves a similar purpose, but, of course, the source of those absolute principles is almost always sectarian and limited to a very particular perspective.) However invaluable as an impersonal ideal, such radical objectivity is impossible.

In defense of science and objectivity, and in defense of impartiality and fairness in ethics, rationality has been described as the ability to imagine oneself as no one in particular, viewing the world or the situation "from nowhere."[14] But since, to state the obvious, we always view our world from *somewhere*, meaning not only from a perspective, but with a lifetime of personal experience, emotions, and values, there is no such rationality, no such possibility of God-like objectivity, strictly understood.[15] Nor does this impossible God's-eye perspective make sense even as an aspiration, an ideal.[16] Attempts to define spirituality this way renders it humanly impossible, thus encouraging by contrast those narcissistic forms of spirituality that are so much in evidence these days. In the face of such extreme and impossible demands, the rejection of reason, in the sense presupposed by such theories, is a natural and tempting alternative. But spirituality, I have suggested, is neither selfishness nor selflessness but rather a perspective that transcends both of these.

This brings us to a truly perverse conception of rationality, now much in favor. In opposition to the overly idealistic and suprahuman theories of reason, some contemporary philosophers and, especially, contemporary economists, have cynically appropriated the honorific "rationality" to refer, often straightforwardly (though sometimes more subtly), to self-interested behavior. This is not quite to say selfishness, but it does very little to block this interpretation and much to encourage it. In opposition to idealistic selfless views of rationality, rationality is now declared to be the ability to get what you want. This is stated, not as a mere interpretation, but as an inescapable insight into human nature. People are essentially self-interested, whether or not they are also selfish. In a world where self-interest is easily measured (by monetary units, for example) so much the better for our theories! Now we can demonstrate their truth. The real test of rationality thus emerges in competitive, non-cooperative situations, a context in which what is rational for an individual (maximizing one's own interests) may be quite at odds with what is optimal or best for everyone. It is easily demonstrated, in the usual restricted experimental conditions, that people thus prefer their own good. It is a model derived from the philosophy of Thomas Hobbes, who summarized a brutal way of life as a selfish "war of all against all."

Philosophers who hold such a thesis take great pains to demonstrate that reason demands maximizing one's desires within constraints that *ideally* might be optimal for all.[17] This "realist" (in fact cynical) version of rationality, sometimes called enlightened egoism, has the virtue of riding on a motivational theory that, these days, usually goes unchallenged. What is motivating is self-interest. Rationality, accordingly, is the pursuit of self-interest, in an enlightened way, of course. The right to pursue happiness is now translated as "everyone has the right to pursue what they want and no one has the right to deny them this (except insofar as it interferes with the equally valid pursuits of others)." Instrumental rationality has never been quite so vulgarly conceived.

Politically, this theory sometimes asserts itself as a particularly virulent form of libertarianism, embellished with a concept of inalienable rights. In philosophy (even more enthusiastically in economics and the social sciences), it gives rise to game theory, an innocent-sounding discipline coupled with a cornucopia of mathematical techniques and paradoxes that hide a hideous vision of life. To be sure, game theorists cover this vision with all sorts of disclaimers. For instance, there is no specification of *whose* goals or preferences are to be satisfied. But the unavoidable suggestion of the theory is that rationality is selfishness and selfishness is rationality, a bleak view that, luckily, most game theorists do not pursue into their everyday social lives.[18]

This use of rationality as *smart selfishness* is diametrically at odds with the older sense of the term, common to Kant and the utilitarians, in which to think rationally in ethics is precisely *not* to think in terms of one's own interests. It is also opposed to that sense of rationality that takes the ultimate good to be not the good of the individual, but the good of the whole, the community, the larger society, humanity. The good of the individual need by no means be excluded in this larger pursuit. Indeed, the good of the individual is both the result and the measure of the larger public good. The fact that "rationality" can refer to such different ends—the strategic interests of a selfish (even if enlightened) individual, the public good, and the principle that says "do not make an exception or special case of yourself"—suggests that the ends of rationality are by no means settled but remain a matter of considerable dispute.[19] The mere fact that rationality can be understood as smart selfishness throws into question just how much of an honorific the concept should remain when it can be so separated from all of our best (and by this theory, often irrational) impulses.

Spirituality as the Rationality of Emotions

> The misunderstanding of passion and reason, as if the latter existed as an entity by itself, and not rather as a state of the relations between different passions and desires; as if every passion didn't contain its quantum of reason!
>
> —Nietzsche, *Will to Power*

Among the many meanings that have been suggested for the concepts of reason and rationality, none has been more destructive than those that systematically oppose reason to emotion, that is, to oppose rationality as reasonableness to being emotional as being *un*reasonable. To be rational is to be dispassionate, "cool," unmoved by emotion. To be emotional, by contrast, is to be blind to reason. I think that this opposition between rationality and emotion needs to be reconsidered, and the priority of dispassionate (or passionless) reason deeply questioned.

With this in mind, let me suggest that we would not go wrong in thinking of rationality and thus spirituality too as *having the right emotions*, or *caring about the right sorts of things*. The right sorts of things would be other people (and animals) to start with, truth, freedom, and justice by extension. Too much of the history of logic and philosophy and too many conceptions of rationality have cut off caring from the more cold-blooded concepts, rules, reasons, norms, principles, symbols, and arguments that make up the basic vocabulary of philosophical rationality. But what if we started to think about rationality not as the philosopher's or the social scientist's special subject matter, but as a matter of cultivated, engaged *sensitivity*?

If we were to view rationality, first of all, as caring about the right things, it becomes obvious that we are no longer talking instrumentally. Rationality, as Aristotle argued, is first of all a matter of ends, not merely of means. Happiness and well-being are constituted, not just helped along, by the right emotions, by caring about the right things. Caring about the right things is an essential precondition of living a good life; it is not a mere means. Aristotle and Confucius agreed (without knowing it) that being virtuous is not just right action but caring about the right things as well. The very notion of the right things opens up all sorts of questions and dangers, but it is the *caring* part of the equation that should draw our primary attention. That points directly to the emotions as an essential part of rationality. Although how one determines what things are right may well be shot through with personal, cultural, and moral conflicts, at least we are now clearly in the realm of ethics and not in the no man's land of game theory, where preferences eclipse values and questions of strategy trump moral intuitions every time. Rationality once again becomes the quest for the good, and the good in turn can be understood in terms of our most important passions.

An emotion is not so much an element or item in experience as it is the *ordering* of experience. Love, quite the contrary of interfering with rational order in our lives, puts our priorities right. Anger, even when it is clearly inappropriate or irrational, does not so much intrude as reorders our priorities. Emotional experience is not a phenomenon in our heads, so to speak; it is the ordering structure of our being-in-the-world. This ordering structure is nothing less than rationality, and emotions might best be viewed as the transient and sometimes enduring reinforcement or re-ordering of our reasons for living. Emotions are not just means or instruments. They concern the ends, the well-earned sense of flourishing that Aristotle called *eudaimonia* (happiness), with all of its rich component passions of pride, affection, and friendship, in short, the meanings of life.

I thus reject the now-prevalent idea that rational criteria are simply the presuppositions of emotion, for example, the idea that fear presupposes the belief that one is in danger but that belief is not itself part of the emotion. I also want to reject the idea that rational criteria are the *external* standards by which emotions and their appropriateness may be judged. That would imply the independent existence of a rational framework *within which* the emotions may be appropriate or inappropriate, warranted or unwarranted, wise or foolish. I suggest instead that emotions constitute the framework (or frameworks) of rationality itself.

Of course, a single emotion does not do this. It fits (or does not fit) into the framework. But together our emotions dictate the context, the character, the culture in which some values take priority, serve as ultimate ends, provide the criteria for rationality and reasonable behavior. Our sense of justice, for example, as well as the grand theories that are constructed as expressions of that sense of justice, does not consist of a single emotion, but rather the systematic totality of our emotions. These are appropriate to our culture and our character, which determine not only particular emotions (for example, hope or resentment), but the standards and expectations according to which those emotions are provoked. But this in turn presupposes a holistic conception in which the whole field of one's experience (or one's culture's) is defined and framed by his or her engagements and attachments, in which truly dispassionate judgment is more often pathological than rational, and detachment more likely signals alienation than objectivity.[20] The conceptual frameworks that philosophers refer to are themselves the product of our emotions and what we really care about. What is rational is what fits best into our emotional world.

Martin Heidegger's punsical conception of mood (*stimmung*) as our mode of "being tuned" (*bestimmen*) to the world is instructive here, both because of its welcome shift in emphasis from detached knowing to holistic personal caring (*Sorge*) and because he emphasizes moods—that are general, diffuse, and devoid of any determinate object—rather than emotion as such.[21] Spirituality, although I have analyzed it in terms of a triad of emotions, might also be analyzed as a matter of mood, that is, the emotions of erotic love, reverence, and trust but without their specific objects, that is, what they are about. But when I say that the objects of love, reverence, and trust are ultimately the world or life as such, the notion of an object, and consequently the distinction between emotions and moods, is rendered rather meaningless. Both moods and emotions thoroughly permeate our experience and are not, as several honorable ancient views would have it, interruptions, intrusions, or brief bouts of madness that get in the way of the otherwise calm and cool transparency of rational objectivity. Indeed, even the distinction between the emotion and the world disappears. The philosopher Wittgenstein (who was often depressed) commented that the depressed man lives in a depressed world. But we might similarly say that the spiritual person, the person who lives with love, reverence, and trust, lives in a spiritual world. As I argued earlier, there is a nonobjectionable sense in which thinking makes it so.

The spiritual life is sometimes defined as a life without the distractions of affections and agitations, a life with minimal commitments and attachments, the supposedly rational approach to a life without loss suggested by a great many ascetics and religious thinkers.[22] Such "eviscerated" lives are the targets of Nietzsche's renowned attack on asceticism in Part III of his *Genealogy of Morals*, in which he claims that ascetics (like everyone) seek power and self-assertion but obtain it, as it were, on the sly, by stealth and self-denial.[23] But Nietzsche's attack is not aimed at self-denial as such, nor is it directed at the hypocrisy that often accompanies it. What he so vehemently rejects is the very idea, much more the ideal, of a life without passion. Of course, caring sometimes requires self-denial, and sometimes the denial of emotions, but it is because one cares. Self-denial is not celebrated for its own sake. It is the caring that dominates, caring that defines the values, caring that defines both rationality and spirituality. Quite the contrary of a life free of affections, agitations, commitments, and attachments, the spiritual life is defined by the most passionate caring, and this is what *defines* its rationality.

What one cares about is defined by one's conception of the world, but one's conception of the world is itself defined by the scope and objects of one's emotional cares and concern. Cultivation, or civilization, is the internalization of the larger concepts of history, humanity, and religion, conceptions of morality and ethics that go beyond personal and provincial self-interests. This is not to say that the emotional nature of these concerns is replaced by something more abstract and impersonal; the emotions themselves become more expansive. Thus rationality is not the defining structure of human experience, and emotions are not just reactions. Rationality is the product not only of thought but of caring, and although the emotions undoubtedly have an evolutionary history that precedes the arrival of the human species by hundreds of millions of years, they evolved not only along with but inseparably from the evolution of reason and rationality.[24]

Emotions and rationality together constitute spirituality and make us capable of an awareness of a larger human and global context in which all of our fates are engaged and our mutual interests are involved. There is nothing particularly human about emotion as such (a dog can be angry or sad), but there are distinctively human emotions. Indeed, some of the peculiarly human emotions, notably romantic love, moral indignation, a keen sense of justice, religious passion, scientific curiosity, and those passions that constitute spirituality are precisely those that are typically designated as proof of our species' rationality.

5

FACING UP TO TRAGEDY

My formula for greatness in a human being is *amor fati*: that one wants nothing to be different, not forward, not backward, not in all eternity. Not merely to bear what is necessary, still less conceal it . . . but *love* it.

—Friedrich Nietzsche, *Ecce Homo*

I opened my heart to the benign indifference of the universe.

—Albert Camus, *The Stranger*

Sooner or later, life makes philosophers of us all.

—Maurice Riseling

The phrase "being philosophical" is commonly used to refer to our ability to cope with misfortune through thought. But it is painfully evident that such coping is usually successful only with the small tragedies in life—a missed promotion, a rained-out ballgame, an unsuccessful dinner date. In fact, one hesitates to call these "tragedies" at all, but rather, disappointments or life's little frustrations, no matter how painful they might seem at the time. The simple truth is, we get over them. We learn from them. But when real misfortune strikes, philosophy is notoriously inept. For instance, there is an enormous amount of philosophical literature about the Holocaust, a modern horror and an overwhelming example of tragedy and evil. But as an illustration of human evil the Holocaust tends to provoke diagnostics, blame, and species self-scrutiny rather than, say, that blameless, awesome silence that follows a natural disaster (an earthquake, a tornado, the sudden onslaught of an epidemic).

If we separate evil, that is, extreme and intented suffering inflicted by human (or divine) agents, and therefore eliminate blame and self-scrutiny, what

74

can philosophy say? How should we cope? Why do horrible things happen to good people? How should we think about tragedy? How should we cope with disease and debilitating "accidents"? What can we philosophers say, beyond the usual platitudes and condolences, to someone who has lost a loved one, or an arm, or the ability to see? How should we ourselves live, and what should we think, when one or another of the ultimately inevitable tragedies happens to us?[1] We have all met or read about those rare sages who have suffered the most profound misfortunes and retained a sense of acceptance, graciousness, humor, and even joy in their lives. Can philosophy help us to do the same?

We might want to distinguish between tragedy and misfortune (or tragedies, a diminutive but widely used way of referring to lesser disappointments and frustrations). Indeed, the whole thrust of modern life has been to redefine tragedy so that it is not necessarily something grandiose, as in the tragedy of Oedipus or the tragedy of King Lear, but something that can happen to anyone in the most ordinary life. (Consider, for instance, the tragedies created by Eugene O'Neill and Arthur Miller.) We have rebelled against the aristocratic theatrical tradition and insist that the suffering and misfortune of a princess or a Princeton graduate is no more (and no less) significant than the suffering and misfortune of a salesman or a barfly. It remains to be seen whether this leveling of tragedy results in greater sensitivity or rather the trivializing of a profound philosophical notion. But looking back at the extravagant outpouring of grief following the deaths of Princess Diana and John Kennedy Jr., it is by no means obvious that people today really accept that all suffering is equal in significance.

Nevertheless, the philosophical point can be made in an egalitarian way. Although what counts as suffering may vary enormously from case to case, from individual to individual, suffering as such is an inescapable part of every life. But as tragedy, suffering has *meaning*. What gives meaning to suffering is what it is philosophy's job to investigate. If philosophy can help us cope with tragedy, it is by giving meaning to our suffering. Spirituality may provide us with an inspiring perspective when our lives are going well, but it is nothing if cannot also find meaning in life that has gone very wrong.

The Tragic Sense of Life

The Spanish philosopher Miguel de Unamuno wrote his classic *The Tragic Sense of Life* just before the first World War.[2] Today, unfortunately, the book and its subject have dropped out of view. Virtually no serious philosophy student ever reads *The Tragic Sense* or has much sympathy for its tragic sensibility. Promoters of spirituality would find it much too dark and joyless. It addresses the poignant questions about death, suffering, and undeserved misfortune, so central to virtually all of the world's religions. Unamuno's own vision was ultimately religious, but in the despairing tones of Dostoevsky, not the "glad tidings for the melancholy" of Kierkegaard. The brute fact of human life is that there is suffering which has no resolution and evil which has no redemption.[3] *So says our reason.*

An early existentialist, Unamuno held a kind of irrationalist line, arguing against any scientific or objective solution to the philosophical problems of suffering and evil. Reason, he argued, can only lead us to skepticism, leaving life devoid of meaning. Unamuno insisted that reason has to be combated by faith and spirituality. But faith and spirituality, although they provide an alternative to reason and despair, never emerge from the shadow of reason. So neither can faith and spirituality escape from skepticism. In that sense, we are incapable of being nonrational.

Unamuno follows Kierkegaard and encourages a leap of faith, beyond reason, beyond objectivity. But wholehearted passionate commitment is always compromised by our rationality. We cannot ignore or deny the facts of unresolved suffering and unredeemed evil, and we cannot ultimately see beyond them. Unamuno sometimes insists that facing up to this "hopelessness" is itself the meaning of human life. (Camus would later insist that the meaning of life was facing up to the "Absurd.") What gives life meaning is a form of rebellion, rebellion against reason, an insistence on believing passionately what we cannot believe rationally. The meaning of life is to be found in passion—romantic passion, religious passion, passion for work and for play, passionate commitments in the face of what reason knows to be meaningless. Philosophy, because it is on the side of reason, is by contrast a kind of resignation coupled with playful distraction and self-deception, the very opposite of spirituality.[4]

The view that I want to suggest here echoes Unamuno's vision, but without buying into his opposition between reason/philosophy and faith/spirituality. I would also like to abandon the morbid associations and the mock-heroic stance associated with this forced opposition.[5] What I agree with is Unamuno's strong existentialist line on personal responsibility and the importance of personal commitment. Whether or not life has a meaning—whatever that is taken to mean—we *make* meaning by way of our commitments. Thus the early Stoics suggested that we could avoid tragedy by refusing to make such commitments. I would argue that the opposite is the case: It is in the context of such made meanings that suffering and evil can be shifted from the center stage of human existence to wait in the wings (from which they will inevitably appear, without direction and oblivious to the plot of the play). It is by making meanings in life that we free ourselves from the meaninglessness of suffering.

If the meanings of life are the meanings we make, we recognize a fatal contingency to our passions and our projects. There is nothing necessary about them. Indeed, there is nothing necessary about us. There is no reason for our suffering and no redemption for the evils that befall us. As Camus and Unamuno both argue, our commitments are thus ultimately limited, there is no ultimate answer to the question *Why?*, and it all ends in death ("the brotherhood of man," according to both authors). As Unamuno argued, reason can prove to be the enemy of our commitments and meanings, especially through *cynicism*. Unamuno finds himself torn between paroxysms of despair and cosmic *chutzpah*. We demand either immortality or identity with God. ("Either all or nothing!"[6]) In his more reasonable pronouncements, Unamuno simply encourages religion, in his own case, a return to the Catholic church. But tragedy, whatever we do and however we "leap," is real and undeniable. Camus, like Unamuno, turns this obvious fact into a heroic stance. He calls it "keeping the Absurd alive" and "rebellion." Sisyphus shakes his fist with scorn and defiance at the gods who condemned him, and thus simultaneously affirms and denies his absurd situation.

There is something both beautiful and pathetic in this quasi-rational, emphatically existential attitude. It is so poignantly human, so pointless, and at the same time unflinching, shaking that puny fist at God or the gods. Of course, such behavior makes no conceivable difference to anything, except in our own attitudes. (Both Unamuno and Camus fail to advocate much by way of social activism in their rebellion.) Our rational, more reasonable philosophical minds want to resist such "absurd" postures. All too often, philosophers simply insist that life is meaningful, without argument, if only because the over-reaching philosophical question (about the meaning of life) is itself meaningless. Life is meaningful, in other words, by default, by not taking seriously the question. But what is beautiful and revealing about Unamuno and Camus (and Jean-Paul Sartre, too) is precisely their refusal to either dismiss the question or despair at the answer. They provoke an irresolvable tension, not the mistaken one between reason and passion, but between our passionate commitments and our awareness that, nevertheless, our lives are ultimately not in our hands.

It is in this unflinching recognition of an essential tension in our lives that spirituality is to be found. It requires the denial of neither passionate commitment nor a certain fatalism, but it nevertheless manages to finesse the opposition. Suffering and death are real. The ultimate frustration of our projects is inevitable. Love entails not only the possibility but, certain romantic illusions aside, the inevitability of loss. We try to hold together our love of life and our dread of what is to come in an uncomfortable philosophical consciousness. Unamuno is right. Our passion can never escape or eclipse our reason, but not for the reason he supposes. There is no passion without rationality. Camus is right as well. There is no viable alternative to this absurd confrontation between our rational, demanding minds and the indifferent universe (however that distinction between mind and universe is to be made). But confrontations can be turned into acceptance, even embracing the opposition. Camus's stranger, Meursault, discovers joyfulness in his final hours before his execution. There is no denying suffering, but suffering can be endowed with meaning. What meaning? Well, suffering has meaning, in short, because life has meaning, and suffering is just part of life.

How is tragedy meaningful? Without going as far as Unamuno and Camus do, we can clear away a certain philosophical presumption. In real life, both justice and rationality have their limits. In the abstract, we may insist that virtue deserves its rewards, vice its punishments, and arrogance its comeuppance. But in actuality we know that life is not fair. We know that misfortunes befall the innocent and the virtuous, that children are killed in natural disasters, that people die before their time, sometimes on the very brink of an elusive success. We also know that villains flourish and sometimes get away with murder. To be sure, we may feel a slightly guilty satisfaction when evil-doing actually gets its due and selfless delight when goodness is miraculously rewarded, but we do not pretend that thus it is always or that life is just and fair after all. Only in philosophy and theology do we dare to argue—or simply presume—that there is an explanation, a rational account, of all that happens. And only in philosophy and theology do we hide behind the demand that there *should* be such a rational accounting. In life, we know that bad things just happen. In this sense, at least, adopting the tragic sense of life is nothing less than accepting reality. Spirituality, whatever else it may be, begins with that acceptance.

Denying Tragedy: The Temptation to Blame

"Shit Happens," says one of the more perpetual and popular T-shirt and bumper slogans among the high school and junior college crowd. Apart from the vulgarity, it is shocking because it is so obviously, undeniably, unavoidably true. Nevertheless, the insight collapses when the shit actually happens. Tragedy gets denied—even by those who have (regarding themselves) a very weak or even negligible notion of personal responsibility—by looking for someone to *blame*. Tragedy does not just happen, in other words. It is brought about, it is the product of *agency*, and someone, or something, must be held accountable.

The denial of tragedy begins in a seemingly innocent philosophical thesis: *Whatever happens, happens for a reason*. Harking back to Aristotle, that notion of reason (or cause) is ultimately to be understood in terms of intentions, purposes, teleology (from *telos*, or purpose). Most immediately, we look for *someone*, someone responsible or, as the case may be, irresponsible: the driver, the manufacturer, the doctor or hospital, the parents. Or, a bit less directly, we blame the institution, the constitution, the country, the culture. We personify nature, thus creating someone who can be held responsible.

(The Chinese still refer to earthquakes as the "anger of the earth." Second-rate evolutionists and compromising creationists still talk about natural selection as if it were a purposive and intelligent process.) And, of course, we personify machines—kicking our cars, slapping our computers. In desperation, we blame "the system." But if no one more tangible comes forward as a plausible candidate, there is always God.

Natural disasters are revealingly referred to as "acts of God." Even people who never think of thanking and giving credit to God for their accomplishments seem to have no hesitation blaming Him for their misfortunes. "It's God's Will" is an all-purpose summary of a philosophy and an attitude that refuses to accept tragedy and insists on rationalization instead. Even without such divine appeal, we look for the good, the *reason*, in everything. Here, we might say, it is reason that is irrational. We edit our narratives to suit our sense of the way things ought to be. And where we cannot find a purpose, we invent our own. Losses are a "learning experience" and a death in the family "teaches us all a lesson."

Conspiracy theorists, working on the darker side of reasoning, will always insist on a culprit, some secretive cabal, communism, the defense department, the Mafia, international bankers, the Jews, the Arabs, international capitalism, the male patriarchy, the CIA, or the all-time favorite, alien visitors from outer space. There is no such thing as "circumstantial," in this view. The blame might fall on whoever is a ready target for suspicion or criticism and might just have a motive, if not the wherewithal, to carry it off. One might say that conspiracy theorists are people with overactive imaginations but limited critical abilities. Everything that happens, they too believe, happens for a reason. It just happens to be a malevolent reason, something to inspire not our gratitude or our worship but our fear, loathing, and hatred. Nevertheless, the logic is the same.

According to "strict liability," blame and responsibility seem to part company. One may be held liable even in the absence of guilt of any kind. The default position is that there can be no literal accidents, that is, events without a cause, an agent and a purpose, without someone to blame. The practical dimension of this position in America involves, by some estimates, $300 billion dollars a year.[7] It is the continuing tort-liability crisis, which is, in a philosophical nutshell, our insistence on blaming others for our misfortunes, sometimes quite apart from any reasonable notion of fault, and claiming compensation ("justice") in return. What gets lost, in addition to billions of dollars and millions of hours of court time and anxiety, is any sense of the tragic life. A loss is never just a loss. It quickly becomes a lawsuit. "Somebody is going to pay for this!"

The tort-liability problem discloses another ugly aspect of the denial of tragedy, one firmly tied to the insistence on blame—blaming others, that is. It is the phenomenon of *entitlement*. There is an irony, here, not to mention some sort of radical inconsistency. We readily blame others for our misfortunes, but we just as readily deny responsibility ourselves, both for our own misfortunes and those which we wreak on others, directly or indirectly. When we suffer, our sufferings are not our fault, and so we deserve compensation. When it appears that *we* are to blame, there are always mitigating circumstances, excuses to be made, and somebody else who is *really* responsible.

The underlying assumption is that we are entitled to a good life, a happy, healthy, comfortable life. (Even the Declaration of Independence claims only that we are entitled to the *pursuit* of happiness.) If we fail to find that happiness, then someone must be to blame. In the case of an accident or (these days) even an illness, there must be someone or some organization that can be shown to have deprived us of the good life we deserve, and he, she, or it *owes* us. The logic of such demands is apparent in the key terms, desert, entitlement, compensation, and debt. This may be the language of justice, but it is not the language of tragedy.

In the big picture, none of us is entitled to anything, much less happiness. That is not to say, which is very different, that happiness is not worth having and promoting. But it is to say that the language of justice loses its place in the larger questions of tragedy, and tragedy, not justice, is the ultimate upshot of life.

Yet, the idea of compensation dies hard with us, even in—especially in— the horrible circumstances of tragedy. A person crippled in an automobile accident naturally sues the other driver, even if it was, literally, an accident. (No one was drunk, reckless or unusually inattentive.) As a bit of social engineering—a device for making sure that the seriously incapacitated have some means of financial support—the goal is unassailable even if the mechanism is inefficient. But that is not what is going on here. The idea that one might be just plain unlucky does not sit well with us. Although we would rather be unlucky than responsible for our own misfortunes, we would still much rather blame someone else. And if they, too, were just unlucky? Well, then they can damn well pay for it. If "they" happen to be a corporation or professional who has been lucky enough to make a profit on the product or practice involved, then so much the better. In Plato's parlance, every citizen deserves his or her due, or at least, his or her day in court.

Some things are within our control, and this is the proper sphere of justice. We live with other people in a society such that they can be held responsible for what they do. Within that social context, we are right to be offended, angered, resentful, and even punitive when they cheat us. But we also live in and are sometimes confronted by an indifferent universe. This is a very different context. We say that nature cheats us, but we realize that we have moved to the land of metaphor. Nature doesn't cheat. There is no one to blame. Even the most pious recognize that some acts of God are not acts of God. At worst,

they are omissions of God, still blameworthy or theologically perplexing, perhaps, but not direct harms for which reasons are expected or an explanation
forthcoming. It is therefore not clear who could be to blame or to what we
may be entitled.

Tragedy is real and by its very nature cannot be explained. Spirituality, accordingly, involves finding or giving meaning to that which cannot be explained or justified. Nevertheless, we balk at this suggestion and insist on
explanations, and if not justifications then someone to blame. But here our
cherished rationality shows one of its more embarrassing aspects: our ability
and readiness to *rationalize*. As Nietzsche said, a universe that is explained
even with bad reasons is better than no explanation at all. But in the face of
tragedy, even the most ambitious explanations turn out to be no more than
denial, a refusal to accept the hard facts of life.

The Problem of Evil

This brings us to one of the most celebrated of philosophy's problems. Six-
teen hundred years ago, the philosopher Saint Augustine worried extensively
about what has since been codified as the "Problem of Evil." I want to consider that "problem" as itself a problem, reflecting our extravagant expectations and demands of the world, and of God, and of our need to explain our
suffering, no matter what the cost. The problem is often interpreted as the
ultimate test of faith, and as such, a serious aspect of spirituality. In fact, the
Problem of Evil turns out to be one more manifestation of our tendency to
blame and our unwarranted sense of entitlement, the very antithesis of that
spiritual sense that foregoes both blame and entitlement.

Belief in God is not a necessary condition for the problem of evil. In the
neat form that I will present below, it may be a problem that turns on the
standard conception of God's personality, power, and goodness. But there is a
"gut reaction" to misfortune and suffering that needs no God to fuel the anguish that expresses itself so logically in theological terms. It is the naturalistic
version of the problem of evil. It is that *Why me?* reaction, when the misfortune is our own and seemingly undeserved. Or simply *Why?* when it is someone else's tragedy, also undeserved. Our tendency to personify the universe
and expect some sense of fair play may be childish, but it also lies deep within
our moral conception of the world whether we believe in God (or anything
like God) or not.

Since ancient times, it has been obvious that bad things happen to good
people. Since ancient times, this has been a source of concern and consterna-
tion, a conundrum and an excuse for extravagant philosophizing, theologiz-
ing and rationalizing. More annoying, perhaps, but no less metaphysically

demanding, is the equally obvious fact that good things happen to bad people, that those who cause harm do not always get their due. In response to this troubling pair of facts, many Heavens and Hells have been discovered or invented, most (but not all) of them dedicated to the proposition that, in the end, there will be justice and so the problem of evil is no longer a problem.

"Life is suffering," teaches the Buddha, the first of his Noble Truths. But where the Buddhists swear off the cravings and expectations that result in suffering, we insist on satisfying them and, when they are frustrated, we ask *Why?* But if life isn't suffering, then suffering requires some external explanation. In the Judeo-Christian tradition, the explanation is the omnipresence of an all-knowing, all-powerful God. But this explanation quickly becomes a paradox: If bad things happen to good people, then it must be because (1) either God doesn't know about it—but he is all-knowing, or (2) God cannot do anything about it—but he is all powerful, or (3) God doesn't care about it—but the premise of the entire argument, the very conception of God, in fact, is such that it is his caring—and ultimately perhaps only his caring—that counts.

There have been many attempts to get around the paradox of an all-powerful, all-knowing, good God who allows evil in His domain. The most prominent of these in Christianity and Islam (though a lesser theme in Judaism) is the dual promise and threat of Heaven and Hell. Despite earthly appearances, there *will be* compensation, reward, and punishment, justice overflowing both in the eternal bliss of the saved and the unending suffering of the damned. This conversion of human tragedy into divine justice takes many forms, both crude and refined, from the crude reward-punishment model of the most offensive television preachers to the sophisticated "moral order of the world" views of Rousseau and Kant. But I do not want to enter into the theological labyrinth to sort them out.

My general attitude, which I am willing to leave undefended here, is that such a belief is understandable. Belief in the afterlife, whether otherworldly Christian or Islamic Heaven or this-worldly reincarnation, ghosts, and joining the ancestors is one of the sweetest and most easily understandable beliefs that people have, and even the most skeptical philosophers ought to respect that. But not all versions of this belief are sweet. Their use as cudgels for thrashing nonbelievers or as excuses to send mere boys to meaningless deaths as "martyrs," for instance, is unspeakable. Less offensive but still problematic is their use as balm for the distraught. Saying "it's God's will" to a bereaved parent, who has suitable religious beliefs, should evoke only sympathy, not philosophical disputation. But what serves as balm does not succeed as a cure, and beyond its role as therapy and from the point of view of *this* life, eternal bliss is no compensation for a life cut short by tragedy. It is not the belief in the afterlife that gets called into question but (as Kant and many other believers have insisted) the appropriateness of any such notion of *compensation*. God does not play tit for tat (nor dice) with His universe.

One of the more ingenious attempts to solve the problem of evil is to weaken the conception of God, suggesting, for instance, that faith only requires one to believe that God is very powerful, not that He is all-powerful, or that it is sufficient that God has vastly superior knowledge rather than, what may be logically impossible, total knowledge.[8] Among the less ingenious attempts is the explanation that we cannot expect to understand God's mysterious ways. Thus the fact that He allows suffering and death in human life need not contradict the idea that he cares, and comparisons with ordinary human sentiments and expectations are beside the point. It has been famously suggested that this creation of his is the "best of all possible worlds" and there is no more evil and suffering than necessary—in some sense that we cannot possibly comprehend. It has even been suggested—in tune with the frantic pace of modern-day business life—that God is, in effect, too busy to look after all of the ills of the world.[9] Then there is the deep green response that we are deceiving ourselves if we think that it is *us* whom God cares about exclusively, whether that "us" refers to a single chosen people or to humanity as a whole.[10]

I have a good deal of sympathy for some of those views, particularly the ecological *Gaia* view, which reaches its most sublime expression in Taoism. But the slip from ecological respect and responsibility to the dismissal of humans as insignificant too readily leads to a rabid anti-humanism in which the interests and needs of mere humans can simply be discounted, or be viewed as counting no more than the interests and needs of mosquitoes. Whether or not such views account for the existence of human suffering in the world (by saying, in effect, it doesn't really matter), they are also views that share all of the potential for viciousness of the Inquisition and damnation crowd. The problem of evil cannot be solved by denying the significance of evil and human suffering.

Contrary to the way it is usually framed, I want to suggest that the Problem of Evil has little to do with belief in the existence of God or in an afterlife. Camus was an atheist, and yet it was the problem of evil, the presence of human suffering, that violated his innate sense of justice and fairness, that evoked his dramatic conception of the "Absurd." Nietzsche was also an atheist ("by instinct," he tells us in *Ecce Homo*), but it is neither God nor Heaven as such that draws his heaviest fire. It is rather the cheap and petty use of theology to deny or rationalize suffering rather than face up to it, like the ancient Greeks he adored.

To challenge the Problem of Evil, we need not call into question either the nature and existence of God or the belief in an afterlife. To challenge the Problem of Evil we must rather remind ourselves of the contingency of our good fortune and how unreasonable we are to deny the inevitability of misfortune and the finitude of our lives. As Bernard Williams writes, "There is a problem of evil only for those who expect the world to be good."[11] We thus call into question those abuses of God and the idea of an afterlife that block our deepest emotional responses by assuring us, against all evidence, that our suffering is well worthwhile.

Blaming the Victims

When a man does not do what he ought, God the Creator is not at fault.

—Saint Augustine

The most powerful responses to the Problem of Evil, even within theology, have come to focus not on the nature of God and his ways or on our own insignificance but, to the contrary, on our own very significant role in the creation of evil and suffering in the world. Disaster happens because *we* are evil, or selfish, or irresponsible. A catastrophe, accordingly, is a *punishment*, not a mere accident. It is an Act of God in the most literal, purposeful sense of the term. According to Augustine, it is our own free will that is the cause and the explanation of evil; God is not to blame. The theological and philosophical tangles that follow, such as whether God is nevertheless responsible for letting us do the wrong he necessarily knew we would do need not concern us here. Such debates only point once again to our tendency to blame God, even if indirectly, rather than face up to suffering "without appeal." What is usually ignored in the invocation of such blame is that it is antithetical to spirituality, because it is the very opposite of acceptance and forgiveness (not to mention love, trust, and reverence).

What makes the assignment of blame so appealing these days is the fact that comparatively few of our disasters and tragedies are natural catastrophes or acts of God. When a statistician wants to indicate how rarely a certain event occurs, he or she compares it with being hit by lightning or dying of a bee sting. Natural disasters are increasingly rare, compared to our own man-made disasters. These are clearly or at least arguably the result of our own doing, our own tinkering with nature, our own manufacturing and experimentation with dangerous machinery and complex biological processes, our love of speed and the internal combustion engine, our love of comfort and convenience despite the terrible though not immediately obvious costs. Earthquakes and hurricanes still occur, but buildings are made to withstand them. When people die in an earthquake, the blame is usually put on the developers, the builders, even the residents themselves. Most people today who are killed in avalanches, rock slides, and blizzards are not innocent, unsuspecting victims, but daredevils, adventurers, sportsmen who have gone out seeking the thrill of danger.

One might hesitate to call the resulting tragedies kin to the Problem of Evil, but, nevertheless, Augustine's free will solution to the traditional problem surely applies in a convincing way today.

The conception of suffering as punishment is not limited, of course, to man-made disasters. In 1755, the philosophers of the European Enlightenment struggled with a particularly gruesome and paradoxical act of God, an earthquake in Lisbon, Portugal that killed thousands of worshippers, many of them women and children, in their churches on a Sunday morning. This calamitous loss of innocent lives was a particularly poignant reminder of the difficulty of the problem of evil, and no amount of self-blame seemed sufficient to explain much less justify this terrible natural disaster. It might be worth noting that a similar disaster, the great Tenmei fire, devastated Kyoto in 1788, with many more dead. But the Japanese, who had no commitment to an omniscient, omnipotent, and gentle God but a well-established belief in fate, responded very differently. In brief, they simply rebuilt the city—as they had done several times before—with remarkable assurance and efficiency.

The free will account of evil seems to leave out an essential distinction that only those obsessed with human depravity would ignore. There are evils that are indeed our own doing, that we bring about directly or indirectly. But there are also evils that do not seem attributable, no matter how remotely, to our acts or intentions. It seems, without question, that they cannot be construed as punishments. But our metaphysics and our social practices continue to do just that. Blaming the victim is not just an element of perversity in our current legal system and our culture. It is a long-standing and still popular metaphysical and theological doctrine.

Much of Hebrew history and so-called Jewish guilt is based on the doctrine that misfortunes are one's own fault. Suffering, accordingly, is punishment. It therefore has a meaning. The theme is familiar: better to blame oneself than to acknowledge that suffering may be meaningless. The troublesome fact that God's punishments seem to be visited not only on the guilty but on the innocent as well must then be explained by the idea—common to many cultures, including the tribes of the Old Testament—that justice is done not just to the individual but to the family, the tribe, the whole society. Whole cities are destroyed by God, although simple demographics would suggest that among the inhabitants of both Sodom and Gomorrah were innocent infants and children who had not yet indulged in the sins of their elders. The idea that only the *individual* is punished for misdeeds is still an oddity in the world, no matter how precious a principle it may be to us. The brutal fact of the matter is that even in our society innocents often pay for their parents', or their neighbors', or their political leaders' crimes.[12]

Even the Old Testament is by no means secure with this radical answer to the problem. Consider the most troubling tale of unwarranted suffering in the Judeo-Christian tradition, the problem—the "test" of Job. Job's God is not so much mysterious as malicious. In any case, He is clearly unjust by any reasonable standard, human or divine. Job was entirely innocent. Indeed, that innocence is the premise of the story, without which there would be no problem, no dilemma, no test of faith. To cause a good man to suffer to prove a point or test his patience is not, in any civilized sense, an act of justice. It doesn't matter that all is restored to him at the end of the story. Compensation is not all there is to justice. The pain of losing one's family is not compensated by the joy of finding them whole again, much less by the substitution of a new family. The suffering of protracted illness and infirmity is not and cannot be compensated by being made well again. But what really raises the problem of evil is not so much the question of God's will or the adequacy of compensation, but Job's own reaction to his suffering. Millions of pages have been written on the "patience" of Job, and how (or whether) he passed the test of faith. But even a casual look at Job's story shows a character who was anything but patient or undoubting. Job was indignant. He was resentful. He did not accept his suffering and did not think of it as justice.[13] He knew that he was blameless, and we know it too.

What Augustine had in mind was that we take responsibility for our own flaws and failures. There is nothing in this good existentialist position that depends upon a belief in an all-powerful God. It is undeniable that we ourselves cause a good deal of human suffering, if only by our extravagant lifestyles and expectations. To tell the truth, in our misfortunes, we often discern a much-deserved comeuppance or delayed retaliation for suffering inflicted on others. The South Asian notion of karma, whatever further metaphysical baggage it may be called upon to carry, is also the recognition that what we suffer in life is in part the residue of our previous actions. Indeed, such rough justice provides the theme of some of the best-loved stories in every society.

We also recognize rough justice in the suffering of whole societies, notably in the aftermath of war. Sartre summarized this harsh vision of extended responsibility without compromise when, at the height of the Second World War and during the Nazi occupation of Paris, he declared that "we all get the war we deserve." One does not need the notion of original sin to understand this idea. It is enough to believe that we are never simply passive observers as life parades before and around us. We are part of it and it is our own responsibility.

But self-blame has its limits. An awful example of our excessive tendency to blame ourselves is the way in which we often regard illness. Instead of viewing disease and bodily malfunction as something natural and, for all of us, inevitable, we tend to tie illness to blame. At least, we do this with respect to other people's illness. When they get sick, we blame them for not taking better care of themselves. Or we blame them for their attitude, their lifestyle, their diet. This is especially true with the most terrifying of all diseases, cancer. In her most personal and perhaps most profound book, *Illness as Metaphor*, Susan Sontag rightly complains about our medieval tendency to interpret all illness as a sign, a punishment, a payback. We refuse to believe, except in our own cases, that people just get sick.

Some tragedies are the result of shortsightedness, sloppiness, or other forms of negligence, but others are not. They occur despite all reasonable precautions, care, and good intentions. We know that a vaccine that will prevent a horrible disease in millions will predictably have some terrible effect on a very few, but we cannot detect who these few will be beforehand. Such calamities are tragic in the classical sense; there is no sufficient reason, no rational and just explanation for them, and no one is to blame. Instead of brutally blaming ourselves, why can't we just leave the matter there?

The Meaning of Tragedy

A few years ago, the mother of a boy who had lost his two best friends in a tragic accident tried to help her son discern some meaning in it all. She wrote up her agony in a popular news magazine, and concluded, "I don't think that tragedies happen on purpose, but, and I echo his [her son's] words, if people learn to value one another more and to appreciate how precious life is, then perhaps some good can come from something so awful." Wise and modest words, and she finished by adding, "In the end, the musings of a nine-year-old boy, struggling to find a reason, are the musings of us all."[14] Those who would give an "answer" to tragedy, or reduce it to blame, lack this wisdom.

There is an answer in such thoughts that does justice to life and justice to tragedy together. It does not deny suffering but does not wallow in it either. One might well say, life is not fair. To that extent, the tragic sense of life is no more than the simple recognition of the obvious. But this is not to say that life is meaningless, nor is it to justify our dwelling on the tragedies of life to the exclusion of its blessings and benefits. Nietzsche quite rightly combined his own keen sense of the tragic life with an unconfined joy (although he is not always convincing) and Unamuno, in his own life, did much the same. We too often opt for victimization or cynicism, the products of our overactive faculty for blame and our extravagant sense of entitlement. Or we take refuge in pessimism. (If we expect the worst, what worse can happen?) But there are better ways to think about life.

Gratitude is one of them. A good sense of humor is another. Spirituality at its best is a combination of gratitude and humor, a dash of that mock-heroic Camusian confrontation with the Absurd, and a passionate engagement with the details and the people in our lives. The important thing is not to deny tragedy, but to embrace it as an essential part of the life we love and for which we should be so grateful. I am not insisting on foolish Pollyannaism here. It is a tragedy of a very different kind that many people lead lives that are so impoverished, oppressed, and full of suffering that no one could possibly expect them to be either grateful or amused. But the always-surprising thing is, many of these people still do. Adopting such a perspective, suffering has meaning because life has meaning, and more than this, perhaps, we have no right to demand of the world.

6

SPIRITUALITY, FATE, AND FATALISM

Oh busy weaver! Unseen weaver! Pause! One word! Whither flows the fabric?
—Melville, *Moby Dick*

The trouble with life (the novelist will feel) is its amorphousness, its ridiculous fluidity. Look at it: thinly plotted, largely theme-less, sentimental and ineluctably trite. The dialogue is poor, or at least violently uneven. The twists are either predictable or sensationalist. And it's always the same beginning; and the same ending.

—Martin Amis, *Experience*

For millennia, and in many cultures, spirituality has been bound up with fatalism, that is, with the powerful sense that our lives are not in our own control and that whatever happens, in some hard-to-pin-down modal sense, *must* happen. Fatalism is typically coupled and often conflated with fate, and, of course, there is a natural affinity between the two concepts. But fate and fatalism are distinct notions. The first refers to some sort of quasi-agency that actually determines the way things have to be. Fatalism, by contrast, is a more abstract notion, requiring only that (some) matters could not be other than they turn out to be, whether or not there is agency or responsibility. Both notions are attempts to give meaning to the world, to see the world in a certain kind of order, something more than the result of mere chance or causal necessity. Both concepts are natural concomitants of spirituality.

But fate and fatalism have gone out of favor. Fate is typically dismissed as a primitive residue of terrified people facing the natural calamities of the world in complete scientific ignorance, converting the inexplicable into something that they do understand, namely their own personalities. This animation of the world, often personified in terms of God or gods, is naturally rejected by most modern thinkers. Indeed, it is worth noting that many Christian theologians have also argued against the notion of fate, despite the obvious kinship between fate and God's will. Fate is identified with paganism, not with Judeo-Christianity. Thus it is often argued that fate (and fatalism) deny what is most human about us, namely the divine gift of free will.

Fatalism is often dismissed as some sort of logical mistake. At its crudest, the argument is that fatalism is a trivial thesis, what will be, will be (or as Doris Day sings, *que sera, sera*[1]), which looks like a straightforward tautology and therefore trivial. But fatalism does not just say that what has happened has happened. It insists that it *had* to happen. Then the charge is that fatalism confuses modalities and fallaciously infers what *must* be the case from what merely is or has been the case. But fatalism is not simply a bad inference from what has happened, nor is it merely rationalization. It involves an outlook that refuses to accept the idea that when something significant happens it "just happened" to happen. It is a rejection, in other words, of meaningless chance. A much more sophisticated charge is that the fatalist conflates past and future, treating future events on a par with past events, whose occurrence really cannot be changed.[2] But the charge itself tends to ignore the fact that, for the fatalist, the necessity of (some) future events is very different from the (undeniable) necessity of past events.

Sometimes, fatalism is simply conflated with fate and ascribed as the power (usually malevolent) of the gods or the fates. But even when it avoids such anthropomorphism fatalism nevertheless gets identified with mysterious forces and primitive animism. Thus Dan Dennett dismisses fatalism (in an unusually entertaining book on free will) as "mysterious and superstitious."[3] For Dennett, fatalism is like one of those "bogeymen" such as the dramatic but ridiculous notion that "life is a prison," or that some neurosurgeon is messing with our brains, or that we are under the spell of a hypnotist or being manipulated by a powerful puppeteer.[4] Thus he finds nothing to recommend fatalism but the "power to create creepy effects in literature."[5]

But our ultimate discomfort with all varieties of fatalism has to do with the apparent conflict with freedom and responsibility. As Dennett puts the matter, overgeneralizing to make fatalism seem absurd, "no agent can do anything about anything." I confess to flatly rejecting fatalism for most of my mature life for just this reason: too many people use fatalism as an excuse not to do anything. The fact that fatalism is also an unscientific thesis may have provided arguments but it did not provide the motivation for my refusal to take it seriously. As an existentialist, I take it that one of the most important messages that philosophy has to give is the importance of individual freedom and responsibility, not as a matter of metaphysics, but as a matter of practical necessity. When people appeal to fate or fatalism they often give up responsibility and refuse to take resolute action. Fate and fatalism thus provide a convenient excuse for what Jean-Paul Sartre calls "bad faith," refusing to act and take responsibility and rationalizing this refusal with an appeal to dubious external circumstances.[6]

I deplore the turn of mind that finds such abstract excuses for personal failings. But I have also come to see that a second and equally important message that philosophy can give is the sense that we are not in complete control of our lives, that there are forces much larger than ourselves that do determine our fates. This is another thing I came to appreciate through reading Hegel. The second message does not cancel out the first but complements it. Freedom, responsibility, and an acceptance of one's fate go hand in hand and in many ways depend upon one another. Even Sartre insists that we are not as such responsible for the situations in which we find ourselves, and we are not free to change the circumstances in which we are both free and compelled to act. ("I am not 'free' either to escape the lot of my class, of my nation, of my family, or even to build up my own power or my fortune or to conquer my most significant appetites or habits."[7]) Even resigning oneself to one's fate need not entail giving up either freedom or responsibility. Fate and fatalism, especially when described as *destiny*, have proven to be among the most powerful motivators of great (and not so great) human beings throughout history.

Fate and fatalism may seem primitive and scientifically unacceptable to philosophers and scientists, but here, as so often, we find that philosophical sophistication runs harshly counter to common sentiment. Ordinary people often rationalize what happens by concluding that this is how it was meant to happen or, with an explicit theological twist, It's God's will. (I do not think that the attempt to divorce divine providence from fatalism, or for that matter the idea that fatalism is incompatible with free will, has any philosophical or theological merit. What moves Christian theologians to make such claims is their effort to separate Christianity from more "primitive" belief systems, thus assuming that fatalism is as such a primitive belief system.) Whether or not they entertain any philosophical theory about it (most, of course, do not), many people find that fatalism and at least some concepts of fate are meaningful notions that enrich rather than degrade their experience and their lives. This is not to deny that fate, as it is often discussed nowadays, is too often abused as an excuse for a lack of effort. Fate is too often construed as banal, New Age kitsch. Thus Vladmir Nabokov aptly called it "McFate," an appropriately mass-marketed notion with minimal spiritual nutrition.[8] Nevertheless, it is intellectual junk food with a long and distinguished pedigree.

To press the point, I have insisted throughout this book that such an outlook should not be taken to mean that we should remain merely passive, or resign ourselves to our fates, or allow ourselves simply to be swept along in the currents of the times, without reflection, without criticism, without resistance. Thus spirituality remains tied up with free will and choice as well as with fate and fatalism. The reverence of spirituality may reside first of all in our recognition of greater powers and higher values than our own. But it also involves our willingness to *act* in accordance with these higher values. The eroticism of spirituality may begin with uncertainty, but it is possible only insofar as we demand and impose some order on our lives. The trust of spirituality may include the confidence that things will work out for the best, but it is also having the resolve to make this so. Spirituality is fatalism and activism together, and neither without the other.

Making Sense of Fatalism

The Moving Finger writes, and having writ,
Moves on: nor all your Piety nor Wit
Shall lure it back to cancel half a Line,
Nor all your Tears wash out a Word of it.

The Rubâiyât of Omar Khayyâm

Fate, in the ancient world, typically involved agency. Thus fate, like some forms of spirituality more generally, involves the animation of the world, an endowment that involves plans and intentions as well as the natural causal order. Thus fate is often personified and treated as an agent, Fate. Thus the later Greeks and then the Romans referred to the fates (depicted as muses) by name. The earlier Greeks took fate to be a unified force, distinct from the gods. In Homer, for instance, not even the gods—not even mighty Zeus— could contravene fate.

There is, to be sure, something comforting in the idea that the world is controlled by anthropomorphic spirits. Even catastrophes are somehow more tolerable if they can be attributed to a jealous God or malevolent Mali. Misfortunes caused by the malicious whims and jealousies of the gods and goddesses are comprehensible, at least. Earthquakes and typhoons are understandable if they are brought about by angry divinities. The destruction of the temple is meaningful if it is perceived as the wrath of a God whom we have let down.

For us scientifically sophisticated moderns, this quaint picture can comfortably be dismissed as so much superstition and nonsense. But the notion of fate need not be so simple-minded. Ancient philosophers were obsessed with the idea that our lives are not under our control.[9] To be sure, we make our daily decisions and seemingly "choose" to go this way or that, but in the larger vision of things those choices are, in one way or another, already determined or at the very least tightly circumscribed. Spinoza says in one of his letters that if a stone thrown through the air were conscious, it would believe that it was flying of its own free will.[10] In *Slaughterhouse Five*, Kurt Vonnegut has his Trafalmadorians reveal to us (by way of the hero, Billy Pilgrim) that they had inventoried hundreds of civilizations on as many planets, and only on earth did they find creatures who believed in "free will."[11] But even the most libertarian among us find ourselves believing in hands other than our own controlling our destinies. In romance, we find the idea of fate irresistible. Indeed, it seems built into our romantic conception of love. ("We were meant for each other."[12]) In economics, we find it hard to get away from Adam Smith's famous metaphor, from *Wealth of Nations*, of the "invisible hand" that assures prosperity despite the narrow self-interested focus of an entrepreneurial society.[13] In biology, all but the few consistent evolutionists still tend to adopt a vision of progress, of purposiveness, for example, when they explain the "function" of this or that adaptation for the survival of a species.[14]

We have choices, true, and we may take responsibility for them. But we also sense some larger destiny, some feeling in which we cannot escape our fate. We are swept along by global forces, the world economy, international politics, the dynamic ecology of our planet, and by more easily identifiable local forces (department and university politics, the threat of crime and violence, the pervasiveness of popular culture, the personalities of our neighbors). Hegel's portrait of the *Zeitgeist* and his view of the relative unimportance of the individual captures this humbling picture so well, as does Tolstoi in *War and Peace* a few decades later. Our lives and fortunes are to a large extent the products not only of our own character but of the more embracing character of the culture and times we live in. Whatever one thinks of the celebrated free will issue, it is undeniable that we are hostages of fate in this larger but more modest sense. We are not the sole authors of our lives or of the circumstances of our lives, and, without denying the role of chance—and just plain luck (good or bad)—our futures are for the most part set out before us. Whatever our libertarian and existentialist pretenses, we find ourselves in them and grow into them rather than make them for ourselves.

Fate as Character

Miniver Cheevy, born too late,
Scratched his head and kept on writing.
Miniver coughed, and called it fate,
And kept on drinking.

E. A. Robinson, *Miniver Cheevy*

Man's character is his fate (*daimon*).

—Fragment #104, in Charles Kahn, *Heraclitus*

How do we save the appeal of fate and fatalism while relinquishing the anthropomorphism and mystery? One way of doing this goes back to ancient times. The Greek philosopher Heraclitus interpreted fate as *character*. In order to make good solid sense of fate and fatalism, one need not bring in any fancy philosophical technology or fanciful metaphysical machinery (and discussions of fate and fatalism are much too often couched in such machine imagery). The notion that someone will very likely turn out in such-and-such a way is a perfectly common sense notion, denied only by those who have such an exaggerated sense of free will (or are so unscrupulous in their pursuit of self-help best-seller status) that they would argue, most implausibly, that anyone can do anything, if only they try hard enough. Thus the concept of fate has a perfectly natural, intelligible home, as character.

Nowhere is this more evident than in the slightly traumatic and amusing experience of attending one's high school reunion. What is so shocking is how *little* most of one's classmates have changed after 10, 20, even 40 years. A few of them will have fallen prey to serious illness or personal trauma, and most will display the wrinkles, extra pounds, and (in men) receding hair lines that naturally come with age. But the majority remain amazingly the same. The metaphor that comes to mind, trite but profoundly philosophical, is that of a sprout growing into a tree. The basic shape and kind, its character, are already established. The rest is all contingency and details. One of one's classmates was, one remembers, destined to be president. Of course, not everyone so destined in the thousands of high schools in the United States can in fact become president, but most of the time that chosen classmate will turn out to be president of something, in some leadership position. One of one's classmates was, one remembers, destined for prison. And the odds are indeed that he (less likely she) will not show up, bound up in another long-term engagement.

Consider some examples: (1) A naughty boy becomes a punk kid, becomes a juvenile delinquent, and turns into a petty then later a hardened criminal. The neighbors and (more or less distant) family members wag their fingers as they say "I told you so." (2) A childhood orator becomes a public speaker and then she becomes an influential diplomat. It is not a surprise, even though she surmounted considerable obstacles on her way to success. (The friends and neighbors say, "I always knew.") (3) A man who never pays much attention to what he is doing gets into accident after years of irresponsible driving. It's not just bad luck. Everyone who knows him concludes, "It just had to happen." There are no mysterious forces or supernatural personalities required here to talk sensibly about fate.

Fatalism should be distinguished from what philosophers call determinism. Fatalism insists only on necessity, *no matter what the causes may be*. Determinism, by contrast, insists on the sufficiency of antecedent causation but gives no particular meaning to how things actually turn out. The standard example of fatalism is poor old Oedipus, who was cursed and doomed to kill his father and marry his mother no matter what he (or his parents) would do to prevent it. There are many philosophical morals and conundrums to squeeze out of that old tale, but the only point to be made here is that the *what* of fate need make no commitments to any *how*.

This does not mean that determinism is false. One might still (reasonably) reply that there must be *some* chain of events and causes leading up to Oedipus's tragic deeds. Can we imagine Oedipus evading the curse, giving way to Laius his father and remaining merely "Platonic" when he moved in with his mother? Of course, but then it wouldn't be much of a story. Could things in our three examples above have turned out otherwise? Of course. But when people speak of fate they are not talking in terms of causal necessity. They are trying to fit what happened into a larger narrative that gives it meaning.

What interests the scientist is not the main concern of the fatalist. Thus the naughty boy who ends up doing hard prison time probably has a nasty biography, but for those who "told you so" the important point is that *this* is how he would end up. (So, too, the intervening successes of the diplomat are, so far as the fatalist is concerned, only secondary.)

Families and cultures have character as well as individuals. This point may have become politically incorrect, but it is still obviously true. Again, this does not mean that the outcome is inevitable (or for that matter, unavoidable). Germany might well have jettisoned Europe's widespread anti-Semitism and somehow propped up both the Deutsche mark and the Weimar Republic, and either not elected, impeached, or ignored Hitler. But it did not, and those who look at Germany's history and speak of Hitler and the War as Germany's fate are not necessarily speaking either racism or nonsense. (Japanese historians come to pretty much the same conclusions looking at the twentieth century history of Japan. It is not unlikely that our turn will come.)

Indeed, looking back (as many are now doing) and retracing the steps of the ascent of man and civilization and rethinking if not human nature then certainly the nature of human progress, there is (and long has been) a fascination with the fate of humanity. There is ample room for speculation and differences of opinion here, but it is the process itself that is of interest. There is something (in fact, a great deal) in the character of human beings, at least considering those who have evolved, developed, and gained dominance on this planet. I do not believe that any particular fate—whether self-annihilation or earthly paradise—awaits us. Indeed, the very idea of a fate *awaiting* us is a matter worth considerable scrutiny. But of the many fates one can imagine, even if they are avoidable (and they are by no means inevitable), it nevertheless makes good sense to call them fate. Our whole history gives meaning to what will come of us in the future.

Character as fate strikes a middle position between determinism and chance. Indeed, the notion of character is employed by a few great philosophers (David Hume, John Stuart Mill) as an answer to the free will–determinism puzzle.

(An act is free if it flows from one's character, but character is determined by antecedent circumstances. And just as character determines future acts, these, in turn, further determine character.) Character can be cultivated, to be sure, but the range of choices, while theoretically unrestricted (I can imagine flying to the moon), is far more restricted in practice than we like to think. Trying to break a simple habit—a small speech defect, a rude spontaneous gesture, an awkward walk, not to mention smoking—can be excruciatingly difficult. Trying to change one's personality, from shyness to socialite, from cowardice to courage, may require a wholesale life change, which, in retrospect, also gets recognized as an essential part of one's character (as resoluteness, as determination).

The fact that character is cultivated over a long period of time prevents us from interpreting who we are as simply a matter of chance, although many coincidences and contingencies go into the formation of character. But one cannot say of one's character, in quite the same way that one can say of one's time of birth or national origins, that it simply happened that way, that it was out of one's hands. To do so ("I am a coward, so I couldn't do anything about it") is a paradigm of what Sartre called bad faith (*mauvaise foi*).[15] But, at the same time, one cannot view one's character as simply a matter of one's own choices. To do so would be, in effect, to deny the notion of character which has a momentum apart from choices. Insofar as a person's future follows from character, we can accept as perfectly intelligible this prominent notion of fate.

Fate and Time

Whether one is worthy is a question of talent and whether one can take action is a question of the person; whether one meets with opportunity is a question of timeliness and life and death are matters of fate.

—Xunzi

All are architects of fate, working within these walls of time.

—Henry Wadsworth Longfellow, *The Builders*

Die at the right time.

—Friedrich Nietzsche (who died ten years too late)

Thinking about our own lives, it is hard not to contemplate the very personal question, *How long do I have to live?* It is not a statistical inquiry about life expectancy ("an average of 72.2 for healthy, nonsmoker males, five years more for comparable females"). Nor is it just a practical question (for instance, in calculating what kind of life insurance to buy, or whether or not to start a multivolume book project). The question, *How long do I have?* has special poignancy, of course, for those who have reason to think that their time is distinctively limited, patients with AIDS or cancer, for instance. Soldiers talk fatalistically of a "bullet with my name on it." It is not so different from the heroes of the *Iliad* and their resignation to their fate (sometimes but by no means always foretold). The same question is readily available—and at times unavoidable—for all of us. It is hard not to think in terms of a certain span of allotted time, what the Chinese call *jie*. To be sure, people die before their time and these days many people outlive their useful lives by several or even many years. But the concept of fate applies just as well to those cases. It is an essential part of the narrative of their lives, the first as tragedy, the second as anticlimax.

Many of us now face the painful discovery that we must care for our aging parents. This is a bit of Chinese virtue (*xiao*) that most of us had never contemplated before. We did not choose our parents, we may have lived a long time away from them, and we had little to do with their current state of health. But whatever our relationship, and however difficult or inconvenient the situation, here is a clear example of a fate that we cannot deny. It is, again, an essential part of the narrative of our lives. And again, to dismiss this as just luck (good or bad), as a matter of chance, is to deny the meaning of such narratives. To be sure, these are not scientific explanations and are not intended in any sense to replace them. But between causal necessity and random chance the narrative of human meaningfulness unfolds before us. Why insist that science must be at odds with this?

Thinking of the ancient agrarian world, it is easy to imagine why the notions of fate and fatalism would become a natural part of the human imagination. Consider the nature of time in a natural setting, the cycles of the seasons, the metamorphoses of lepidoptera and amphibians, the inevitability of change in nature, the passages of human development, the sacraments, the cycles of life and death. Ancient conceptions of time and existence as a wheel or a circle were quite reasonably based on such evidence, long before the linear arithmetic of Christianity and the complex calculations of Einstein were on the horizon. In our own urbanized, increasingly global and virtual world, when we sometimes don't step outside or see the sky for days at a time, it is easy to lose sight of the obvious. Nietzsche's great thought experiment, eternal recurrence, is based on such a conception, abstracted and then personalized as an existential imperative.[16] Time is a circle, and fate is just the passage of time.

Our sense of time (and here I am not referring to what philosophers or physicists may think about time) is built around our projects, our aspirations, finishing college, law school, internship or residency. Only secondarily do we tend to think in terms of generations and the suprapersonal cycles of life and death. But thinking beyond the bounds of one's own life, it is hard not to think of the tumbling of generations, the epochs of evolution, the larger narratives within which our lives are embedded. In the context of these larger narratives, it is difficult to avoid revising our personal narratives and seeing our lives under the auspices of a certain sense of necessity, which is quite different from holding that the events of our lives (and our deaths) have a causal explanation.

The Chinese point with some reason to the fate of the individual in the context of the times (*shi ming*—what Hegel captured in his notion of *Zeitgeist*). A quick look at the awesome expanse of Chinese history, with its various periods of Warring States and churning upheaval makes it quite clear that *when* one is born has an overwhelming effect on the life one lives. Just think of the twentieth century, from Sun Yat-sen's revolution that created the Republic to the Japanese invasion in the thirties, to Mao's revolution in the forties, to the horrors of the Great Leap Forward and the Cultural Revolution of the fifties and sixties. (Zhang Yimou's brilliant movie, *To Live*, traces the fate of a single family through these tempestuous years, making it brutally clear how personal initiative is bound and geared to larger necessities.) In such circumstances, it is virtually impossible to avoid thinking of one's life as bound and determined by forces much larger than oneself, however one may rail against that fate or resolve to make one's way in the face of it. As the controversial Confucian philosopher Hsun Tse (Xunzi) wrote (fourth century B.C.E.), "Whether one meets with opportunity is a question of timeliness."[17]

But even in our considerably more stable and secure existence the truth about *shi ming* becomes self-evident along with the more localized notion of opportunity (*jie*). Think of the difference between what Tom Brokaw calls the greatest generation that fought (willingly) in World War II and the generation that fought (bitterly, resentfully, regrettably) in Vietnam. Then think of the present generation of college students, for whom Vietnam is just history. Think of the opportunities enjoyed by my generation (college and university positions for the asking in the largest expansion of higher education since Confucius, life-time employment in corporations without a hint of downsizing) or that slim window of opportunity enjoyed by fortunate Internet entrepreneurs at the very end of the nineties. Being in the right place at the right time is a conception of fate that we all recognize from time to time, especially when it really counts. So, too, being in the wrong place at the wrong time. Quite the contrary of a feeble excuse to do nothing, fate is the recognition of an opportunity to *do something*.

In ancient China, as in most societies, being born into wealth and privilege as opposed to hardship or poverty was considered definitive of one's fate. Of course, there were mainly these two extremes and little socioeconomic mobility in ancient China (as in most societies), so the idea that one was blessed or condemned to a life of one kind or another seemed both obvious to most people and conducive to social stability.[18] Today, of course, any such notion runs into serious political obstacles and abuses. Most Americans belong to that enormous, amorphous middle class. They insist, against a great deal of evidence, that they are free to become rich, and we no longer dismiss poverty as unavoidable, as most people did until the late nineteenth century. But the price of this precious mobility for most people is an enormous amount of envy and resentment and a perilous sense of social satisfaction. This is awkwardly combined with enticements to the spirit of charity and reminders that "there but for the grace of God go I." This humbling and essential ethical realization tends to be as close as most of us come to the recognition of our "lot" in life as an acceptance of fate.[19]

We often expect things to work out in a certain way. This may be a residuum of our more or less secure upbringing, parents who made promises and protected us, who served us and made sure that everything came out all right, who soothed us when we were hurt, made excuses for us and consoled us for our failures with ready-made rationalizations. When we suffered from our own mistakes, the ready response was "I told you so," and when we succeeded, praise was always embellished with "I knew you could do it." The future seemed laid out for us, and to a certain extent assured. We came to expect a rational universe, and we never got over it. This, of course, was Freud's thesis about religion in *The Future of an Illusion*, and Albert Camus's view of the "Absurd." But we all feel it, at least whenever something bad happens to us. We can't help but ask, *Why me?* as if the universe owes us some sort of an answer. We know that we ought to ask such questions when something extraordinarily good happens for us as well. That is why some sense of fate and fatalism are not only appealing, they are virtually inescapable as expressions of philosophical and humane sensitivity.

Thus the notion of fate gains respectability in our modern-day world, not as the expression of any mysterious agents or as an inexplicable necessity, but as an essential aspect of the narratives in which we live our lives. Naturalized spirituality, as I am conceiving of it, is just such a narrative, just such a broad-based conception of time.

Fate and Luck as Two Modes of Meaning

Luck be a lady tonight.
— Frank Loesser (*Guys and Dolls*)

The notion of fate is charming not because it takes away our sense of responsibility, but because it makes the future—and thus our responsibilities—seem more real. It is as if one's grandchildren are already waiting, as if one has already earned that Ph.D. toward which one is now but a fledgling graduate student, as if the salvation of the world is already settled and it is just up to us to find the means. Belief in fate is thus the equivalent of a kind of optimism, a way of seeing the future as promising. (Of course fate can also be conceived as a kind of pessimism with the idea of the future as doom.)

Regarding the past, fate is the larger narrative in which a present choice or an event that might otherwise seem meaningless can be seen to have profound significance. Fate is, in that sense, a *teleological* phenomenon, the ascription of purpose *in addition to* the causal explanation of what has happened. Fate may refer to the future, but it can be realized only retrospectively. Thus a couple may say, even on a first, wonderful date, "we were meant for each other." Whether that is true, or perhaps just a bad joke, will be evident only years later. We act in ignorance, but we always act with an eye on the future, in the light of the past, in a fatalistic narrative that gives meaning to our actions.

Fate is not the only conceptual vehicle in this quest for meaningfulness. A kindred concept, and one that seems better suited to our current scientific outlook, is the concept of *luck*. But it is important to distinguish luck from fate. The two are often conflated, even though, looking at them closely, they have what would seem to be diametrically opposite meanings. Fate, as we saw, is a kind of explanation. Luck refuses to ascribe to an event any further explanation. Familiar examples are the fall of a coin, heads or tails, the random pick of a number or a card in the deck, the odds of being number seven in a radio program quiz call. There may or may not be such an explanation *in practice,* but a detailed microanalysis of the surface and weight distribution of the coin, the precise torque of the flip, the distance to and nature of the surface, might well provide a full account and an accurate prediction of the coin toss. Coins, unlike quanta, do obey deterministic laws. But for all intensive purposes, the possibility of an explanation is excluded. It is chance that the coin lands this way or that. It is luck (good or bad) that one wins or loses the bet on that particular outcome. Within the scope of the reference to luck, no further explanation is called for (whether or not one is available).[20]

We run into problems when this theme is generalized or extended beyond the well-circumscribed domains in which such talk of luck makes sense. On an all-too-familiar everyday level, this happens when something that is clearly our responsibility is attributed to luck (usually bad luck, for obvious reasons). On a far more profound level, it happens when physics fans generalize the problematic findings of quantum mechanics to all of physics, ignoring the fact that Newtonian mechanics (that is, *real* mechanics) still governs most of our world as we live in it. Such generalization also occurs on a lay level when philosophers and secular-minded folk argue that the world is based on chance. Contemporary Darwinists, for example, argue (against those who insist on "intelligent design") that evolution has proceeded by way of blind chance.[21] But to accept Darwinism and deny creationism is not to relegate all explanation to chance. It is an unfortunate choice that is left to us, when our only options are belief in a very particular God or blind chance, which is to say, there are no explanations (other than the supernatural or stochastic probabilities) at all.

Fate, we saw, provides a different kind of explanation. It does not exclude or conflict with causal explanations but provides a narrative with meaning. We can and inevitably do supplement the evolutionary story with our own perspective. Darwinian theory may assure us that there is no reason for us to suppose that we are the end of the evolutionary story, but looking at evolution from our perspective it is impossible not to perceive natural history in terms of luck if not in terms of fate. That is, the perspective might be very much like that of the "argument from design" theologian who finds the world miraculous.[22] We find ourselves extremely lucky to be here, and even more so if there is no good reason for that being so. Or, we can see fate at work, an invisible hand behind evolution. This is not to invoke either a creator or some other mysterious force but rather to insist on seeing the world and our being in it as something special, something that may or may not have a complete causal explanation, but is in either case not without meaning.

Luck, unlike fate, allows for no explanation. But to see our lives in terms of luck is nevertheless to see our lives as meaningful, even if inexplicable. To put the matter bluntly, the notion of luck makes sense *only in the context of outcomes whose meaningfulness has already been ascertained*. Thus heads not tails is lucky for the person who has called heads, but apart from such activity it is a matter of utter indifference how the coin falls. Sometimes we realize, to our horror, that we have averted tragedy or disaster just by luck. For instance, when driving a car or some other fast-moving vehicle, a split second's difference may make *all* the difference. But such a realization is a complex matter. We are aware that it is our own driving (or simply the fact that we are driving) that has put us in harm's way to begin with. In that sense, perhaps, we make our own luck. We are also painfully aware of the enormous number of unanticipated events that might make all the difference between life and death, and that is what makes the discussion of luck relevant. (We can simply assume here that the outcome of the near miss, living as opposed to dying, is of value.) Thus luck is parasitic on meaning while fate helps to create meaning.

Luck is another missing ingredient in most contemporary philosophy.[23] Volumes have been written on probability and chance, of course, and recent literature has brought out the complexities of "moral luck."[24] Typically, it is lumped together with the impersonal notion of chance. But luck is not merely chance. In the infamous free will problem, luck is dismissed along with chance as a nonstarter in the explanation of the causes of human action (if only because it is neither a cause nor an explanation).[25]

In the philosophy of science, chance and probabilities, but not luck—that has an ineliminable meaning component—is the substance of scientific explanation. But it is important to distinguish luck from mere chance. Luck is a very human notion, loaded with hopes, fears, and regrets, in other words, with personal meanings. Chance, by contrast, is an utterly impersonal notion, a matter of mere probabilities. Modern science has reduced the world to matters of chance, indeterminism rather than determinism, quantum statistics rather than classical mechanics. For today's physicists, contrary to Einstein, God (if there is one) does play dice with the universe. But for the rest of us, there would be no point in talking about God—or for that matter about life itself—if it were not for concerns about meaning.

Luck has another advantage, a political advantage. In his recent series on Australia, *Beyond the Fatal Shore*, Robert Hughes (speaking with ex-Prime Minister Bob Hawke) makes note of the unusual emphasis on luck in Australian society. For one thing, Australians gamble more than any other people in the world (and Hawke suggests that the best way to understand Australian society is to go to the races). But in a more profound and obvious way, luck is the ultimate egalitarian notion. Australians are very hesitant to ascribe merit, and they refuse to acknowledge that they have anything like a class structure. (Using England as their contrast, one can understand why that might be.) A multimillionaire is interviewed and ascribes his success to luck. Hughes comments that "It's better than having to admit that one bloke is cleverer than another." Fate is often employed (e.g., among the Chinese) to explain and justify vast differences in power and wealth. But here one can quickly appreciate the very real differences between fate and luck and the differences in meaning they represent. Both provide narratives that go beyond (or simply ignore) the scientific explanation of events to bring out their *personal* significance.

Fate provides an explanation, even if a vacuous one. ("It is fate that has brought us together.") But such explanations do not pretend to account for a phenomenon the way a causal analysis would. They rather underscores the narrative significance of an event. Luck, by contrast, refuses an explanation but rests content with the significance (good or bad) of the outcome. Luck would point to the fact that we had a preference in the coin toss, but suggests nothing about its necessity. The reference to fate suggests that in some sense it was meant to come out that way. Fate is necessarily part of a larger, more all-encompassing narrative, and although its explanatory value may be slight to nil, its ability to convey meaning is extraordinary. People who believe that nothing happens by chance lead incredibly rich (if overburdened) lives. But if fate enriches luck, too much emphasis on luck tends to diminish life. This is so not only in the case of the pathetic gambler whose sole ambition in life is to win the jackpot and loses everything, but in the more philosophical case of those scientistic fanatics who insist on seeing everything as *nothing but* a matter of chance. They therefore reject the search for meaning and lead not only a spiritually but an intellectually impoverished life.[26]

To see how luck and fate provide two alternative interpretations of a single event, consider this romantic example: Two people meet by chance on a train, they talk, have coffee, later meet for dinner, then fall in love. To say that it was luck is to say that it was a good thing but there was no reason for it. It just happened, happily. To say that it was luck is to say that there is no explanation. On the other hand, one can view a seemingly chance meeting as fate. Film-maker Claude Lalouche made a movie (in 1975, called *And Now My Love*) in which he shows three generations of two families, virtually at opposite ends of the world, and how their lives slowly converge until—during the last scene of the movie—their two grandchildren happen to meet on a plane. The romance of the story is that what seems utterly coincidental, indeed utterly insignificant ,otherwise is made to appear predestined. This is a narrative of fate, not luck.

Gratitude: The Idea of Life as a Gift

Gratitude is a sign of a noble soul.

—Aesop

A businessman in Dallas was interviewed on television, at the height of the eighties Texas boom (just before the eighties Texas bust). He said, "I just thank the good Lord that I came of age when I did and that I was born and live in Dallas, Texas." But it was amply clear from what else he said that he did not see himself as lucky at all, but as a man who had been responsible, smart, and hardworking. He *deserved* his considerable fortune, in his humble opinion, and as he made clear he saw no obligation to share it with anyone. So, too, successful athletes ritually thank the Lord for their talents, but they leave no doubt that it is by virtue of their years of practice and their special abilities that they and they alone are responsible for their success (though often with the encouragement of their mothers).

Such testimonials are not hypocrisy, but they are carefully, philosophically edited versions of life. They are narratives that focus on and take credit for what we can control and ignore what we cannot. We do not see the world or society, for example, as a strictly shared enterprise, in which the talents of one are properly speaking the talents of all, in which rewards are to be shared and credit is to be taken lightly. We do not and perhaps cannot see that it is mere luck that some of us have talents, abilities, and resources and others do not. If we were to think of this as fate, however (and giving thanks to God would seem to indicate some such supposition), then it becomes more than just luck. It is clearly out of our hands, but now it becomes a *gift*, in effect, something to be *thankful* for, a good reason for humility mixed with our good fortune and our pride.

The reintroduction of luck and fate into philosophy brings with it at least one very important consequence, and that is a renewed sense of *gratitude*. Luck, fate, and chance suggest intriguingly different views of the world. To see one's good fortune in terms of sheer chance is to wave away any sense of obligation to be grateful or thankful for it. To see one's good fortune in terms of luck, by contrast, is, or should be, to be appreciative, at least if the luck in question is *good* luck. To see one's good fortune in terms of fate, however, is to see one's whole life in a much grander context. It would seem, accordingly, that our appropriate response would be an emotion too little appreciated in ethics or in philosophy more generally, gratitude.

What does it mean to feel gratitude, not for this or that particular favor from another person or even (as in the case of one's parents or a great teacher) for setting the course of one's entire life, but (in some sense) to life itself, to the universe as a whole? Insofar as one personifies fate, for instance in the personality of God or some guardian angel, there is a straightforward interpretation of gratitude. One is grateful to God or one's angel because he (or she) has done something for which gratitude is appropriate. But it seems to me that we naturalists have given up a great deal by relegating gratitude to the supernatural dump just because there is no particular person to feel grateful to. This does not mean that there is no need for gratitude.

This naturalistic conception of gratitude or thankfulness is an extension of our more usual, interpersonal emotion. In this case it is the emotion and not the specificity of its object that ultimately determines its meaning. Whether or not there is sufficient personification of fate to warrant personal thanks, the recognition of fate in any sense implies that we are the beneficiaries of a (more or less) benign universe, or even the lucky beneficiaries of good fortune in a cruel universe. This should dictate gratitude, even if there is no one or nothing in particular to whom that gratitude is directed.

Unfortunately, it is not as if belief in fate and the acceptance of one's fate naturally leads from enjoying one's good fortune to gratitude. Our Dallas businessman made that quite clear. On the other hand, for those who adopt an overly rigid concept of fate, the predetermined nature of fate may make gratitude seem unnecessary. One need not be thankful for that which is going to happen anyway. One need only be thankful for that which might not have happened but did, or for that which did not happen but might have. The portrait of fate I have tried to paint is not one of inevitability or mechanical causality. I have said repeatedly that it is not as if it couldn't have happened otherwise. To the contrary, I want to suggest that belief and acceptance of fate has to do with embracing a larger narrative in which one's actions and fortunes have meaning and make sense of one's life. Part of that meaning and making sense, an essential aspect of that acceptance, is our willingness to feel and show our gratitude.

Gratitude, I want to suggest, is not only the best answer to the tragedies of life. It is the best approach to life itself. This is not to say, as I keep insisting, it is an excuse for quietism or resignation. It is no reason to see ourselves simply as passive recipients and not as active participants full of responsibilities. On the contrary, as Kant and Nietzsche, among many others insisted, being born with talents and having opportunities imposes a heavy duty on us, to exercise those talents and make good use of those opportunities. It is also odd and unfortunate that we take the blessings of life for granted—or insist that we deserve them—then take special offense at the bad things in life, as if we could not possibly deserve those. The proper recognition of tragedy and the tragic sense of life is not shaking one's fist at the gods or the universe in scorn and defiance but rather, as Kierkegaard writes in a religious context, going down on one's knees and giving thanks. Whether or not there is a God or there are gods to be thanked, however, seems not the issue to me. It is the importance and the significance of being thankful, to whomever or whatever, for life itself.

When Nietzsche asks us to consider the eternal recurrence of life, the unending repetition of our lives just as we have lived them, he makes an appeal for gratitude. This is partially eclipsed by they fact that Nietzsche toys with the idea that eternal repetition is a physical hypothesis and thus renders it far more mechanical than he intended. In fact, he was well aware that it was an image borrowed from ancient Vedic, Persian, and Greek religions and its significance was spiritual and existential rather than (in the narrow nineteenth century sense) scientific. Nietzsche intended his thought experiment as a test for one's acceptance of life, and in his best-known presentation of eternal recurrence he asks, "Would you not throw yourself down and gnash your teeth and curse the demon who thus spoke? Or have you experienced a tremendous moment in which you would have answered him: 'You are a God and never did I hear anything more divine!'"[27] What Nietzsche doesn't quite say is that one should, in the latter case, have *thanked* the demon, or rather thanked the universe for thus granting him life, *this* life. Nietzsche talks throughout his philosophy about the affirmation of life, but affirmation means little if it is not accompanied by some larger sense of gratitude, not necessarily to any one (and for Nietzsche, certainly not to God), but to life itself. We might say that one is grateful not only *for* one's life but *to* one's life—or rather to life—as well.

Why did Nietzsche not just say this? I think that there is in him as in most self-creators an enormous suspicion of gratitude, not because of its theological temptations, but rather because one does not want to admit to one's own limitations, much less the fact that one owes one's virtues to someone or something other than oneself. In a study some years ago, Boston psychologist Shula Sommers found that American men, in particular, found gratitude to be the most discomforting and humiliating emotion, worse than fear. It is not hard to understand why. Gratitude recognizes the fact that we are not, in fact, the authors of our own destiny, that we owe our good fortune to others and, perhaps, to luck. Fate further complicates this picture by suggesting that we are not only lucky in our lives but serving some greater necessity, God or no God. (I sometimes hypothesize that the need to think of God as all-powerful and so on has much to do with our unwillingness to admit gratitude to anything or anyone who is not *infinitely* more powerful than we are.)

As Milan Kundera repeatedly states in his magnificent novel, *The Unbearable Lightness of Being*, borrowing his theme from Beethoven, the recurring motif of our lives is *Es muss sein* (It must be). Nevertheless, this necessity is shrouded in contingency, and one should always add to the fate-filled question *Why me?* the philosophical question *Why is there me at all?* Kundera's novel is a tragic novel (the heroes die just as they find true happiness), but it is one of the most uplifting tragedies I have ever read. The lightness of being also underscores its preciousness (even though Kundera ironically uses Nietzsche's eternal recurrence to make the opposite point, that a life lived just once is of no significance at all). Life, in the final analysis, is a gift that once or eternally recurring none of us deserves. Nevertheless, it is a gift that can be earned. And for that very reason, we should feel not only acceptance but gratitude, gratitude for, if nothing else, life itself.[28]

If one were to think in terms of the abstract possibility of being any one or another of the many human beings on earth at the moment, the odds are that one would be born impoverished, raised malnourished and ignorant, and find oneself living in the middle of a famine, a civil war, under a harsh dictatorship, without real hope or possibilities. That we were not so condemned to a miserable life and an early death is surely, whatever our virtues, a matter of luck. Though we may acknowledge this in the abstract, it seems almost impossible to live with, much less base our lives on, this profoundly disturbing realization. What would we owe, and to whom, if all of our successes and even our health and our talents had to be credited? How could we tolerate misfortune in others if we knew, and really believed, that "there but for the grace of God [or fate, or luck] go I?" On the other hand, how different would our understanding of our own misfortunes and setbacks be if we accepted the idea that this is fate, or "just the way it turned out," or that all in all we really have been extremely . . . lucky?

LOOKING FORWARD TO DEATH?[1]

When Chuang-Tze's wife died, Hui Shih came to console him. As for Chuang-Tze, he was squatting with his knees out, drumming on a pot and singing.

"When you have lived with someone," said Hui Shih, "and brought up children, and grown old together, to refuse to bewail her death would be bad enough, but to drum on a pot and sing—could there be anything more shameful?"

Not so. When she first died, do you suppose that I was able not to feel the loss? I peered back into her beginnings; there was a time before there was a life. Not only was there no life, there was a time before there was a shape. Not only was there no shape, there was a time before there was energy. Mingled together in the amorphous, something altered, and there was the energy; by alteration in the energy, there was the shape; by alteration in the shape, there was the life. Now once more altered she has gone over to death. This is to be a companion with spring and autumn, summer and winter, in the procession of the four seasons. When someone was about to lie down and sleep in the greatest of mansions, I with my sobbing knew no better than to bewail her. The thought came to me that I was being uncomprehending towards destiny, so I stopped.

—Chuang-Tze

It is ironic, perhaps, that while spirituality is often associated with the eternal, it is our undeniable sense of finite mortality that seems to draw us to it. Of course, there need be no irony. Spirituality may simply be conceived as an escape from mortality, an alternative to finitude, a denial of death. But I consider this a cowardly motive for spirituality (although it is easy enough to understand it). Spirituality is rather the acceptance of death as the completion of life, as the closure that gives an individual life its narrative significance in a larger whole. One's life may be over but life goes on. (This is the absolute horror of what Robert Jay Lifton years ago described—with reference to the bombing of Hiroshima and Nagasaki—as the "second death," the destruction of not only oneself but of one's entire world.[2])

In Picasso's last years, when he was still very active and creative, art historians became impatient for him to die. They wanted to "sum him up," for the story to be completed. Such ghoulish behavior reinforces not only the prejudice that most academics feel comfortable only with the dead, but the sense we all share that "it isn't over until it's over." Life, no matter how predictable, always allows for new possibilities. But even the least predictable life is predictable in this: One is going to die.

It has been suggested that death is the ultimate philosophical topic in the sense that death, along with serious suffering, provokes even the most practical person to philosophical reflection. This may be true, but it is overstated. Martin Heidegger's famous if not always crystal clear thesis that our very existence is that of a Being-towards-Death has received many respectful nods, as has the much older view of Boethius (480–526), that the "consolation of philosophy" is the transcendence of death.[3] Although philosophers certainly have something to think about in the inevitability of death, I think it is a mistake to exaggerate the importance of this. It is just another version of what I call death fetishism—making *too much* of death and refusing to see it in the larger context of life.

I have heard many people say that death is the ultimate tragedy. This seems to me to be trite and also false. One might well fear (and rightly) that the death of his or her spouse or child would be much more of a tragedy than one's own death (restricting the field to personal tragedies and ignoring the collective horrors of war, mass murders, nuclear accidents, and holocausts). One might retreat to the claim that death is one's *last* (and in that sense ultimate) tragedy, but even this supposed truism seems to be false without trivializing qualification. Aristotle, in a famous passage quoting Solon, argued that "No man should be called happy until after his death."[4] I think that this is a true and valuable spiritual insight, an excellent antidote to the mindless solipsism of the "when I'm gone, I'm gone" view of death.

At first glance, Aristotle's statement seems like nonsense, both as a statement about happiness and as a statement about death. What sense could it possibly make to speak of a person's happiness after his or her death? And what would it mean to call a dead man happy? But Aristotle's argument, rendered in full, makes good sense. Once we have given up our modern hedonistic sense of feeling happy and taken up Aristotle's much more embracing sense of living and having lived a good life, we realize that tragedy is by no means limited to the living. Humiliation and scandal that affect a person's good name, even after death, nevertheless reflect back on that life and the way it was lived. It is not just the fate of one's family, but of one's community and ultimately of all humanity that matters. What does it mean to say that some tyrant in the ancient Shang dynasty led a happy life, if by way of his hedonism and self-indulgence he lost the mandate of heaven (*tian ming*) and brought ruin to his people for generations?[5]

"X must be spinning in his grave" is but one of several poor poetic allusions to the obvious fact that our lives and our happiness go on after we are gone. This has nothing whatever to do with any more ambitious belief in immortality, reincarnation, or life after death. One's own death is not the ultimate tragedy. There may be much worse, whether before or after one's death, even from the perspective (vicarious though it may be) of the dead. It is this, for many people, that makes spirituality in the face of death both possible and necessary.

The Denial of Death: A Brief History

Almost 30 years ago, Ernest Becker wrote his classic treatise—as he was dying—on *The Denial of Death*. The phrase and the theme quickly became a watchword of the more depressed intelligentsia and found its way into several (at one time almost all) Woody Allen films. Becker's thesis, in fact a familiar existential thesis, was that we Americans had so busied and buried ourselves in the everyday world that we had not so much lost as purposively denied the basic facts of life, death in particular. Becker, who succumbed to cancer, busied himself with his book through his final days, almost as if living out his own thesis. But the word hit home, and intelligent, healthy Americans started worrying more and more about whether they should be worrying more about their eventual demise. *Incipit* Woody Allen.

Of course, there were good reasons, not at all of them metaphysical or spiritual, why Americans should have been timid about facing death. Jessica Mitford wrote her wonderful and horrifying exposé of the funeral industry in 1963. The death scam was not confined to America, of course. (A good cynic could no doubt trace it back to the Egyptians.) Evelyn Waugh had satirized the same industry in *The Loved One* in 1930, which was made into a high-grossing movie in 1965 (screenplay by Terry Southern and Christopher Isherwood). By the mid-1960s, with Vietnam looming in the background, death had come of age in America. The denial of death had become virtually a cliché, but like most oft-spoken denials, it seemed to be contradicted by its very exposition. One of the most popular music groups of the era, The Grateful Dead, were in this as in so many matters perfectly tuned to the times.

What began as a lament became a celebration, not of death but of the denial of death. Indeed, all of the talk about the denial of death itself became a convenient way of ignoring death. In place of existential angst and reflection, it became—sociology. There were increasingly heated arguments about the depiction of lethal violence in movies and cartoons and, as the baby boomers got older, there was more concern about retirement and social security. People exercised more, ate healthier, stopped smoking, and started to plan to live to be 90 or 100 years old. Death, according to contemporary thinking, is thus deferred. Perhaps that is not the same as denial, but it seems to me rather close. However, just what does it mean to deny death anyway?

Elsewhere in the world, and throughout most of history, death has been hard to deny. It was everywhere, unhidden and all-too-evident to the senses. Ever since the discovery of death (and when and how would that have been?), the denial of death—death once and for all—has been an unavoidable temptation. One hundred thousand years ago, the Neanderthals practiced ceremonial rituals for the dead. We have no way of knowing what they believed, but it is not unreasonable to suspect that they were hedging their bets, both appealing to and protecting themselves from the dead.

Throughout history, virtually until the twentieth century, death was more dramatic than birth, and almost always more of a disruption for the survivors. Babies were born all the time and fewer than half survived. But the death of an adult left children without parents, tribes without leaders, hunters without trackers. Whether the Neanderthals feared their own deaths or just acknowledged and coped with the mortality of others is a question we cannot answer. What must have been absolutely clear was that death was a part of life. It had to be dealt with. Presumably there were no Neanderthal nurses, hospitals, or undertakers to hide or remove that unpleasantry from daily life. Nor were there lawyers to further complicate matters. Death was death. But, even then, maybe not.

So-called primitive people since at least the Cro-Magnon have developed detailed strategies for placating and warding off the spirits of the dead. The dead, in other words, were not wholly dead, even after giving up most of their earthly pleasures and powers. The oldest known epic (at least a century before the Hebrew Bible), the Babylonian tale of Gilgamesh, is largely set in the land of the dead. The Egyptians were exemplary but not unique in their full-scale preparations for the afterlife. They looked forward, not to death, perhaps, but to the life that followed. Death and its details, accordingly, were given enormous, even obsessive amounts of attention. It was not only life after death that received so much attention, nor was it the nasty business of dying. It was the nature of death itself, the gateway or the transition, that received the attention. Life after death, we infer from many funereal findings, was pretty much a continuation of the life one had already lived.[6]

The ancient Hindus of the Vedas and later the Buddhists and the Jains were concerned that the soul (or *jiva*) would not die but would continue to carry on (in some other body) well into the future. In contrast to their colleagues to the west, however, they were not delighted by this prospect. They viewed life as suffering, as a burden to be relieved by ultimate liberation (which was very different from mere death). Death was taken quite seriously, something of a mix of cosmic graduation and karmic condemnation.

The Greeks, by contrast again, assumed the survival of that pathetic shadow called the breath (*psyché*), banished from the body but nevertheless not nothing. The depictions of Hades are by no means enticing, and though the Greeks did not deny death they certainly did not celebrate it either. Two millennia later, Friedrich Nietzsche would speculate that the great virtue of the Greeks was their fatalistic acceptance of death and suffering as the ground of human existence. It was this acceptance, he enthusiastically proclaimed, that made them and their lives "so beautiful!"[7]

It was Socrates who transformed the soul into a philosophical phenomenon, as he fantasized being freed from the body to do nothing but think for the rest of eternity. In Plato's *Apology*, he more or less obliges the jury to give him the death penalty, declaring that he would rather be dead than stop doing philosophy. Socrates' (Plato's) vision of the soul is a matter of much philological debate, but what is amply evident is that he did believe in the soul, and a mighty substantial soul at that. However little personality the liberated soul might have, it was clearly capable of thinking. Socrates imagined that, as an unencumbered soul, he could spend eternity thinking, nothing but philosophy. In this he broke ranks with most of his predecessors and opened the way to a rich life after life. (He also hinted at some form of reincarnation, which he probably got from Pythagoras, who in turn adapted it from the Egyptians.) It was only a matter of a few centuries before this aspect of the Platonic philosophy would ignite one of the greatest religious awakenings in the ancient world.

In Palestine to the east, the Jewish Pharisees believed in an afterlife, although the full significance of this belief was largely unspecified until the Christians came onto the scene. Indeed, one of the most appealing promises of early Christianity was Christ's anticipated conquest of death. This went far beyond the hopes of any previous peoples. Not only was there life after death, life eternal, but it would be more glorious, more righteous, than even the greatest of great empires, and it would be free of suffering. The travel brochures made the promise of Heaven irresistible. Life was but a short sentence, and death was barely even punctuation. Given the pervasiveness of such thinking, one might almost conclude that death would no longer be an issue. It was only a gateway to the kingdom of God. Nevertheless, the most passionate of beliefs has to cope with the evidence of the senses, and while the plain fact of death was obvious, the existence of the promised hereafter was not.

The Denial of Death: An Analysis

The main thing is to start talking about death and dying. In our society, death is a taboo subject. One of the main things that [we] want to do is change our culture so that death is not seen as a failure.

—Rosalynn Carter, *Newsweek*

The problem for us now is that we have outgrown the fantasy of a personal life eternal and now we have to cope with the aftermath. This is not just the realization that death might actually be the end of us, but the contrast between those pretty pictures of eternal bliss (or whatever) and cold reality. This does not imply a rejection of spirituality, but neither does it permit the adolescent illusion that the future will go on forever. It is not as if a promise of an afterlife has been broken, but many people certainly react that way. The nonexistence of Hell is little compensation for those good people who happily anticipated going to Heaven. So, the most common approach to death is one of denial. We are all adolescents, perhaps, when it comes to the hardest questions of life.

What does it mean to deny death? It is to refuse to believe that *it* will *happen* to you. To think of death as an it, and to think of yourself as its victim, is but another strategy of denial, another way of putting it at one remove, of abstracting it, of denying responsibility, if not for one's death (that is more often the case than one thinks), then for facing up to one's death. In its most mundane but pervasive strategy, to deny death is to focus on the hurly-burly of the everyday world and never look up to the horizon, to one's own mortal limits.

I suspect that we all do this. We plan our projects, stretching indefinitely into the future. We believe, every day, that "tomorrow will be another day." We act and feel as if we have all the time in the world. Of death we simply say, "it will come when it comes." This comes out in our priorities, putting off the truly important until we "clear the path" and "put out a few fires," take care of the urgencies.[8] But the path is never clear, and the fires keep burning, and someday there is no tomorrow.

The most effective denial of death, of course, insists that death is not really death, that life goes on in some more or less self-identical medium. This might be the survival of the soul pure and simple. It might be the survival of one's mind, one's memories, one's sense of self. It might be the reincarnation of the soul into another creature, perhaps another person. It might be something much grander, unification with the Godhead or joining the divine Inner Circle. I watched the Reverend Billy Graham's son on television a few years ago, and he was asked by his interviewer what he would feel when his father died. He carefully explained that he would feel terribly sad when his dad retired from the ministry, but he would feel nothing but joy when he "departed," knowing that he would then be far happier than he had ever been before. That, surely, is the denial of death plain and simple. But what, you might ask, could possibly be wrong with that?

I do not doubt the appeal of such beliefs, nor do I have any good arguments to prove that they could not possibly be true. Indeed, I worry a bit about those who take it as their mission to debunk them. Nevertheless, I can think of no reliable evidence whatever in favor of such beliefs, wishful thinking and multiple reports of bright lights and long tunnels during oxygen-deprived medical emergencies notwithstanding. Insofar as it makes any sense at all to talk about probabilities in this area, I will say without hesitation that it is most improbable that anything remotely resembling the persons we are continues in any relevantly similar form after death. True, it is always possible (in the enormously stretched sense in which that term is used in philosophy and religion) that there may be some significant sense in which the person survives the loss of his or her body. Personally, I do not believe it, although this, I would be the first to insist, is of no interest or importance to anyone but myself. Indeed, it may well be my loss. In my case *any* experience after death would come as a rather remarkable surprise.

Nevertheless, the belief in an afterlife—any afterlife—is a denial of death in the sense that most concerns me here. Perhaps there is an afterlife. But *What happens after death?* is not a substitute for the question, *What is death and how should I think about it?* It is that confrontation that counts, not evasive or easy answers to it. To think that life after death answers our concern about death is just another form of denial. What happens after death is quite another matter.

Death Fetishism

Nothing, nothing mattered, and I knew why. . . . Throughout the whole absurd life I'd lived, a dark wind had been rising toward me from somewhere deep in my future, across years that were still to come, and as it passed this wind leveled whatever was offered to me at the time. . . .
We're all elected by the same fate, me and billions of privileged people. . . . Everyone was privileged. There were only privileged people. The others would all be condemned one day.

—Albert Camus, *The Stranger*

Death has often been considered a trial, a test, a definitive event in a life that often flirted with fatalities. In Homeric ethics, notably, the mode of a man's death was considered a definitive mark of his character. To die bravely in battle was virtuous. To die young of the flu or pneumonia was—not to be too unkind—pathetic. (Alexander the Great and Lord Byron are cases in point.)

113

To die of old age was commendable, but only if one had the full background of battle scars and near misses. In classical cowboy ethics, to jump 30 centuries, it was considered essential "to die with your boots on." Death was a ritual, and if it meant that you lost the fight, it also signified that you put up a good one. (Being shot in the back not only meant cowardice on the part of your assassin, it also deprived you of your chance for an honorable death.) Dueling rituals of the American South and contemporary urban gang fighting maintain similar codes of honor, loyalty, and death, in which death is not only a part of life but its ultimate test. Death is an evil but also inevitable. *How* one dies means everything. The biology of death is of little importance.

In much of the Christian tradition, the aim is to die with a clear conscience, whether by reason of right behavior or by way of well-timed repentance. Throughout the Middle Ages, warrior ethics joined the ethics of salvation in an uneasy collaboration, as Christianity and Islam joined in battle in the Holy Land. To kill and be killed for God but die with absolution was as much of the chivalric ideal as the languor of love and the oath of undying loyalty. Death remained a highlight of a person's life, because of the significance of the manner of exit as well as the promise of another life to come.

A woman's death, through much of the same history, was thought to be a simpler thing, preferably quiet and uncomplaining, or tragically in childbirth. Just as women were denied the right and the capacity to a full life, they were denied the right and the capacity to a full death as well. Only rarely was a woman's death an exceptional act of honor, heroism, or patriotism (Joan of Arc, for example). One of the dubious achievements of the women's equality movement is that women are inching closer to combat positions in the modern military, while their street-fighting sisters in urban gangs are now accumulating rap sheets as lengthy as those of their male comrades. From such evidence, one might conclude that at least some young people have lost their fear of death and do not in any sense deny death at all. Perhaps this is a phenomenon to be explained by socioeconomic disadvantage, as a class phenomenon, but the evidence points elsewhere. I would suggest that the love affair with death transcends class and signifies something more.

In recent philosophy (and in a great deal of avant-garde poetry, theatre, and lifestyle pretensions, for example, in the death warmed over fashions of Calvin Klein), death has become the ultimate *experience*. One thinks immediately of the French: Foucault, depicted so vividly by Jim Miller in his recent biography; Artault, so celebrated by Susan Sontag in some of her more intoxicated writings of the seventies, Rimbaud and his exalted status among French poets, mainly because of his deliciously early death.[9] One thinks of Heidegger and his always carefully qualified notion of "Being-unto-Death." For Heidegger himself, of course, this was emphatically *not* to be thought of as an "experience"—indeed, Heidegger had not much to say, except sarcastically, about experience in general.[10] But as Heidegger has been read, first by the French and now by the Americans and some Australasians, "Being-unto-Death" has certainly become the focal point for a certain kind of experience, an *authentic* experience.

Strictly speaking, the idea of death as the ultimate experience may be nonsense. Death isn't an experience. As Epicurus assured us two millennia ago, it is nothing. But now *nothing* too has been elevated into a life-defining experience, and the process of dying, the moment of dying, the keen awareness of one's dying, the recklessness with which one lives in anticipation of dying, all of this has come to be regarded as a kind of heroic sensibility. Of course, all too often, the most dramatic characters exit prematurely in a drug-induced haze, like the artist Basquiat or Kurt Cobain, the lead singer of the rock group Nirvana a few years ago. A great deal of emphasis has been put on the notion of *choice* in dying, inspired perhaps in part, by the dehumanizing medical and hospital practices of the past few decades.

The new-found emphasis on *choice* in dying may be a dramatic realization of the Heideggerian emphasis on making one's death "one's own." This, I think, is the more philosophically significant explanation of the explosion of youth violence around the world. In a world without jobs, in which relationships are problematic, in which big-screen heroes come to life by continuously challenging death, facing death, and dying becomes emblematic not of escapism but a mode of self-expression. Stunt pilots crash alone in the mountains on a drunken or foolish run and come to be seen as heroes, not fools. Criminals who throw their lives away in a hopeless shootout are lionized. (Consider the undeniably charming characters in *Breathless* and *Butch Cassidy and the Sundance Kid*.) There are many sociological and psychological dimensions to such phenomena, but we should not underestimate the power of the philosophical rage for free will, for dying on one's own terms, even (if necessary) by one's own hands.

Making death one's own, savoring (or believing that one will savor) the experience has become a powerful existential motive. In his very important book, *After Virtue*, Alasdair MacIntyre bemoans the fact that his contemporaries generally express the opinion that they would prefer to die instantly, without warning, and not suffer the slow, lingering death that allowed people in earlier times to reflect and ruminate on their lives and sins, to assemble the story and meaning of their existence.[11] This topic has become part of popular discourse.

In the wake of the explosion of TWA flight 800 out of New York (in July of 1996), the conversations were revealing. On the one hand, the passengers were said to be victims. (It is a degradation of the language and not an expression of sympathy to insist, as politicians often do, that they are "heroes.") But, on the other hand, there were many anguished, quasi-empathetic discussions about what it would mean to be such a victim. What is often commented on, given the suddenness of the explosion, is the awful fact that (for the victims) not only was there no choice, but there was no time, no time to savor or anticipate the experience, no time for anything more than shock and fear, no time, in other words, to make death one's own.

Then news was released that some of the passengers (those towards the back of coach) continued to fly through the air, presumably in full consciousness, for another 10–12 seconds. That inspired horror of exactly the opposite kind. Some people insisted that it is better to just go all at once ("not knowing what hit you"). Others declared it far preferable to have those precious seconds—to come to an understanding, to collect one's soul, so to speak, and to live if not savor the experience. In this detached, petty squabble on the heels of a horrible tragedy, one can see the whole history, indeed the very nature, of the human preoccupation with death. How should we think about death? What does it mean to prepare for death? Would it be better not to think of it at all, even when it is immediately upon us? Is it even possible to make one's death one's own?

Death fetishism is the glorification of the death experience. It is an extreme but perverted version of the heroic warrior mentality in which death is the critical moment in life. But the hero and the warrior do not think of death as an experience. For death fetishists, on the other hand, it is the *ultimate* (and not just the last) experience. Unlike the heroes who face death but hope to avoid it in battle, the death fetishist flirts with death on his or her own terms. Indeed, the verb "flirt" seems perfectly proper to the phenomenon, both because death fetishism is undeniably an erotic if not also sexual phenomenon and because one is never quite certain of one's intention to go through with it. Thus death fetishism is a familiar ingredient in some of the more dangerous, even lethal sexual practices of the S and M crowd.

A fetish, in many religions, is a sacred object, perhaps one endowed with magical powers. Since Freud, the word also describes an erotic and arousing object, although one could argue that the distinction between the religious and the erotic is itself the product of Judeo-Christian mischief and Freud one of its latter-day seducees. However, in secular and quite sexless terms, a fetish is any object of excessive attention and devotion. Thus Marx quite rightly pointed out the fetishism for money and commodities in present-day capitalism, and pop-culture historians talk with considerable nostalgia about that all-American fetish, the automobile (at least before the 1980s, when most of the cars became not only Japanese or German, but so loaded with computer gadgetry that intimacy under the hood was no longer possible for most amateur enthusiasts).

In America then—and now in the rest of the world—the automobile is not only useful and sometimes necessary, but also a sign of status. It also represents the concretization of one's powers, one's personality, one's very *self*. Yet, it is just a piece of machinery. Death fetishism similarly converts death, one moment in the machinery of life, into the meaning of life, the ultimate test of life, even the *point* of life. At the very end of *The Stranger*, Camus's character Meursault declares, "There was only one class of men, the privileged class. All alike would be condemned to die one day." Meursault goes on to note that nothing else, none of a person's choices, none of his or her actions, made any difference in that "dark horizon" from whence "a "slow, persistent breeze had been blowing toward me, all my life long."

In his *Myth of Sisyphus*, Camus similarly notes, in his own voice this time, that "By the mere activity of consciousness I transform into a rule of life what was an invitation to death." Refusing to commit suicide, according to the young Camus, is what gives meaning to life. If Camus's philosophy is throughout a kind of celebration of life, one cannot help but notice that it is always also a fascination with death, as he more or less admits himself in his most autobiographical works.[12] The "passion for life" he so celebrates is often indistinguishable from an obsession with death. One can make *too much* of death, but death is not the focal point of our existence. We are not Being-unto-Death, despite the inevitable fact that we are going to die.[13]

Death is one fact of life among many (birth, the appetites, excretion, and, according common folk wisdom, taxes[14]). We can accept that fact without thereby viewing everything else in its shadow. Death fetishism deserves recognition as a rebellious opposition to the denial of death, but I think that we need to be more critical both about the very idea of denial of death and death fetishism. Beneath the bravado of death fetishism, there is too often terror and irresponsibility. Much of what is included in both obsessions with death seems to me no more than an implicit appreciation of life.

"Death is Nothing"

> Become accustomed to the belief that death is nothing to us. For all good and evil consists in sensation, but death is deprivation of sensation. And therefore a right understanding that death is nothing to us makes the mortality of life enjoyable, not because it adds to it an infinite span of time, but because it takes away the craving for immortality. For there is nothing terrible in life for the man who has truly comprehended that there is nothing terrible in not living.
>
> —Epicurus, *Letter to Menoeceus*

Admittedly, we know no greater game of chance than the game of life and death. Here every decision is faced with supreme suspense, concern, fear. In our eyes, it is all or nothing. On the other hand Nature, ever honest and open, does not lie. It speaks very differently on the theme, much as Krishna does in the Bhagavad Gita. Its testimony is that nothing at all rides on the life or death of the individual.

—Arthur Schopenhauer, *World as Will and Representation*

The rejection of death fetishism naturally turns to one of the most classic of the classical bits of wisdom on the subject, the idea that "death is nothing." Therefore, it follows, there is nothing to fear—and nothing to deny. Whole schools of philosophy have been dedicated to the pair of propositions, that death is nothing and therefore nothing to fear. In this context, the most famous name is Epicurus (340–270 B.C.E.), followed by his Roman successor, Lucretius (98–55 B.C.E.). Thousands of miles to the east, Chuang-Tze (369–286 B.C.E.) and other Taoists also insisted that death was nothing, a view defended later by many Buddhists and, in modern times, Schopenhauer. For the Epicureans, death was nothing in a rather straightforward way: "Accustom yourself to the belief that death is of no concern to us, since all good and evil lie in sensation and sensation ends in death. While we exist death is not present and when death is present we no longer exist."[15]

Lucretius, like Epicurus a follower of Democritus, suggested that the human soul was nothing more than an arrangement of atoms, which on death dispersed, leaving nothing. Chuang-Tze endorses a similar image, even though Taoism is a holistic as opposed to an atomistic philosophy. Like the Western philosophers, the Taoists placed enormous emphasis on the idea that human beings are part of nature. Our individuality is something of an illusion, and one of the ideals in life is to regard both life and death with equanimity and serenity. Chuang-Tze leaves us with a series of beautiful images, for example depicting the death of an individual as a drop of water joining all of the other drops of water in a stream. Thus death is nothing and nothing to be afraid of.

The thesis that death is nothing need not be a denial of death. It accepts death, and it accepts death *as* death, not as a gateway to an afterlife. The Epicureans and the Taoists did not deny that death was inevitable (although some later Taoists toyed with the idea of personal immortality.[16]) It was just that death did not matter, and in some sense it was unreal. The dispersal of atoms, or the merging of what was never really disconnected in the first place, why should such matters matter? But the serious charge is that the view that death is nothing feeds on or leads to the idea that life is nothing, or nothing significant, or even that life is a burden, something unwanted. This is suggested (but much disputed) in the four Noble Truths of Buddhism and sometimes seems to be lurking in Taoism as well. It is central to the notion of "liberation" in all three of the great South Asian religions, Hinduism, Jainism, and Buddhism and, of course, it plays a central role in Schopenhauer's pessimism.

The idea that life is pain is particularly poignant in the Judeo-Christian-Islamic tradition. In both Judaism and Christianity, there is the continuing urge to transcend suffering and "conquer" death. But isn't this also a way of deprecating life? To view life as essentially pain and suffering and death as relief from pain and suffering may soften our fear of death, but at considerable cost to our appreciation of life. Several versions of Christianity are pretty straightforward about this. It is one's eternal life that counts, not mere earthly life. This, Nietzsche charges, is the nay-saying of otherworldly thinkers, beginning with Socrates, who (Nietzsche claims) hated life and dreamed of other, better worlds instead. The Epicurean and the Taoist, by contrast, do not promise any such Otherworld. But if death is nothing, just the dispersal of atoms, or the substance of our bodies, or our souls rejoining that nature from which they have never really been separated, is life then anything more than atoms or souls conjoined?

I think that the Epicurean and the Taoist can be cleared of such charges. What we must understand is the context in which the idea that death is nothing was introduced. The idea that death is nothing should be seen as a reaction to the idea that death is a terrifying (and unending) experience. In place of increasing panic about the nature of the afterlife and the punitive nature of the gods, Epicurus strikes us a sign of sanity. He did not so much take aim against death (or the concern with death) as against the gods and worry about the vindictiveness of the gods. He simply insisted that there were no gods, as well as no afterlife in which gods could act on us. There was, in this context, nothing to worry about. One can only imagine, against the terrifying religious backdrop of the times, that what Betty Sue Flowers calls the "Bald Scenario" must have been a tremendous relief.[17]

What is worrisome about this whole line of argument, from the ancients to the New York and Parisian moderns, is that it really evades the poignancy if not the point of the question, *What is my death to me?* One can appreciate the contexts in which Epicurus and Chuang-Tze tried to neutralize the hysteria that surrounded death in their cultures, but in the contemporary context of death denial and death fetishism, I think a very different dialectic is in order. Someone concerned with the spiritual significance of death might well argue that "death is nothing" just misses the point, but a point is precisely what there is not. The fear of death is rather a web of concerns and confusions, not only about the possibility of an afterlife but about the life that is brought to an end in death. The meaning of death comes down to the meaning of life, nothing less, and nothing more.

Spirituality and the Social Dimension of Death

I know it is common; all that lives must die, passing through nature to eternity. My father lost his father, and my children will lose theirs, and their children (this is immensely onerous to contemplate) will lose theirs.

—Martin Amis, *Experience*

Much more important for our discussion of spirituality than his "death is nothing" philosophy is Epicurus's emphasis on the social significance of death. This is not to be confused with the obvious observation that death affects the survivors as well as the deceased. It is rather to say that death should be conceived of as an event in a social nexus rather than that morbid solipsism that dwells on death as a personal confrontation with nothingness. Death is through and through a social phenomenon, despite that existential pretension that each of us "dies alone." Even the most cowardly among us worries about how he or she will die, that is, how to behave and comport oneself with dignity. We worry about the disposition of our bodies after death. But most of all, we worry about the people we care for.

All too often, we approach death with the self-indulgent thought that my death is a bad thing because it *deprives the universe of me*. I picture the world without me, like Sartre's characters in *No Exit*. I see them talk about me, laugh about me, pity me. I watch someone date and marry my wife, raise my children, refute my books. Or worse, I see that they ignore me. This is not grand metaphysics or fundamental ontology, but petty selfishness wrapped up in enigma. What I call "morbid solipsism" is an approach to death solely in terms of the self. But what spirituality is all about, and what takes the sting out of death, is looking at death in a larger, non-self-centered context and in particular the social dimension of death. Our lives are not only tied to but defined in terms of other people. Our exit is thereby defined as well.

To appreciate the importance of this, it is not necessary to compromise our robust sense of individual life or to denigrate our personal worries about death. It is to say that we are, first and foremost, social animals. One's own death is always, except in the most lonely of cases, a disruption (one hopes not too minor) of a network of relationships. Even in those lonely cases, one's death is, in one's own thinking, a disruption of past or possible relationships or, at the outer reaches of pathos, a lament that one is, quite *unnaturally*, dying all alone.

What Heidegger marks off as the uniqueness of Being-unto-Death seems to me to be a just another version of morbid solipsism. But when I think of my death, I cannot help but think of how others will see me, how others will think of and remember me. When I imagine myself at my own funeral, a la Freud, it is through the eyes of others that I am imagining, not my own, whether or not my perspective is, logically and irreducibly, mine and mine alone. When I imagine my body on a slab, or bloodied in the street, or frozen from terminal pain, it is others I imagine thus seeing me, not I. When I worry about how I will die, it is for others as well as myself (my pain, my humiliation) that I am concerned. Of course, I also worry about my reputation, but here, more dramatically than anywhere else, the social nature of the self is in evidence. After all, what difference could it make *to me*, posthumously, whether I exited the hero, the coward, or the clown?[18] But it obviously makes a great deal of difference to me *now*, precisely because I anticipate the thoughts and reactions of other people.

Most societies, of course, would consider this obvious. Their mourning rituals take it for granted. Death is a spiritual concern not just because of concerns about the fate of the soul, but insofar as spirituality and consequently death are irreducibly social and interpersonal concerns. But in our advanced decadent philosophies, such thinking is all but ignored, or explicitly denied. Death is something we go through alone. What we fear about death is our own impending nothingness. But it is important to look at grief and mourning as aspects of death rather than as mere cultural artifacts that properly belong to the anthropologists. It is essential that we force ourselves to think, no matter how dramatic or grizzly the death, that the proper moment of death is nothing less than the whole narrative of a life. (In this context, we might consider the morbid Silenus, for whom all of life was dying.)

In cartoon wisdom, it has long been a cliché that, as one is dying, the whole of one's life flashes before one's (inner) eyes.[19] In place of the "death is nothing" argument, we should argue that it is the richness of life that provokes the pathos surrounding death. I want to live because of my wealth of friends and social responsibilities. I want to live because I love. I want to live because I am steeped in my projects, virtually all of which are social projects, as Sartre above all would be the first to appreciate, no matter how solipsistic their practice (writing, for example). I want to live because others need me, and because I care for and about others. I am definitive of their world as they are of mine.

The idea of death as putting an end to life's plans and projects should not be interpreted as simply self-interested, as referring only to *my* projects. Many of my plans and projects essentially involve other people, not just their connection with me, or their opinions of me, or their affections for me, but rather their own plans and projects and, in general, well-being. Thus, however unphilosophical this might seem, one central concern in the fear of death is *What will happen to them?* Such protectionism may be self-aggrandizing. One may not be as necessary as one thinks, and there is a plausible chain of thought that goes from "my family will starve without me," to the somewhat reassuring "someone else will take care of them," to the deflating realization "someone else will take my place," to the awful "they will eventually forget about me."

Of course, this is so. One does tend to become a mere memory, and, after a generation or two, not even that. It is probably a good thing for most of us that we are not left around to see that this is so. We would all be like the Jimmy Stewart character in *It's a Wonderful Life*, screaming, "Don't you know me?!" And then, perhaps, get a second chance, together again with one's loved ones.

In thinking about death, it becomes clear to me that what I really care about is the people I leave behind. This is, in part, because of my interests, my pride, my vanity. My concern is not just altruism. It also self-interest, vanity, pride, shame, and the fear of loss of control (the real horror of Sartre's *No Exit*). So it is not all about spirituality. Death is what individuates us only insofar as it targets the vulnerability of intimate and significant relationships. In itself, death is nothing and dying nothing worth celebrating. It is ultimately significant only because our lives are significant and our significance is entirely wrapped up in other people. Even the hermit imagines the impact his death will have on others and how he fits (by excluding himself from) the collective stream of life that he then, like a Taoist drop of water, rejoins.

Death is not nothing, but it surely can be made into something, a noble death, a death not just one's own, but with others in mind and for the sake of others. According to Heidegger, this may be an inauthentic death, but it is death such as the Homeric heroes would have contemplated. That is where a philosophy of spirituality should once again take us—away from death fetishism, away from morbid solipsism, away from obsessions with nothingness, and back into the richness of our lives. We fear death because it brings an end to our lives. That much is a truism. But we can appreciate death insofar as we identify with the people around us, with our culture, with humanity, and with *life*. To the extent to which we can do so, death is not the end at all, so long as we do not cheapen our spirituality with the idea that *as individuals* we will in the end cheat death and gain some sort of eternal personal life.

8

THE SELF IN TRANSFORMATION: SELF, SOUL, AND SPIRIT

The Chinese philosopher awakened with a start, for he had been dreaming that he was a butterfly. And for the rest of his days, he did not know whether he was a Chinese philosopher who had dreamed that he was a butterfly, or a butterfly who was now dreaming that he was a Chinese philosopher.

—Chuang-Tze

In Chapter 1, I suggested that spirituality, though thoroughly concerned with the self, is not to be confused with selflessness. It might better be construed as an enlargement of the self. This phrase is subject to all sorts of misunderstandings, of course, beginning with the vulgar interpretation of an expanded selfishness, taking the world as one's oyster, as one's personal domain. Or, it might be mistaken for a merely expanded narcissism. But the enlargement of self that I have in mind owes very much to Hegel and before him to a hundred generations of mystics and Asian thinkers who saw quite clearly that our routine conception of the individual self is in fact quite tenuous and fragile. One does not have to buy into mysticism in order to defend such a view. It is available to us in perfectly naturalistic forms, notably, in our various experiences of love and our identification with nature writ large and in our appreciation of the different notions of self-identity evident in various non-Western societies. The self is, as the French anthropologist Marcel Mauss suggested in 1938, a "delicate category," subject to substantial variation.[1]

The focus on the self and the soul that is so central to spirituality emerges from mixed motives. On the one hand, the search for self is an expression of our search for meaning and the existential angst that characterizes our need for personal significance and a definitive role in the world. It is the natural outcome of reflection and self-consciousness. On the other hand, the celebration of the soul is too often motivated by the impossible desire to evade death, to indefinitely continue, in however tenuous a form, some semblance of one's consciousness or at least one's identity and one's life. These are often conflated and confused, but the desire to evade death, I have suggested, is ill-conceived. Death is simply a part of life, and life goes on, for a short time anyway, in the hearts and minds of those who have loved or been affected by us. This is enough. But the former, the search for significance, could not be more central to the human project. The self (or soul) as a focus of meaning is indispensable for any conception of spirituality.

"Who are you?" Self and Soul

> Self is that conscious thinking thing, which is sensible or conscious of pleasure and pain, capable of happiness or misery, and so is concerned for itself, as far as that consciousness extends.
>
> —John Locke, *An Essay Concerning Human Understanding*

Spirituality is a mode (or many modes) of being-in-the-world. It begins with our knowing our place in the world. To be sure, spirituality also requires a large dose of ontological humility, which is wrongly interpreted as a sense of our ultimate insignificance. But spirituality is not a self-dismissive or self-abandoning leap into the fullness (or Buddhist emptiness) of the cosmos. It begins with and is anchored by our concrete sense of self and is characterized by the transcendence, not abandonment of the self. Here again, transcendence should not be understood as a leaving-behind (transcendent as a realm beyond this one), but rather as a *reaching* beyond, an expansion of self. Soul is both a (misleading) way of characterizing that expansion of self and a denial (by way of a contraction) of that expansion.

What is the concrete sense of self that is expanded and in that sense transcended through spirituality? It is our sense of personal identity. But personal identity raises very different issues in different cultures. In conversation, *Who are you?* in China most likely means, *Who is your family?* Whereas *Who are you?* in the United States most likely means, *What do you do (for a living)?* Indeed, it raises very different sorts of questions for different individuals, depending on their lot in life, their temperaments, their talents and their possibilities. *Who am I?* asked by a jaded but still scrupulous entrepreneur facing down a potentially lucrative dirty deal implies a very different concern than *Who am I?* asked by a student selecting a major or the *Who am I?* asked by a frustrated mother and housewife who has never had the opportunity to test her talents in the marketplace. In the context of spirituality, by contrast, the *Who are you?* question quite quickly leads to speculation about the eternal soul and the loss of self to the enormity of the universe. But I want to say, *Whoa*. Let's slow down. The spiritual "Who" may not need to be so conceived and in any case probably should not be conceived in terms of either eternity or loss.

Starting with concrete personal identity, we should note that every human being has *some* conception of him- or herself, and that conception can be called into question in both its scope and contents. Taken at its minimal face value, the question *Who am I?* would seem to be a request for a name. Occasionally, such a request may be dramatic, for example, after an accident or a long drugged sleep. A name in turn implies a history and a place in a social nexus. In moments of moral crisis, the same question can be a cry of despair or deep existential confusion. *Who am I?* means *What am I now to do?* My history and my social place and position have been called into question. What concerns me is not what I have been but what I should be. Such existential crises evoke the angst much celebrated by Kierkegaard, Heidegger, Sartre and all of those millions of Ericksonian adolescents. But in a spiritual context, which is not the same as an existential crisis (and is not, *contra* some spiritualist traditions, akin to a long-drugged sleep), the question seems to require something more than the ordinary self and a merely social self-identity. The difficult question is, how much "more?" Here again we should resist the temptation to take a leap into the transcendent and the divine.

In some philosophical or ecumenical moments, we think of this expanded personal identity in abstract species terms, "I am a human being." Such thoughts are already a step towards spirituality, for we (momentarily, at least) cease to think of ourselves as particular beings with our own interests and instead think of ourselves in a community of essentially similar beings. This idealized sense of self is well represented in classical art, for instance the art of the Greeks, where heroic figures are depicted as ideal types and not as individuals ("warts and all"). The obvious contrast is the sculpture of the Romans, a famously unspiritual people, in which we do indeed get the warts. This idealized sense of self can also be located in such different religious sources as Christianity and Confucianism in the thesis that *humanity* is to be found in each and every individual. Unfortunately, the usual answer to *What is it to be a human being?* is neither so abstract nor ecumenical. The idealized Greek looked—Greek. Humanity is typically depicted in terms of one's own type. In most cultural contexts, not excluding Europe and North America, to be a human being means to be a person *much like us*, where "much like us" (and "person") refers in one instance to Aristotle's fellow male Athenian aristocrats, in another to Clifford Geertz's Javanese, in another to George W. Bush's faithful Republicans, and in still another to the Chinese. The definition excludes as well as includes. Such exclusion becomes all the more vicious when it is absolutized as the "Beloved of God" or the "Chosen people." So used, the word "human being" is no longer a biological category. It is a clumsy and sometimes oppressive political weapon. A spiritual conception of the self must first of all reject any such conception while nevertheless retaining the concrete personal self as its ontological anchor.

This concrete personal self should not be confused, however, with *individuality*. There is a popular sense in which every person is significant because he or she is "unique," but this is as irrelevant to personal identity as it is uninteresting. (Think of those Roman warts!) There is more to be said in favor of our significance insofar as we are *not* unique, but share (with our ideal prototypes) our most significant features. As Hegel and Nietzsche both argued, the category of the individual is one that has been carved out, in certain sorts of societies, in an often false or trivial way. For instance, in Western philosophy and religion there has been a crescendo towards pure *subjectivity*, already evident in Augustine's *Confessions* and solidified in Descartes's *Meditations* 1300 years later. The idea is that the concrete self is to be found "inside" of us, to which we have "privileged access," and it is therefore directly knowable through "introspection." The ancient concept of the individual soul is then recast as introspectable, and, indeed, by the time of Descartes it has already become more or less equivalent to the mind.

But in many cultures, one's sense of self and personal identity have little or nothing to do with introspection and that oddly "private" sense of individuality that follows from this. By contrast, one's sense of self and personal identity have everything to do with one's place in the family, the group, the community. In other words, the day-to-day conception of self is already enlarged, encompassing not only the individual, but all of his or her relations and connections to other people and, often, to the land and its natural richness. Even in Western philosophy, we find such luminous thinkers as St. Exupery declaring "man is but a network of relations, and these alone matter to him." Nevertheless, Western philosophy remains notoriously individualistic and is too often saddled with a narrowly introspective paradigm of selfhood, the metaphorical notion that the self or soul is something to be found inside, in contrast to its outward expression in behavior and in the "external world."

How important is self-reflection in the conception of self and soul? We sometimes talk about "looking into one's soul," but does this make sense, given the fact that we are also told that the soul is something distinct from the particularities of our experience? Or, perhaps, one looks inside one's soul precisely to the extent that one looks at oneself *not* as consciousness but as a person behaving in such-and-such ways, expressing such-and-such feelings, that is looking at yourself as you would look at another person? Or, more obscurely, suppose that one looks inside one's soul precisely to the extent that one looks at oneself *not* as an individual but only insofar as one is conscious and aware of being-in-the-world? This is what Heidegger called *Dasein*, simply "being-there." Heidegger (like Hume before him) would be quick to say that there is no soul to be found there. Thus even through introspection it is by no means obvious that what one finds in one's consciousness is one's self or soul, and one might push much harder (as Heidegger does) to question whether the metaphor looking into even makes sense. Pushing even harder, one might identify oneself not as a particular human being, nor even as human, but as something undefined, perhaps even an all-encompassing cosmic or general consciousness that just happens to be specifically situated. This is what Hegel called "Spirit," but Spirit, unlike the metaphysician's soul, might be quite the contrary of something very individual and inside of us and it is certainly not *mind* or *subject* as distinct from body and the biophysical world.

Thus what once seemed simple (each of us has his or her own soul and is immediately aware of it) evokes a blizzard of questions: What is the relationship between the self, the soul, and the mind? Are these three different names for the same thing (as in Descartes, for example)? Or is the self something *in* the mind and the soul something transcendent and not "in" the natural mind at all? Once we begin to question the one person, one soul assumption, what are we to make of the notion of a multiplicity of selves, which has now moved from the annals of psychiatry into mainstream personality theory (and Hollywood fantasy)?[2] What are we to make of the notion of the "de-centered" and "fragmented" self that is the love of so many French postmodernists? What are to we to make of the notion of "no-self" (*Anatman*) so central to several forms of Buddhism? And most important for our exploration of spirituality, what are we to make of Hegel's Spirit (*Geist*, often mistranslated into English as "mind") and many mystics' claims that the true self is not ultimately individual but cosmic? Do we have to abandon subjectivity and individuality, or are they just a misleading focus on a much larger and more complex phenomenon?

Beyond Descartes: Mind and the Mind-Body Problem

> Although I certainly do possess a body with which I am very closely con-
> joined, nevertheless, I have a clear and distinct idea of myself, in as far as
> I am a thinking and unextended thing, and as on the other hand, I possess
> a distinct idea of body, in as far as it is only an extended and unthinking
> thing, it is certain that I [as mind] am entirely and truly distinct from my
> body, and may exist without it.
>
> —René Descartes, *Mediations*

One of the long-standing problems in philosophy that bears directly on the concept of self and personal identity but blocks progress towards a naturalization of soul and spirit is the Cartesian conception of the mind and the so-called mind-body problem. The mind-body problem is usually traced back to the musings and meditations of René Descartes and Cartesian dualism. Descartes took the mind to be a special sort of substance, an immaterial and unextended thing not located in space and wholly distinct from the (extended) body. But, then, how is the mind connected to the body—or, more precisely, to the brain?

Today it has become a matter of general consensus, shared by such diverse interest groups as French-styled postmodernists and neurology-loving cognitive scientists, that Descartes made a stupid mistake. He separated what obviously should not have been separated and led philosophers to struggle for 300 years to put Humpty Dumpty together again.

. But, then, we should pause to consider that the distinction between mind and body in one form or another goes back to ancient times, perhaps to the beginning of human self-consciousness. It can be found in many if not most philosophical traditions. It is the recognition that people (and many if not most other animals) have at least two different aspects, obviously linked but not identical: their merely material or physical being and something else, their life, their spirit, their animus, their soul, their mind. After death, the material being remains. The life seems to be gone. Viewed in this way, "mind" and "body" are two short but clumsy English words that point to these two different aspects. And some such distinction is built into virtually every language and every known way of thinking.

Although mind and soul were pretty much interchangeable for Descartes, it is by no means clear to what extent he thought that the survival of the soul after death carried with it many aspects of the mind, for instance, particular memories and emotions. He was intrigued by neurology (that is, the relation between consciousness and the brain). But it is quite clear that what ultimately moved Descartes was not the physiological intrigue so much as it was the often violent confrontation of religions and the seemingly perennial conflict between religion and science. "*Soul*" was the name of a domain that could be known and explored though subjectivity and independently of both science and religious authority.

It is too rarely appreciated, in the ferocious debate over "sensations and brain processes,"[3] to what extent the traditional separation of mind and body has protected the relatively safe operation of two very different spheres of human inquiry and concern. This was evident in early Christianity, and it had certainly become a major concern by the end of the medieval era and when Descartes was writing. Descartes' distinction between two substances safely protected the physical sciences from the dogmatic authority of religion, and, in the centuries to come, it protected religion from the physical sciences. Immanuel Kant nicely summarized that dichotomy years later when he insisted that we "limit knowledge, to make room for faith." The separation of mind and body was no philosophical "error."[4] For many centuries, it rather made Western philosophy—as the study of human freedom and faith and their consequences—possible.

This is a very different way of approaching the "problem" than the now current conception of the mind-body problem as a technical, quasi-scientific set of questions. I say quasi-scientific because there is some real tension between those who do the empirical research on the brain and those philosophers who theorize about it. Descartes would not have raised the mind-body (or mind-brain) problem without the flourishing of seventeenth century scientific knowledge about the brain (about which he was as knowledgeable as any of his contemporaries). The discovery of the neuron at the end of the nineteenth century and increasing knowledge of brain function and physiology at the end of the twentieth now puts the problem on the front burner, for neuroscientists and many philosophers alike. Perhaps that is why, one might suggest, there is no such problem in Aristotle, in Confucius, or in the Upanishads, despite ample concern in all three traditions for the nature of the person and the nature of the soul. They did not know diddly about the brain. And, of course, they had no desktop PCs to compare minds to.

But let us move away from the particularities of mind-brain research to ask a far more general and more radical question: How are minds distributed among the beings of the world? Hegel and many Vedic philosophers would say that there is only one mind, one consciousness, for all of us. Many traditional tribal religions would grant some sort of mind to every thing, including rocks and plants as well as animals and human beings. A few pathological cases and a good deal of postmodern rhapsodizing would suggest that there might be several minds per human body. Descartes viewed animals as machines without souls and therefore without minds as well. We, of course, worry about how far throughout the animal kingdom one finds minds (as opposed to mere "sensitivity"). Dogs, cats, horses, elephants, dolphins, and whales, certainly. Sparrows, of course, lizards and frogs—arguably, bees and ants—questionably, worms and mollusks—dubious. But this all depends on what we think of as mind. If mind were to mean mere sensitivity—the ability to feel pain or sense light or heat, for example, then mind goes all the way down the list. If by mind we mean the capacity to have feelings, that is, emotions, then the line probably gets drawn between lizards and frogs.[5] But if mind means what Descartes and many other philosophers think it means, the capacity for reflective self-consciousness, then not all human beings would seem to have minds. Indeed, having a mind might be a relatively rare human achievement.

By contrast, if mind means only some sort of animation or self-movement, as in Aristotle's *anima*, then the way is open to attribute mind or minds to not only living things but much of the earth (and, perhaps, the earth itself) as well. Thus Aristotle said that all living things and even the universe itself had an *anima*—typically translated as soul. Such a notion has everything to do with the question of spirituality—and again this does not oppose spirituality to science—and it has to do with a more radical suggestion about how mind or minds is/are distributed among bodies in the universe.

If mind or soul can be attributed to the world or the universe as a whole as well as individual creatures within it, then the attribution of minds to individuals on a one-to-one basis can be called into question. Here, of course, is where Hegel as well as the ancient Vedas and other classic spiritual texts come into the picture. They do not deny the existence of individual consciousness. (Indeed, what would be the point of doing so, except to say something palpably absurd?) But they do raise the question, Why do we insist on individuating minds (or consciousnesses) *only* on an individual basis? If Aristotle, Hegel, or the Buddha is right, couldn't there be One Mind that we (in some sense) all share?

Body, Mind, and Soul: Some Asian Perspectives

> The self which is free from evil, free from old age, free from death, free from grief, free from hunger and thirst, whose desire is the real, whose thought is the real, he should be sought, him one should desire to understand. He who has found out and who understands that self, he obtains all worlds and all desires.
>
> —*Chandogya Upanishad*

It is an oft-stated observation in comparative philosophy: in Indian philosophy, in Chinese philosophy, in other philosophical traditions, the mind-body problem—at least in the form stated by Descartes and treated by his successors—did not arise. This does not indicate any inadequacy on the part of those traditions. On the contrary, the fact that they lack any appreciation of the truncated concepts of mind and body in the Cartesian sense is now taken as a sign of their superiority from a spiritual point of view. They do talk, in different ways and with different concerns, about *persons*, and, in Indian philosophy in particular, there is remarkably subtle and complicated concern with different senses of *soul* or *self* and its relation to persons (*parusha*). There is *jiva*, which represents the individual self. There is *Atman*, which represents the larger, cosmic self we all share, and then there is *Brahman*, the one, all-encompassing reality. There are also several distinctive senses of the social self, which differ (but are ultimately identified with) all of these.

Persons have different aspects, some of them indisputably physical (one's weight, one's warts), others having rather to do with perception, awareness, consciousness, thoughts, beliefs, desires, and emotions. But what is important in discussions of the self or soul is not so much the relation *between* these as their *significance* for higher-order spiritual knowledge. Perhaps the most personal and enduring controversy throughout Indian philosophy is, Is the individual self (*jiva*) real? Or is it an illusion? Jains and Buddhists, in particular, come to very different conclusions about this. Throughout the Vedic tradition, it is clear that the ultimate identity of a person lies in the one ultimate reality. But whether or not this should be construed as cosmic soul (Atman) or not (Anatman) remains the Vedic bone of contention. Discussions of the senses and the appetites as well as discussions of perceptual and conceptual knowledge are all geared to this realization.[6]

In Indian philosophy, the mind is continuous with the body, not, as in Descartes, opposed to or distinct from it. There is no one dualism that hovers over Indian philosophy as Descartes's dualism hovers over Western philosophy. Indeed, an appreciation for the complexity of the world coupled with a strong resistance to reductionism defines a great deal of Indian philosophy. Spiritual monists would argue that mind, and body too, are nothing but aspects of spirit (another identifiable Western view, usually associated with Spinoza, Hegel and the remarkably unspiritual "neutral monism" of Bertrand Russell). True, there are those in Indian philosophy who would agree that the relationships (note the plural) between mind and body are peculiar, but the Nyaya, Mimamsa, and other Realists would add that there are many peculiar relationships in this spectacularly rich and complex world, that this one is nothing special. South Asia also has its materialists (Carvaka) who would argue that there is *nothing but* continuity and that consciousness is what William James calls an epiphenomenon. The Carvakas even ridicule the very notion of soul or consciousness, drawing a famous analogy between consciousness and the brewing of beer. ("And from these (material) elements alone is consciousness produced, like the intoxicating power produced when kinwa etc. are mixed together [to form beer]."[7])

In Chinese philosophy, identifying spiritual analogs to the mind-body problem is even more difficult, although, again, there are surely distinctions that could be interpreted in terms of the "mental" and the "physical." It would be utter nonsense to deny that the Chinese recognize anything like consciousness or subjectivity, but the holistic complementarity of Chinese philosophy, summarized as *yin* and *yang*, already suggests that anything like an opposition of incommensurable substances would not play a prominent role. In Mencius (a contemporary of Aristotle), what is called "mind" is "moral mind" or what we would call "ethical character," the locus of compassion and humanity.[8] The mind is not to be distinguished from the person. Indeed, the distinctions to be found in Chinese philosophy are much more reminiscent of Aristotle than Descartes. The mind is not to be distinguished from either the person or the body but, especially, it is not to be construed as an amoral phenomenon, a mere subject for scientific investigation.

In the neo-Confucians, for example, Chinese *li* (principle) and *ch'i* matter (literally, "instrument") resemble Aristotle's form and matter far more than they do Descartes' mind and body. "*Li*" is primarily the term used for ritual action, indicating not thoughts as such but appropriate behavior. That "*li*" does not refer to mind is exemplified in the following exchange (from Chu Hsi): "Do things without feeling possess *li*? Certainly." *Li*, like Aristotle's *anima*, is the form or principle of all things. Human nature includes the *li* of humanity, and in all men it is the same. It is the *ch'i* that makes them different.[9] But mind exists only when *ch'i* is united with *li*. "The case is similar to that of the flame of the candle . It is because the latter receives this rich fat that we have so much light."[10] Other such dichotomies are similarly complementary. In Tung Chung-shu, for example, human nature is said to be made up of two elements, *hsing* (man's nature) and *ch'ing* (*emotions or feelings*), which in a narrow sense might be opposed but, in a broader sense, *hsing* embraces *ch'ing*, where *ch'ing* means something like "basic stuff."[11]

In Chinese philosophy, even more than in Indian philosophy, *holism* is a viable alternative to Descartes's dualism.[12] Yet, this is no "identity theory," in the sense still defended in contemporary Anglo-American philosophy. It is neither a solution nor mere neglect of Descartes' problem. It rather depends on an entirely different context, a context in which neither the body nor the brain is considered as a discrete object. Moreover, the individual mind as such is of relatively little interest because the isolated individual "soul" or "consciousness" is of only secondary interest as well. The dominant concept in Confucian philosophy is *jen* or "the whole person" in his or her social context. It was a context in which the exercise and manipulation of the body and its energy (*ch'i*) is seen as one with as well as a means to the cultivation of one's person in community.[13] This, I would suggest, is the much-touted "wisdom of the East," not any particular conception of soul, or spirituality but an openness in which self, soul and spirituality are contextually conceived as a negotiable aspect of nature and society.

The Rise of the Western Soul

The Greeks, from Homer to Democritus, believed in the soul only to a minimal extent. They admitted that something, call it "breath" (which is the original meaning of the word *psyché*), was needed to animate the body, which departed the body with death. But, according to this picture, the soul needed the body just as much as the body needed the soul. Without the soul, the body was dead, but without the body, the soul was just a pathetic shadow, (the shades of Hades), with no meaning and no value. This is, perhaps, a gloomy version of the pagan view I am defending here, except (here is the upbeat part) the shadow in question is one that lives on in the minds and the hearts of those who survive us. This was the understanding of the ancient Hebrews, and it is worth asking what sort of interpretation and what kind of wishful thinking combined the Hebrew and the Greek into such a radically different conception of a bodiless soul enjoying a blissful independent and eternal existence.

Part of the answer, of course, is Socrates. Socrates held that the soul outlives the body in a far more significant sense than any of his predecessors, even the ancient Egyptians, who clearly had a keen picture of the survival of the soul. But the Egyptians, anticipating precisely this point, could not conceive of the soul apart from the body. And so the resurrection of the body was essential to the survival of the soul.[14] (There are remnants of this in early Christianity, and the spiritual body plays much the same role in Buddhism.) But in the *Apology*, where Socrates fantasizes the joy of thinking philosophy all of the time in the afterlife, without interruptions or distractions, it is as if he faced death as the prospect of a vacation, even treating it as a cure for life.[15]

Plato's later vision only reinforces this conception of the soul. The soul, unlike the rest of us, belongs (in part) to the World of Being, the eternal world. The loss of the body is therefore only a partial loss (or no loss at all, depending on how you look at it). That is why, according to Socrates, a truly good man can ultimately suffer no evil, despite physical harm or even death. His good soul survives any and all of the outrages and misfortunes visited upon the body. In the *Phaedo*, Socrates says, "In order to know anything absolutely, we must be free from the body and behold actual reality with the eyes of the soul alone." The soul thus becomes the conduit of personal as well as intellectual and moral life. Quite literally, it is the one thing in life truly worth worrying about.

But for Socrates, it was not as if the soul was deep inside of us. This was the product of the long course of Christian theology, as the soul became more and more identified with a "deep" conception of self. The first step, perhaps, was Aristotle's bold but innocent insistence on the "inner" workings of the self, that is, those movements of an animal or human soul (*anima*) that are self-moving rather than engineered from without. But with that simple discovery of the "inside" of the soul, it was only a matter of time until what began as a simple description of self-movement turned into the invention of a vast and largely unexplored inner cavern. The metaphor of depth suggests that the soul is indeed within, presumably in the same metaphorical sense that the mind is "in" the body (or in the brain). But as I have suggested, I do not think that this long-standing metaphor is very productive or illuminating. Nor do I find anything intelligible in the idea that the soul is part and parcel of some *other* world, whether it is Plato's World of Being or the Christian Heaven and Holy Spirit. But this is not the only concept of soul, nor is it one that helps rather than hinders our self-understanding.

Although the notion of the soul dates back as far as the very beginnings of philosophy and religion, it should not be supposed that the metaphysical and otherworldly interpretations of soul are the last word. In addition to the excessive individualism of the soul idea—what Kant (who believed in it) disdainfully called the "soul thing" and Nietzsche (who did not) called "soul atomism"—the very virtues of the soul hypothesis turn out to be its undoing. Its independence from the vicissitudes of life also render it *irrelevant* to life, and the very fact of its profound interiority cut it off from the one thing that really matters to it, those connections to the world and to other people that make the soul spiritual. Instead of thinking of the soul as deep and inside of us, why not look in another direction, outward, and think of the soul as that which transcends our individuality and joins us with other people and the world at large?

Soul and Society (Kafka's Identity Crisis)

> When Gregor Samsa woke up one morning from unsettling dreams, he found himself changed in his bed into a monstrous vermin. . . . What's happened to me he thought. It was no dream.
>
> —Franz Kafka, *Metamorphosis*

The mind-body dichotomy can be cut in many different ways, not only through a metaphorical pineal gland in which mind stuff and brain stuff supposedly meet, but by way of a rich variety of moral and social contexts in which it is the whole living person in his or her society that remains the primary focus. In the preceding chapter, I commented on the solipsistic nature of a good deal of Western thinking about death, the Christian conception of the afterlife as individual soul-survival being just its most obvious instance. But much of Western thinking about life and the nature of the self tends to be individualistic to the point of solipsism, the lone, true self in isolation from (or antagonistic with) other people and community, what Nietzsche and Kierkegaard in agreement called the "herd." But individual soul-survival is not the only conception of the continuation of the soul after death, and the isolated individual soul is not the only or the best instantiation of soul.

In Judaism, the ancient conception of continuity is firmly tied to community remembrance. In many ancient Asian and tribal religions around the world, continuity is to be found through spirits that survive only through a living social medium, for instance, a new generation. The soul may survive the death of a particular body, but it cannot survive without bodies and it cannot survive alone. In many religions, the survival of the soul is firmly tied to past behavior, in other words, to ethics and morality. In Indian philosophy, the soul survives the body as the residue (*karma*) of one's previous self. The psychological idiosyncrasies that defined the person before his or her death are not of lasting importance, but his or her moral behavior is definitive. Reincarnation would be a very different prospect if one maintained one's particular memories and individual sense of self-identity, but this is the stuff of fairy tales. It may be good Kafka, but it doesn't play in Calcutta. In Indian philosophy as in Jewish theology, the self is a social self, and the Indian soul survives as the holistic One rather than as one individual. (Indeed, individuality is conceived as a burden, not a blessing.)

If we reject (or at any rate do not give a privileged place to) the Cartesian notion of self as mind as introspective individual consciousness, what we discover is that our concept of self, too, is social. With a hint of paradox, one might note again (following Hegel and Nietzsche) that the individual self—that is, our conception of an individual self, even our conception of individual consciousness—is a social product of a certain sort of society with a certain kind of language and certain distinctive individuating concepts. To be sure, there are more primitive notions of self that have to do merely with the organism in its organized engagements with the world (as in works by biologist Lewis Thomas and neurologist Antonio Damasio[16]), but the reflective self of self-consciousness, in which *conceptions* of the self become relevant, is something distinctively human. Understanding this, and understanding the many senses in which the self is open to all sorts of interpretation and transformation, is an essential step in coming to terms with an adequate concept of the self as soul and as spirit in naturalized spirituality. The self as soul is not an eternal nugget but an ever-changing, always negotiable part of the world.

Consider, in this regard, poor Gregor Samsa, turned (in the very first sentence) into a cockroach by his creator, Franz Kafka. As a consequence, Gregor had an identity crisis, a confusion about who he is. But an identity crisis is not, for the most part, self-contained. Despite its existential focus, it is essentially a social problem. How can poor Gregor make it to the office today? How can he deal with the horrified screams and disgust of his sister? What is he to do with long-habituated conceptions of himself as a loyal, hardworking employee, a good provider, and an innocuous, perfectly ordinary citizen, once he finds himself turned into a vermin?

Waking up as a giant insect in a world all his own, Gregor might still have to cope with the problem of getting off of his back, but what the story is about is his social embarrassment. Similarly, an adolescent is at an awkward age not so much because his or her body is out of control as because of his or her intolerable social position—no longer a child, incompetent as an adult. Again, Camus's Meursault (in *The Stranger*) has great difficulty getting used to being called a criminal, not because of the negative meaning of the term but because he has never understood what it is to be called or classified as anything. He is strange in part because he has no inherent sense of self-identity, his rich sense of subjective experience notwithstanding.

One's identity is a social construct. An identity crisis is a social crisis. That is why Jean-Paul Sartre, after 300 pages on the dualistic dialectic between Being "in-itself" (bodily thinghood) and "for itself" (consciousness) insists on introducing "Being-for-Others" as a third basic category.[17] In just plain English, what one *is* is a function of not only the facts and what one thinks of oneself but what others think and what they make of those facts. Indeed, one can read the third part of *Being and Nothingness* as a systematic undoing of what has been going on before. The facts that constrain personal identity are neither given nor determined by the subject. They are a matter of social construal, dependent on the context as well as the (often malevolent) motives of others. (Thus Garcin, the character in Sartre's play *Huis Clos, No Exit,* tries desperately to construe himself as a hero despite his cowardly performance in front of the firing squad. He then finds himself the victim of his two eternal roommates, Estelle, who could not care less about his *post facto* identity crisis, and Inez, who already despises him.)

This picture of mutually construed personhood is borrowed from Hegel (from whom some of Sartre's awkward Teutonic terminology is also taken). In his master and slave parable in the *Phenomenology,* Hegel suggests (the text is too understated to do more than suggest) that personhood essentially depends on what he calls recognition by another. The general suggestion is that one would not be a self at all without mutual recognition, and this recognition obviously refers to oneself as publicly embodied (as opposed to the Cartesian model of introspective self-identification). The argument is rendered somewhat more complicated by virtue of the fact that Hegel refers to the individuals involved as self-consciousnesses, indicating that they already have some sense of self-awareness,[18] but the primacy of recognition of *persons* rather than the purely mental self is evident enough.[19]

Hegel also suggests that the self and self-consciousness are first of all a matter of *status*, and status can be obtained, again, only through mutual recognition. In the stripped-down world of the parable, the proto-persons engaged in mutual recognition have not much to rely on, since they are presumably without social rank, bank accounts, a wardrobe, good upbringing, philosophical wit, or any of the other pedestrian virtues by which we compare and measure ourselves. So, Hegel says, they fight, "to the death" if necessary, but, of course, the death of one would defeat the aim of the other, namely, to be recognized. Hegel then describes the curious inversion that confuses all questions of status and, consequently, compels both master and slave to more philosophical attempts at self-understanding.[20]

Hegel's point is that personal self-identity is not just the abstraction, self-consciousness. It is concrete and it is social, even when it perversely rejects both the concrete and the social.[21] One's identity is never just as a person, a human being, or an organism of a particular animal species; it is as a *particu-*

lar person, defined by where we fit ourselves into the world. Anything less is just, as Hegel would say, an "empty universal." Thus Kafka's Samsa is defined neither by his consciousness nor by his grotesque physical transformation, but by his concrete social relationships.

Nevertheless, being a particular person (or a particularly bookish cockroach) is not the last word for Hegel. Not only are our selves formed only in interaction with others, our selves ultimately *are* that interaction, that network of relations. But interdependent selfhood is not the end of the story either. Cultural identity gives us our first sense of spirit, but it still falls short of spirituality. Cultures in conflict—even in the name of spirituality or spiritual matters—are hardly examples of spirituality. Hegel's own philosophy was largely motivated (at the height of the Napoleonic Wars in the early nineteenth century) by the notion of international community and harmony. But even this is too limited. So in our search for comprehension and harmony with the world, we are drawn to Hegel's grand conception of self as Spirit, not as opposed to individuality or culture but as an ever-larger, more comprehensive understanding of ourselves.

Spirituality, Soul, and the Transformation of the Self

> Let us get rid of *soul atomism*. [But] between ourselves, it is not at all necessary to get rid of "the soul" at the same time, and thus to renounce one of the most ancient and venerable hypotheses—as happens frequently to clumsy naturalists who can hardly touch on "the soul" without immediately losing it. . . .
>
> —Friedrich Nietzsche, *Beyond Good and Evil*

The very word soul has long suggested something deep and enduring, something transcendent and divine. Does our naturalistic spirituality wipe out any possibility of such a soul? I think that Nietzsche has an important insight here. Getting rid of transcendent and unworldly notions of soul does not eliminate the most spiritually significant aspects of soul, and once we give up what he calls soul atomism—the notion of soul as a metaphysical nugget deep inside of each one of us—the concept of soul begins to look more or less identical to the concept of spirituality. In Indian philosophy, from which Nietzsche took a lot more (via Schopenhauer) than he let on, the notion of *Atman* fills this very role. It is one's true self and in that sense one's soul, but it need not be opposed to either one's ordinary self or the more profound religious conceptions of soul. It is very here and now, yet something much *more*—and not deeper—than the self of everyday life. If deeper means simply profound (the same metaphor, but with an implication of insight and special significance), then, of course, one's true self is indeed deeper than the often petty, obsessive, or frivolous self of everyday life. But if deeper means deep inside, then we have given good reasons why such an introspective framework falsifies both the self, which is "out there" in the world rather than "in here" in our minds, and the passions that (in part) constitute the self, which are also about the world and not merely the psychic rumblings of our own interiority. I propose that we shift our understanding of soul to focus on this sensitivity to and participation in the world. There need be no interiority, and there need be no transcendent selflessness.

Thinking of soul as selflessness, or as metaphysical eternal nugget, leaves out what is most essential to soul as spirituality and that is *passion*. I refer not necessarily to those noisy, explosive passions, but those that are all-embracing and pervasive: caring, love, reverence, and trust, for instance. Thus there is a street-level conception of soul (for example, at the core of the blues as a musical and philosophical genre) that is closer to the mark than the dispassionate conception of a transcendent nugget that in some sense resides deep in the heart of every one of us. To have soul is to experience profound emotions in one's intimate engagements in the world, not just as pertaining to one's own individual woes but as exemplary of the human condition. To have experienced a great deal and to have digested and accepted it, is to have soul. Thus the soul is not something other than the ordinary self, but it is the ordinary self filled with extraordinary feelings, none of which need to be directed toward anything outside of life. Indeed, one could argue that such transcendent focus tends to be a distraction.

In philosophical terms Aristotle's great-souled man (*megalopsyche*) is a person complete with all of the virtues. Nietzsche follows with his view that such a character (exemplified by his imaginary *Übermensch*) overflows himself. What Aristotle does not say but clearly holds, and what Nietzsche makes amply clear, is that the *megalopsyche* and the *Übermensch* both represent someone with extensive and profound experience, including a good deal of suffering, and it is through such suffering, together with virtue, that soul develops. Hegel's conception of Spirit, which is nothing less than the collective soul of all of humanity and nature, develops through experience and suffering. This, of course, is the critical point: that spirituality and the naturalistic conception of the soul *develop* from the more ordinary concept of self rather than constitute a radical break or leap away from the mundane, daily self. Thus many wisdom traditions insist that spirituality is to be found in the details of everyday life—or it is to be found nowhere. The idea of a mystical experience or a sudden spiritual breakthrough is dramatically appealing—and it nurtures our desire for immediate and uncompromising gratification—but I doubt that it is a very sensible aspiration for most of us.

A much more practical and worldly approach to the development of soul is through the interpersonal sentiment of compassion. The Buddhists (and

Schopenhauer in the West) identified compassion as the key to the conjunction of the individual self and all of the other selves with which it is conjoined, and for many Buddhists it also signaled the shift to spirituality. Very few Buddhists ever experience the nirvana described by the greatest sages, but every good Buddhist daily experiences the compassion for suffering that ties him or her to the world and to other people. So, too, very few Christians or Sufis have experienced that mystical bliss described, for instance, by Meister Johannes Eckhart, but every good Christian or Sufi daily experiences the compassion for suffering that ties him or her to the world and to other people. This fits in well with our earlier characterization of spirituality as a passion. Compassion is a keen awareness of our interconnectedness with others, not just on the level of intellectual realization. but on the basis of immediate *feeling* as well (where feeling obviously includes understanding). Through compassion, even those of us with amazingly fortunate and comfortable lives can share in the suffering of others, not just vicariously but (as in the Blues) through the passionate comprehension of how we all in some sense share life and its difficulties. It is through compassion that we can get beyond Sartre's slightly paranoid notion of "being-for-others," in which other people are viewed as a threat rather than as an extension of ourselves. It is also through compassion that we place ourselves firmly in the world's community of souls (animal as well as human). Indeed, Nietzsche makes much of this point and it was only his own hypersensitive nature that provoked him to condemn pity and compassion (*Mitleid*) so roundly.

When I say that spirituality is the enlargement and not the negation of the self, it is this communal sense of self as soul, instantiated in its most immediate form as compassion, that I have in mind. But it need not just be negative, a painful awareness of the suffering of the world. It can also be the positive sense of the joy of the world, the euphoric sense of sharing life and sharing in the happiness of others. Soul and spirituality find their natural base in this concept of an enlarged and enhanced sense of the compassionate ordinary self. It is our ordinary selves, not some idealized vision of human nature, that naturally seeks community and harmony and embraces the natural world. It is thus a distortion of ourselves that we get locked into petty tasks and competitions, and selfishness—that cynics always seem to think lies at the heart of human nature—turns out to be nothing of the kind but rather a constriction and a cramping of human nature. Thus soul is both something natural and something to be striven for, perhaps not so much our truer selves as our *better* selves. And to speak of soul is not a rejection of the ordinary individual self but rather the full realization of it.

The most important reason to "believe" in the soul is not the possibility of life continuing after death but rather the possibility of an essential *transformation* of the self during life. This is put in different ways by different religions, whether in terms of salvation or enlightenment, whether through faith, good works, prayer, group song, or private meditation. The self of everyday life, we are assured by the various traditions, is not necessarily the real self. The self that is too often selfish, that is too readily caught up in its own personal ambitions and interests, may in fact be—as we sometimes suspect it to be—a distorted self, a deluded self, a self that is neither one nor at peace with itself. It is a mistake, however, to insist that this mundane self be sacrificed or replaced by some other self rather than transformed through discipline and spirituality. Thus Socrates sought the transformation of his self through philosophy, the Buddha and Jesus through their own understanding of suffering.

In many spiritual traditions, the purpose of life itself becomes the achievement of such a transformation. For some, it could happen in a moment, like Saint Paul's conversion on the road to Damascus. For others, it may take a lifetime of ritual and practice, like those Tibetan monks whose self-discipline is legendary. For most people, the transformation of self may be nothing more than total immersion in a group and a tradition. But for those of us who enjoy the mixed blessing of seeing beyond all traditions and thus finding ourselves without an anchor in the world, spirituality is rather an arduous process, filled with doubts and misgivings, skeptical of glib formulations and platitudes, frustrated with the limitations of the personalities we have worked so hard to create over the course of a hard-headed lifetime. But if the self to which spirituality and philosophy refers is nothing *other* than the everyday self, neither is it *just* the everyday self, and the tremendous effort to discover or realize our better selves is what spirituality is all about. Thus, to borrow an old observation from Hegel, spirituality is a process rather than a result. This may seem to be far less than the true enlightenment that spirituality often promises, but this naturalized notion of spirituality is, in this narcissistic and materialist age, something well worth striving for.

Thus soul meets spirit and spirituality, not only in suffering but in cosmic joy and humor as well, what Nietzsche famously referred to as the Dionysian aspect of human life.

CREDITS

Many of these chapters are based on my book, *The Joy of Philosophy*, (New York: Oxford University Press, 1999). The first chapter was written exclusively for this book. The prior incarnations of pieces upon which the other chapters are based are:

Chapter 2: Spirituality as Passion was partially drawn from "The Virtues of the Passionate Life," which was originally published in the Bowling Green State University Center for Social Philosophy and Policy journal, *Social Philosophy and Policy* (vol. 15, no. 1, 1998), "The Politics of Emotions," in P. French, ed., *Midwest Studies in Philosophy*, vol. XXII (*Emotions*), and "Beyond Reason" in J. Ogilvy, ed., *Revisioning Philosophy* (S.U.N.Y. Press, 1993).

Chapter 3: Spirituality as Cosmic Trust was adapted from *Building Trust*, which I co-authored with Fernando Flores (Oxford, 2001).

Chapter 4: Spirituality as Rationality is partially based on a talk at a conference on "Culture and Rationality" at Mount Abu, Rahjistan and subsequently published as "Existentialism, Emotions, and the Cultural Limits of Rationality," in *Philosophy East and West*, vol. 42, no. 4, Oct 1992 pp. 597–622. My thanks to the editors for allowing me to use and considerably amplify parts of that essay.

Chapter 5: Facing Up to Tragedy is adapted from *The Joy of Philosophy*.

Chapter 6: Spirituality, Fate, and Fatalism is based on some ideas in *The Joy of Philosophy* but much developed since then.

Chapter 7: Looking Forward to Death? was originally written for a conference in northern New Zealand in January of 1996 and first published as "Death Fetishism, Morbid Solipsism" in J. Malpas and R. Solomon, eds., *Death and Philosophy* (London: Routledge, 1998). This chapter is a radical abridgment of that essay.

Chapter 8: The Self in Transformation: Self, Soul, and Spirit is based on *The Joy of Philosophy*, and on an article I published in Ames, Wissanyake, Kasulis, eds., *Self as Person in Asian Theory and Practice* (State University of New York Press, 1994), and an earlier Oxford book, *A Short History of Philosophy*, co-authored with Kathleen M. Higgins (New York: Oxford University Press, 1997). The section on the mind-body problem is adapted from my critical review of William Lyons's book, *The Philosophy of Mind* (London: Dent, 1995), published in *Philosophy East and West*, vol. 46., no. 3, 1996.

NOTES

INTRODUCTION

1. It was Fichte who famously said that "a philosophy is not something that one can try on at will. The kind of philosophy one chooses depends on the kind of man that one is." *The Vocation of Man.* Trans. P. Preuss. (Indianapolis: Hackett, 1987).

2. James Crabbe, *From Soul to Self* (New York: Routledge, 1999).

CHAPTER 1

1. Nietzsche, *Gay Science*, sect 257. Trans. W. Kaufmann. (New York: Random House, 1967).

2. Both of these theses have a long philosophical history. The Socratic and Stoic emphasis on self-examination had a lot to do with the elusiveness of our own thoughts and motives, and Jean-Paul Sartre famously argued (in *Being and Nothingness*) that other people's consciousness is a source of great anxiety to us. ("The other has a secret— the secret is what I *am*.") *Being and Nothingness.* Trans. M. Barnes. (New York: Philosophical Library, 1956).

3. Richard Bergh, quoted in the Catalog of the permanent collection at the Thielskad Museem, in Stockholm (that includes a marvelous portrait of Nietzsche by the great Norwegian artist, and Nietzsche enthusiast, Edvard Munch).

4. For example, Irving Singer, *The Harmony of Nature and Spirit* (in his *Meaning of Life* trilogy, Baltimore: Johns Hopkins, 1996) and Richard Dawkins (author of *The Selfish Gene*), *Unweaving the Rainbow* (New York: Houghton Mifflin, 1998).

5. I have in mind here Friedrich Hölderlin's poetry, which inspired both Hegel and Nietzsche (and later Heidegger as well). *Poems and Fragments 1778–1843*. Trans. M. Hamburger. (London: Anvil Press, 1994).

6. Noticeably absent from this expanding humanism are the atheists, who do not have merely a different name for God but see no need to believe in any such being in the first place. Thus the public ritual that preaches tolerance for everyone who believes in a "supreme being," while attempting to be all-embracing, is highly discriminatory, not only excluding atheists but any number of polytheistic and "godless" forms of spirituality.

7. See Robert T. Pennock, *The Tower of Babel: The Evidence Against the New Creationism* (Cambridge: M.I.T. Press, 2000) for a good critique of this.

8. *History and Human Nature* (New York: Harcourt Brace, 1979), *Continental Philosophy Since 1750* (Oxford: Oxford University Press, 1988).

9. See my *Joy of Philosophy* (Oxford: Oxford University Press, 1999).

10. According to studies by the Center for Reproductive Law and Policy and by Jean Ruth Schroedel, associate professor of political science at Claremont Graduate University, *Is the Fetus a Person? A Comparison of Policies in the Fifty States* (Ithaca, NY: Cornell University Press, 2000). "The data," Schroedel writes, "showed that anti-abortion states do not consistently value fetal life." Reported by Katha Pollitt in *The Nation,* 2001.

11. Immanuel Kant, "The Idea of a Universal History" (1794), reprinted in P. Gardiner, ed., *Theories of History* (Glencoe, IL: Free Press, 1959).

12. p. 9 in his *How Are We to Live* (Prometheus Books, 1995). See my "Peter Singer and the Expanding Circle" in Dale Jameson, ed. *Peter Singer and his Critics* (New York: Blackwell, 1999).

13. "Saint Peter" *Inside Magazine* (Philadelphia: December 1999).

14. Watty Piper, *The Little Engine that Could* (New York: Platt and Monk, 1930).

15. Julian Jaynes, *The Origins of Consciousness in the Breakdown of the Bicameral Mind* (Boston: Houghton-Mifflin, 1976).

16. Ned Block, 1981, accuses Jaynes of making what philosophers are fond of calling a "use-mention" mistake, that is confusing a phenomenon with the name or concept of that phenomenon. Jonathan Miller maintains that Jaynes places far too little weight on social and cultural factors in the origination of consciousness. On the first point, I think the argument here—that owes something to Daniel Dennett—absolves Jaynes of that particular philosophical sin. On Miller's criticism, it seems to me to be quite compatible with the general thesis I take Jaynes to be making, leaving aside his very controversial hypotheses about brain evolution. *Canadian Psychology,* vol. 27, 1986, 149–54.

17. G.W.F. Hegel, *Introduction to the Lectures on the Philosophy of History* (also known as *Reason in History*). Trans. L. Rauch. (Indianapolis: Hackett, 1988), 12.

18. Such a view has been defended, for example, both by Daniel Dennett in his work on consciousness, "Julian Jaynes's Software Ideology", *Consciousness*

Explained (Boston: Little Brown, 1991), and by Dennett's nemesis John Searle in his *Construction of the Social World* (New York: Free Press, 1997).

19. See Tara Smith, *Viable Values* (Lanham, MD: Roman and Littlefield, 2000).

CHAPTER 2

1. Sam Keen, *The Passionate Life* (New York: Harper and Row, 1983).

2. See my "In Defense of Sentimentality," *Philosophy and Literature*, Fall, 1990, 304–323.

3. There is, no doubt, some neurophysiological explanation of such behavior, probably in terms of such exotic brainstem spots as the locus coerulleus and the deficiency or excess of such chemicals as norepinephrine/seratonin. I do not doubt that a good deal of "the passionate life" is chronic rather than cultivated, but the question—if we are not to beg such questions as whether a virtue must be something "under one's control"—is whether the passionate life can be considered virtuous and, if so, what those virtues might be.

4. E.g., O.H. Green, "Emotions and Belief," *American Philosophical Quarterly Monograph* no. 6 (1972).

5. Of course, a new and different "character" may be revealed or emerge from that lapse, as when one falls in love or is overwhelmed emotionally by the birth of a new baby. Nevertheless, the virtue lies in the having of the emotion, not the disposition of character that may follow. In fact, several recent authors have rejected the strong sense of disposition and character as illusory. See Gil Harman, *Explaining Value* (Oxford: Oxford University Press, 1999) and John Doris, *Lack of Character* (Cambridge: Cambridge University Press, 2002).

6. If love is a virtue, for instance, there may yet be instances in which love is folly, although one would balk at the idea that love could sometimes be vicious. There are such passions, of course, but perhaps they should not be called "love," rather "obsession." For example, Heathcliff's destructive passion for Cathy in *Wuthering Heights* would seem to be like this. We might insist that love is a virtue even when it is foolish or destructive, however, just as we insist on calling justice a virtue even when the results are disastrous, or just as we insist on calling honesty a virtue even when the outcome is much worse than it would be with a simple "white" lie. But then, I think, we would want to draw some careful distinctions within the arena of virtuous behavior, adding some other measures that are independent of virtue-talk. I owe this clarification to a good question by Robert Audi.

7. Confucius, in emphasizing what we would call "the unity of theory and practice," repeatedly stresses the "virtuosity" of the virtuous person (*jen-ze*). There is no coincidence that this is also a familiar term in music, and, given Confucius's sense of the centrality of music in life, "virtuosity" is not a mistranslation.

8. See Luc Bovens, "The Value of Hope," *Philosophy and Phenomenological Research,* vol. 59, no. 3 (September 1999) where he discusses the film *The Shawshank Redemption* in this regard.

9. Deepak Chopra has widely promoted this sleazy thesis, ignoring the considerable wisdom of his native Tantric philosophy (that prolongs or abjures orgasm as the termination of the spiritual-sexual experience) and confusing the phenomenology of spiritual devotion with that of mere joyful obliteration.

10. The term has been banalized. It now refers to a friendship without sexual involvement. It originated, however, in the Renaissance, when it referred to the love of God *through* the love of another person. The origin, of course, is Plato's view that it is through the love of another person that one comes to love the Good.

11. The shift of attention from action and character to feelings can be argued to have occurred in Europe in the eighteenth century, in the works of Rousseau, most obviously, but also in the work of the Moral Sentiment theorists. There is an ancient argument against the passions, raised by Julia Annas, that holds that passion leads to excess. But what is meant by "excess," and is it not the desirability of such "excess" that is brought into question here? If "excess" means bad behavior, then there are plenty of arguments, in utilitarianism and in virtue ethics, to condemn such behavior. But if "excess" refers to the passions themselves, the ancient argument begs the question. My argument is that being passionate is, in a qualified sense, good in itself. And if that is so, then an "excess" of passion is impossible in just the same way that an excess of any virtue is impossible, according to Aristotle.

12. This is not to deny, however, that love might take inappropriate objects. Plato anticipates this possibility when he insists that love (*eros*) cannot be merely desire but must be desire for the Good. I take it, in a pedestrian illustration, that this means that one cannot love a person for features that are evil. This conflicts with some current popular wisdom, for instance, in the many too many movies in which one morally perverted character supposedly loves another precisely because of his or her moral perversions. (For instance, in Chodoros Laclos's epistolary novel, *Dangerous Liasons* (*Liasons Dangereuses*), and the several movie versions of this, most recently with Glenn Close and John Malkovich, directed by Stephen Frears (1988). I owe this clarification to a difficult question from Robert Audi.

13. E.g., Bernard Williams, "Morality and the Emotions."

14. Amelie Rorty, *Explaining Emotions* (Los Angeles: University of California Press, 1980) 103f.

15. This is not an a priori argument and it is subject to obvious empirical counter–examples, for example, the soaring divorce rate. But the fact that love often ends does not undermine the thesis that love is an emotional process that is (or can be) intensified and "deepened" with protracted intimacy, fa-

miliarity, knowledge, understanding, and shared experiences. The most poetic description of this process is the French Romantic M.-H. B. Stendhal's description of "crystallization," as the beloved accrues more and more charms and virtues. Stendhal (Marie-Henri Beyle), *On Love*, Trans. C.K. Scott-Moncrieff. (New York: Liveright, 1947) 28–34.

16. See my *About Love* (Lanham, MD: Rowman and Littlefield, 1994), chap. 2.

17. The term "intensity" is overly one dimensional and quantitative and is often confused with (and then measured by) physiological arousal. But the most powerful passions may be "calm" (Hume's term) while the most petty irritations can become "violent" (also Hume's term).

18. This is defended in detail in my *About Love*, 194ff.

19. This section owes a great deal—in fact, its very existence—to Paul Woodruff's *Reverence* (Oxford: Oxford University Press, 2001). I am greatly indebted to Paul for helping to inspire the very idea of this book and an appreciation for reverence in particular. Our simultaneous appreciation of the importance and the similarity of the Greek virtue of reverence and the more Hegelian-romantic notion of spirituality and our shared antipathy for the proselytizing, reactionary sectarianism we saw all around us prompted both of us, I think, in directions we had never before considered.

20. The expression "Will to Power" appears in *Daybreak* (1881) and culminates in Nietzsche's last philosophical work, *The Antichrist* (1889, published 1895).

21. Nietzsche, *Daybreak*, section 548.

CHAPTER 3

1. The ideas in this chapter have been adapted from a book, co-authored with Fernando L. Flores, *Building Trust* (Oxford: Oxford University Press, 2001).

2. *Ecce Homo*. Trans. W. Kaufmann. (New York: Random House, 1967). "Clever" 10.

3. There is good reason to suppose that Schopenhauer's basic distrust toward the world had much to do with the fact that his mother, a successful author and free spirit herself, largely neglected him. See Rudiger Safransky, *Schopenhauer and The Wild Years of Philosophy* (Cambridge, MA: Harvard University Press, 1990).

4. Martin Seligman, *The Optimistic Child* (Boston: Houghton-Mifflin, 1995).

5. See, for example, Annette Baier, "Trust and Anti-trust," who argues such a thesis (without any reference to religion or to God). (Annette C. Baier, "Trust and Antitrust," *Ethics* 96, no. 10, 1986, 231–260. Reprinted in her *Moral Prejudices*, Cambridge, MA: Harvard University Press, 1994.)

6. The history of the concept of God's grace and its relationship to trust and faith is a fascinating story in its own right. The concept of "grace" goes

back to the ancient Hebrews, and its central thesis is that God is autonomous and without obligation. He can give or refuse to give grace without regard to faith or merit, and while the ancient Hebrews were obliged to trust God they recognized that they had no *right* to His grace. Augustine famously argued a similar thesis against Pelagius and denied the relevance of "good works" to salvation. Similar theses are familiar to us from the Reformation, when Luther and Calvin again emphasized the irrelevance of deeds to "earning" God's favor. Indeed, Luther initiated the Reformation as a protest against the idea that one could buy (bribe) God for salvation, and Calvin adamantly denied that faith was either a condition or a guarantee of salvation as one of the "Elect."

7. Given the central place of guilt in several major religions, one might well challenge this exclusion of guilt from the realm of the spiritual. To be sure there is at least one version of guilt, perhaps also of shame, that is sufficiently cosmic in scope (whether or not it involves the monotheistic conception of a morally authoritarian God) to warrant consideration as a spiritual emotion. But I do not want to pursue this suggestion here.

8. F. Nietzsche, *Genealogy of Morals* (New York: Random House, 1967) Essay I, sect. 10.

9. Helmut Schoeck, *Envy* (New York: Harcourt Brace, 1969).

CHAPTER 4

1. Jamie James, *The Music of the Spheres* (London: Springer-Verlag, 1993).

2. Plato, *Republic*. Trans. G. Grube. (Indianapolis: Hackett, 1974), book 4.

3. Hume, *Treatise of Human Nature* (Oxford: Oxford University Press, 1974), book 2, 3.3.

4. *Will to Power*, 387.

5. Hume, *Treatise*, book 2, 3, p. 416.

6. Jamie James, *The Music of the Spheres*.

7. Courtesy of Jay Garfield of Smith College.

8. This is by no means simply a philosophical matter. The justification for mistreating and slaughtering animals has long been their lack of rationality, in one or another of these rather sophisticated senses. Similar arguments, of course, have supported racism, exploitation, and even slavery ever since Aristotle. Jeremy Bentham answered such self-serving claims over two centuries ago: "The question is not, can an animal think, but can it suffer?"

9. Nietzsche, *Gay Science*, no. 360. cf. David Glidden, who in a fit of populist rage once argued that "many in our profession are successful reasoners precisely because their emotions are defective." An accomplished Plato scholar, he argued that "many of us follow Plato's path because we are far more comfortable with our reasoning than we are with our own feelings." ("Philosophers on a Train"—read at the Portland A.P.A. meetings in 1988).

10. Max Weber rejected instrumental merely procedural rationality because he thought that such bureaucratic emphasis on efficiency had co-opted rationality as such. Although he became one of the dominant theoreticians of rationality in the twentieth century, he favored the distinctively emotional, the nonrational and perhaps even the irrational powers of spirituality.

11. Richard Bernstein, "The Rage against Reason." For a popular example of this rage see, e.g., Redfield's best-selling *Celestine Prophesy* or even the usually excellent Thomas Moore's uncalled for rage against scientific understanding, *The Re-enchantment of Everyday Life* (New York: Harper Collins, 1996).

12. Alan Sokal (1996a) 'Transgressing the Boundaries—Toward a Transformative Hermeneutics of Quantum Gravity', *Social Text* 14 (#1 &#2), 217–252; reprinted in Sokal and Bricmont, *Fashionable Nonsense* (New York: Picador, 1998), 99–240. And Sokal, A. (1996b) "A Physicist Experiments with Cultural Studies," *Lingua Franca* (May–June), 62–64; Robert Nola, "Postmodernism, a French Cultural Chernobyl: Foucault on Power/Knowledge," *Inquiry: An Interdisciplinary Journal of Philosophy*, vol. 37, 1994. 3–43.

13. Without getting all exotic and entering into the controversial arenas of magic and other supposed alternatives to Western science, I would point to the rich literature in feminist epistemology of the last decade or so and the sometimes striking arguments that do not reject science as such but point to very different ways of conceiving of its practices. See, for example, Allison Jagger and Sandra Harding. Jane Duran, ed. *Philosophies of Science/Feminist Theories* (Boulder: Westview, 1998).

14. Thomas Nagel, *The View From Nowhere* (New York: Oxford, 1986).

15. This is, I confess, one of my main reservations with Hegel, anticipated by Kierkegaard: From what perspective does Spirit view the world?

16. Cf. Nagel, *View from Nowhere,* 186.

17. David Gautier, *Morals by Agreement* (New York: Oxford University Press, 1986).

18. R. Solomon, "Game Theory as a Model of Business," *Business Ethics Quarterly*, vol. 9, no. 1, Jan., 1998. But research by Robert Frank, one of our more humanistic economists, suggests that people who believe such theories (e.g., his economist colleagues) in fact tend to act more selfishly than their "less rational" brethren.

19. It is worth noting at exactly what point philosophers themselves dispense with argument and insist on simply seeing the point. Indeed, one common claim for rationality—dating back to Plato's *nous* (intellectual intuition)—is that beyond procedural rationality (clarity and careful use of evidence and argumentation, for instance) there is that sort of rationality that "sees" veridical or apodeictic certainty. Edmund Husserl gives us elaborate phenomenological procedures, but ultimately, he tells us, if we do not see the truth there is nothing more to be said. Bloomsbury philosopher G.E. Moore is said to have treated anyone who did not share his intuitions of the Good

with a withering stare. As clever in argument as he was reputed to be, Moore was famous among philosophers for his moral dogmatism. In this light, too, we might want to pay close attention to the actual role of what John Rawls variously calls "intuitively appealing accounts," "various reasonable and natural presumptions," and "initial convictions" in his discussion of "reflective equilibrium." To what extent is the rationality of this most painstakingly methodical theoretician just a well-argued but nevertheless unsupported assertion of his own political preferences? (Rawls has as much as admitted such, in his subsequent works, notably *Political Liberalism*, in which he restricts his once universally rational claims quite explicitly to the claims of rationality inherent in his own—liberal democratic—way of seeing things.

20. See Michael Stocker, "The Schizophrenia of Modern Ethical Theories," *Journal of Philosophy*, vol. 73, 1976.

21. Martin Heidegger, *Being and Time*. Trans. J. Stambaugh. (Albany: SUNY Press, 1996).

22. For a very positive view of the Stoics, see Martha Nussbaum, *Therapy of Desire* (Princeton: Princeton University Press, 1994). On a-Kindi, see L. E. Goodman on "Medieval Jewish and Islamic Philosophers," in Biderman and Scharfstein (Eds.) *Rationality in Question: On Eastern and Western Views of Rationality* (SUNY, 1989) 95–99. On Schopenhauer, by all means read Schopenhauer, *World as Will and Representation* (New York: Dover, 1966).

23. Friedrich Nietzsche, *On the Genealogy of Morals*, 1967, essay 3.

24. Antonio Damasio, *Descartes' Error* (New York: Putnam, 1994).

CHAPTER 5

1. "The horrible stuff will happen," says the Danny Glover character in *Grand Canyon*. Indeed, this is so obvious that it usually need not be said. Nor do people want to hear it. Despite critical acclaim, the movie quickly died at the box office.

2. Miguel de Unamuno, *The Tragic View of Life (Del sentimento tragico de la vida en los hombres y en los pueblos)* (New York: Dover, 1954) 29. Unamuno (1864–1936) was perhaps the greatest philosopher of Spain, and he took great pride in the fact that his philosophy was distinctively Spanish, which may explain his neglect by French, German, English, and American philosophers. He wrote elegant poetry, novels and literary commentary as well as philosophical essays.

3. See Peter Koestenbaum's good little essay on Unamuno in *The Encyclopedia of Philosophy*, P. Edwards, ed., (New York: Macmillan, 1967), vol. 8, 182–5. See also J.J. Ellis, *The Tragic Pursuit of Being: Unamuno and Sartre* (Tuscaloosa: University of Alabama Press, 1988).

4. "[Man] philosophizes either in order to resign himself to life or to seek

some finality in it, or to distract himself and forget his griefs, or for pastime and amusement." *Tragic Sense*, 29.

5. Don Quixote was Unamuno's paradigm example of the existential hero, but there was nothing mock heroic about Unamuno. He supported the Allies against Germany in the World War and opposed Franco's fascist regime. He was put under house arrest in 1936 and died a short time after.

6. But, as Camus came to realize in his retelling of the Sisyphus story, eternal life is no answer to the meaninglessness of life, the Absurd. Of course, if life is thought to be without meaning because of death, then this would be an appropriate antidote. But if life is without meaning because of the inevitability of suffering, then a life of eternal suffering is surely without meaning.

7. Peter Huber, *Liability* (New York: Basic Books, 1988).

8. John Bishop, of Auckland University, has recently been devising alternatives to what he calls the "Omni-God," the God that provokes the Problem of Evil.

9. Rabbi Harold Kushner, *When Bad Things Happen to Good People* (New York: Avon, 1983).

10. Bill McGibbens, *The End of Nature* (New York: The New Yorker Press, 1989) and Greg Esterbrook, *A Moment in the Earth* (New York: Viking, 1995).

11. Williams, *Shame and Necessity* (Berkeley: University of California Press, 1993) 68.

12. Current tort law shares in this ancient sense of collective responsibility. Punishing the innocent may be an idea that seems to us intolerable in questions of criminal law (so, too, guilt by mere association), but in tort law and civil proceedings, the intentional punishment of the innocent is simply given another name: strict liability. It is, in fact, a version of punishing a person or an organization for merely being associated with or otherwise connected to a person who has done something wrong. When that associate has "deep pockets," this unjust practice of punishing the innocent can become lucrative indeed. Huber, *Liability*, esp. 98ff.

13. C.G. Jung, *Job*, J. Singer, ed., *The Portable Jung* (New York: Viking, 1989); see also John T. Wilcox, *The Bitterness of Job* (Ann Arbor: University of Michigan Press, 1989); and Bruce Zuckerman, *Job the Silent* (Oxford: Oxford University Press, 1991), which treats the book as parody.

14. Jane Brooks, "Pondering an Act of God," *Newsweek*, "My Turn," 29 April 1991, 10.

CHAPTER 6

1. In Alfred Hitchcock's second version of *The Man Who Knew Too Much* (1956). The song won an Academy Award that year. The phrase, of course, is not a tautology at all, but a minimalist statement of fatalism.

2. Mark H. Bernstein, *Fatalism* (Lincoln: Nebraska, 1992).

3. Daniel Dennett, *Elbow Room* (Cambridge: M.I.T. Press, 1984), 104.

4. Daniel Dennett, *Elbow Room,* 123.

5. *Elbow Room,* 104.

6. One can imagine Sartre thus responding to his one-time friend Albert Camus's conception of the Absurd as just another version of fatalism.

7. Jean-Paul Sartre, *Being and Nothingness.* Trans. H. Barnes. (New York: Philosophical Library, 1956) 619.

8. In his *Lolita* (New York: Pantheon, 1956).

9. Martha Nussbaum, *The Fragility of Goodness* (New York: Cambridge, 1986).

10. Quoted by Schopenhauer, *World as Will. . . .*

11. Kurt Vonnegut, *Slaughterhouse Five* (New York: Dell, 1969).

12. Aristophanes' lovelorn half-creatures serve as a metaphor here. The concrete sense in which they are two halves of a former whole gives a literal twist to the "meant for" or "made for" imagery. Plato, *Symposium* (Indianapolis: Hackett, 1989) p. 25ff.

13. Robert Nozick offers us a catalog of "invisible hand" type explanations in his *Anarchy, State and Utopia* (New York: Basic Books, 1974), 20–1.

14. But even strict interpretations of evolutionary theory, in terms of random mutations, natural selection, and so on, follow "invisible hand" type patterns of emergence. J. Crow and M. Kimura, *An Introduction to Population Genetics Theory* (New York: Harper and Row, 1970).

15. Jean-Paul Sartre, *Being and Nothingness,* chap. 2.

16. Bernd Magnus, *Nietzsche's Existential Imperative* (Bloomington: Indiana University Press, 1978).

17. Xunzi 103/28 Translated by Lisa Raphals in her "Fatalism, Fate and Strategem in Ancient China and Greece," in Shankman and Durrant, eds., *Thinking Through Comparisons* (Albany, NY: SUNY Press, 2001).

18. Confucius is particularly interesting and important in this regard. On the one hand, he was a serious reformer who insisted on learning and merit as the hallmarks of social position and advancement. A man's fate lay in his talent and ability, not solely in his ancestry. Nevertheless he was not so egalitarian as to question the necessity of social hierarchy.

19. "There but for the grace of God go I" is one among many variations on that imaginative reminder to be empathetic that has come to be known as the "Golden rule." It can be found in Confucius as well as in Buddhism and the Old and New Testament.

20. "Is this a game of chance?" asks the sad sack sucker in the poker game in *My Little Chickadee.* The W.C. Fields character answers, "Not the way I play it."

21. Richard Dawkins, *The Blind Watchmaker* (New York: Norton, 1996).

22. The classic example is Reverend William Paley, in the eighteenth century, who drew the classic analogy between finding a watch on the beach and concluding that God is the creator of this miraculous world.

23. A notable exception is the prolific philosopher Nicholas Rescher, who has written on "Luck." Presidential address to the American Philosophical Association, Atlanta Georgia, 29 December, 1989. Published in the *APA Proceedings*, vol. 64, no. 3, 5–19.

24. Bernard Williams, "Moral Luck." Reprinted in his book, *Moral Luck*. Thomas Nagel, "Moral Luck" in his *Mortal Questions* (Cambridge University Press, 1979).

25. Chance, in these arguments, is typically converted to indeterminism, a purely scientific, more neutral notion. E.g., see Robert Kane, *The Significance of Free Will* (New York: Oxford, 1997).

26. Whether people who believe that everything ultimately happens by chance, lead meaningful or meaning-impoverished lives depends on how seriously they in fact take their stochastic model of life. I know one excellent physicist who gets incensed by people who do not accept the "everything is chance" model, but that is only because he does not for a moment think that their accepting it (or anything much else) is in fact a matter of chance. It is only, it turns out, a theory (a good one indeed), but not a philosophy of life.

27. F. Nietzsche, *Gay Science*, sect. 341.

28. I hasten to emphasize that this is not to say that *any* human life is worth living or worthy of gratitude. There are, to be sure, tragic and miserable lives, lives that are a curse and worth cursing rather than a blessing deserving of gratitude, But for most of us—certainly for most readers of this book—life IS a blessing, whether or not it has been "blessed" by anyone.

CHAPTER 7

1. This chapter was originally written for a delightful conference on this most morbid of topics held in the Bay of Islands in northern New Zealand in January of 1996. My personal thanks to Peter Kraus, for hosting the conference, and for his friendship. This chapter is dedicated to him. Peter described life—on the breathtakingly beautiful Bay of Islands—as a "holiday from death." I'm not very good at holidays (even my honeymoon was a "working honeymoon"), but the idea hit home. I'm now thinking of my life as a "working holiday," and writing about death is (for a philosopher) an essential part of it.

2. Robert Jay Lifton, "The second death" in *Death in Life: Survivors of Hiroshima* (Chapel Hill: University of North Carolina Press, 1991).

3. Martin Heidegger, *Being and Time*. Trans. J. Stambaugh. (SUNY Press, 1996), esp. Division II, sect I. 213–246. Boethius, *The Consolations of Philosophy*. Trans. J. Walton (London: Oxford University Press, 1927).

4. Aristotle, *Nicomachean Ethics*. Trans. W.D. Ross. (Oxford: Oxford University Press, 1948), 1, chap. 10. I argued this in my essay, "Is There Happiness After Death?" *Philosophy*, vol. 51 (1976).

5. For a good discussion of *tian ming* in the conception of Chinese history, see P. J. Ivanhoe, *Confucian Moral Self-Cultivation* (second edition, Indianapolis: Hackett, 2000).

6. Christine Hobson, *Exploring the World of the Pharoahs* (London: Thames and Hudson, 1999).

7. Friedrich Nietzsche, *The Birth of Tragedy*. Trans. W. Kaufmann. (New York: Random House, 1967).

8. Stephen Covey has a well-known quadrant of couplets, from the "Important and Urgent" to the "Unimportant and Not-Urgent," pointing out, correctly, that many of us, much of the time, find ourselves moved by the urgency rather than the importance of things to do. *The Seven Habits of Highly Effective People* (New York: Simon and Schuster, 1989).

9. James Miller, *Michel Foucault* (New York: Simon and Schuster, 1993). See Susan Sontag on Antonin Artaud (Los Angeles: University of California, 1988), Enid Starkie on Arthur Rimbaud (New York: Norton, 1968).

10. Heidegger, *Being and Time*, 46–9.

11. MacIntyre, *After Virtue* (University of Notre Dame: 1981), 120.

12. Notably, *The First Man*, published posthumously, unpolished, by Camus's daughter in 1995. Trans. D. Hapgood. (New York: Vintage, 1996).

13. The outline of this argument is similar to Sartre's argument in *Being and Nothingness*, 680–707.

14. One can too easily imagine a crypto-Heideggerian accountant, perpetrating the concept of Dasein (a.k.a. *Homo Economicus*) as Being-Unto-Taxes, for whom all of life's practices should be sorted into such existential categories as "tax deductible," "employee business expenses," and "capital gains." (Unfortunately, that sounds not unlike the lives that the I.R.S. imposes on most of us good citizens already.)

15. "Letter to Menoeceus," in Epicurus's *Letters, Principle Doctrines and Vatican Sayings*. Trans. Russell M. Geer. (Indianapolis, IN: Bobbs-Merrill, 1981), 54

16. "Wei Boyang and his loyal disciple, together with their dog, revived, became real immortals, and went away." *Shenxian Zhuan*, fourteenth century.

17. Betty Sue Flowers, "Death: The Bald Scenario," in Malpas and Solomon, eds., *Death and Philosophy* (London: Routledge, 1998).

18. One might object that surely my pain and anxiety are for me and for me alone a concern, apart, that is, from empathetic friends and relatives and the medical staff who must figure out how to deal with them. But, again, I think pain and anxiety management are issues quite separate from death, not in the analytic sense of separateness that I have been questioning but in the more obvious sense that these are features of our experience that are unpleasant in any situation, and more so when the prospect is unending rather than terminal. Death and dying are not necessarily painful, and the anxiety must be understood, I am arguing, in a much broader and more social frame than "Being-unto-Death."

19. Pluto (Mickey's dog) whizzes from puppiedom through bones and frisbees as he faces death by drowning in an old Walt Disney comic book.

CHAPTER 8

1. M. Mauss, "A Category of the Human Mind: The Notion of Person, the Notion of Self." Trans. W. D. Halls. In M. Carrithers, S. Collins, and S. Lukes, eds., *The Category of the Person: Anthropology, Philosophy, History* (Cambridge: Cambridge University Press, 1985), 1–25.

2. See, e.g., Owen Flanagan, *Self Expressions* (Oxford University Press, 1996). Hollywood examples abound, from the classic *Three Faces of Eve* (1957) to Jim Carrey's more recent and ridiculous *Me, Myself, and Irene* (2000).

3. "Sensations and brain processes" was the phrase of choice in the middle of the last century, when the debate almost wholly focussed on the conditions of contingent identity that would apply to the basic units of experience (according to traditional empiricism) and then unknown goings-on in the brain. See, for instance, J. J. C. Smart, "Sensations and Brain Processes," (1959) reprinted (with other such works) in William Lyons, *The Philosophy of Mind* (London: Dent, 1995).

4. I intend this to add a perspective but not to contradict neurologist Antonio Damasio's ground-breaking thesis in his *Descartes Error* (New York: Addison-Wesley, 1997). Indeed, Damasio's research supports the radical claim that I made in Chapters 2 and 4, that emotions and reasons are not so distinct, *even on the most basic neurological level*. But his demonization of Descartes, typical of contemporary cognitive science, needs to be balanced with historical and cultural considerations.

5. Michel Cabanac, of the Université de Laval, on the basis of various measures, concludes that reptiles have emotions, amphibians do not. "The Phylogeny of Emotion." (International Society for Research on Emotions Proceedings, August, 2000).

6. I am greatly indebted to my colleague and friend Steve Phillips for virtually all that I understand (*if* I understand) about these matters in Indian philosophy.

7. Madhava, Sarva-darsana-samgraha is the source. Thanks again to Steve Phillips.

8. Wing-tsit Chan, *A Sourcebook in Chinese Philosophy* (Princeton: Princeton University Press, 1963), 49–83. See also *The Mind of Mencius*. Trans. D. C. Lao. (New York: Penguin, 1970).

9. Fung yu-lan, *A Short History of Chinese Philosophy* (New York: Macmillan, 1968), 302. I am indebted to my good friend Roger Ames for much of my introduction to Chinese philosophy.

10. Fung yu-lan, *A Short History*.

11. Fung yu-lan, *A Short History*, 195.

12. Roger Ames, the introduction to Chinese section and a chapter in T. Kasulis, *Self as Body in Asian Theory and Practice* (Albany: SUNY, 1993), 149–177.

13. See classic articles by U.T. Place and J.J.C. Smart in Lyons's collection.

14. The link between Socrates and the Egyptians was the great and mysterious philosopher Pythagoras, who brought from Egypt the doctrines of immortality and transmigration of the soul.

15. His dying words were, "I owe a chicken [a sacrifice, a gift of thanks] to Asclepius," the god of healing. (Plato, *Phaedo*).

16. Lewis Thomas, *Lives of a Cell* (New York: Viking, 1974); Antonio Damasio, *The Feeling of What Happens* (New York: Harcourt Brace, 2001).

17. Jean-Paul Sartre, *Being and Nothingness*. (New York: Philosophical Library, 1956).

18. *The Phenomenology of Spirit*. Trans. A.V. Miller. (Oxford University Press, 1977) part B, chap. 2, 109ff. In the dialectic of the *Phenomenology*, the master-slave chapter follows the very short chapter on "Self-certainty," which, along with much else, entertains and rejects as question-begging the Cartesian certainty of self. Hegel also considers, with equal brevity, the importance of the notion of desire in self-consciousness and, echoing Fichte, the ultimate awareness of oneself as *life*. These more rudimentary forms of self-consciousness are then carried over (and *aufheben'd*) in the parable of master and slave. (There is also a short discussion of the "I" as a matter of immediate acquaintance in the first chapter of the book, Sense-certainty.)

19. Cf. more recent work by P.F. Strawson, *Persons* (London: Methuen, 1959) and Mark Johnston "Human Beings," *Journal of Philosophy* (1987). Philosophers often distinguish between first-person and third person accounts of the self. What Hegel is bringing out, in contrast, is what we might call a second-person (or confrontational) conception of self.

20. These are the philosophies of Stoicism and Skepticism, respectively, but eventually the dialectic turns to an entirely different sense of personal identity that involves group identification (*Sittlichkeit* or ethical substance) rather than the dubious independence of a competitive State of Nature. I have defended the idea that Hegel's discussion constitutes his contribution to the ongoing state of nature debate (and the nature of the so-called social contract that is formulated therein) in my book, *In the Spirit of Hegel* (New York: Oxford University Press, 1983), chap. 7.

21. Subsequent chapters of the *Phenomenology* spell out these various versions in the form of indifference to or withdrawal from the world, as hedonism, the Rousseauist "Law of the Heart" and the Pascalian "Way of the World."

INDEX